UNIVERSALIZABILITY

SYNTHESE LIBRARY

STUDIES IN EPISTEMOLOGY,

LOGIC, METHODOLOGY, AND PHILOSOPHY OF SCIENCE

Managing Editor:

JAAKKO HINTIKKA, *Academy of Finland, Stanford University, and Florida State University*

Editors:

ROBERT S. COHEN, *Boston University*

DONALD DAVIDSON, *University of Chicago*

GABRIËL NUCHELMANS, *University of Leyden*

WESLEY C. SALMON, *University of Arizona*

VOLUME 141

WŁODZIMIERZ RABINOWICZ

UNIVERSALIZABILITY

A Study in Morals and Metaphysics

D. REIDEL PUBLISHING COMPANY

DORDRECHT : HOLLAND / BOSTON : U.S.A.
LONDON : ENGLAND

Library of Congress Cataloging in Publication Data

Rabinowicz, Włodzimierz.
    Universalizability: a study in morals and metaphysics.

    (Synthese library)
    Bibliography: p.
    Includes index.
    1. Ethics. 2. Metaphysics. I. Title.
BJ1012.R28   170   79-13674
ISBN 90-277-1020-1

Published by D. Reidel Publishing Company,
P.O. Box 17, Dordrecht, Holland

Sold and distributed in the U.S.A., Canada, and Mexico
by D. Reidel Publishing Company, Inc.
Lincoln Building, 160 Old Derby Street, Hingham,
Mass. 02043, U.S.A.

Printed in Sweden by Almqvist & Wiksell, Uppsala, 1979

To Ewa

Acknowledgments

I welcome this opportunity of expressing my gratitude to some of the persons who have given me their help and support in writing this book.

Special thanks are due to my advisor, Professor Lars Bergström, whose constant interest and encouragement have made this book possible. I am deeply indebted to him for his acute and illuminating criticisms and for innumerable constructive suggestions.

I have benefited greatly from many discussions with my teachers and colleagues in Uppsala: Thorild Dahlquist, Sven Danielsson, Kaj Børge Hansen, Stig Kanger, Sören Stenlund, Bertil Strömberg and Jan Österberg, among others. I am grateful to all of them for their friendship and intellectual support. I also wish to express my thanks to my former teacher, Professor Ingemar Hedenius. His fascinating seminars awakened in me my interest in moral philosophy.

Sections of the manuscript were discussed at two philosophical seminars at Stockholm University, led by Professors Harald Ofstad and Dag Prawitz, respectively. I wish to thank the participants of these seminars for their interesting remarks and suggestions. Professor Prawitz has pointed out a significant difficulty in my approach, which I try to remedy in the Appendix.

Preparation of this book has been forwarded by much able assistance made available to me. Professor Stanley Bender corrected my English. Mr Jan Österberg and Dr Paul Needham assisted me in the reading of proofs. The manuscript was typed by Mrs Gloria Bender and Miss Marianne Carlstedt. Professors Jaakko Hintikka, Stig Kanger and Ingmar Pörn assisted me greatly in connection with publication. I am deeply grateful to all these persons.

My main debt of gratitude is to my wife, Ewa, to whom I dedicate this book.

Uppsala, June 1979

Włodzimierz Rabinowicz

ABSTRACT

Rabinowicz Włodzimierz, 1979. Universalizability. A Study in Morals and Metaphysics. *Synthese Library*, vol. 141, 190 pp. Dordrecht, Holland.

In this dissertation, we consider the so-called Universalizability Principle. As applied to 'situations' (= possible worlds) and their 'obligation-structures' (specifications of the states of affairs which are obligatory /permitted/ forbidden in a given situation), this principle asserts the following:

Situations which possibly involve different individuals but otherwise are exactly/relevantly similar to each other exhibit exactly/relevantly similar obligation-structures.

It is shown how to represent this principle as a formal condition on a set-theoretical model.

Since the concept of (moral) relevance is notoriously unclear, this lack of clarity extends to the relevant-similarity variant of the Universalizability Principle. At the same time, the exact-similarity variant of the same principle becomes trivial if we accept the Leibnizian thesis about the identity of indiscernibles: no two distinct objects are indiscernible from (exactly similar to) each other. We argue that there exists a formulation of the Universalizability Principle which avoids both these difficulties. It is shown that, from the *anti*-Leibnizian point of view, the formulation in question is equivalent to the exact-similarity variant of the Universalizability Principle. The equivalence disappears, however, as soon as we adopt Leibnizianism. While the assumption of *identitas indiscernibilium* trivializes the exact-similarity variant, this triviality feature does not extend to the formulation proposed by us. At the same time, the formulation in question does not in any way depend on the concept of relevance.

While the Universalizability Principle is an ethical thesis, analogous conditions may be found even outside the ethical domain. (To illustrate: Similar *causes* have similar *effects*.) One could ask, therefore, whether one can derive all such 'universalizability claims' from some underlying metaphysical intuition. We argue that such a derivation is, in fact, possible and show how the intuition in question may be expressed in our formal framework.

Włodzimierz Rabinowicz, Philosophy Department, Uppsala University.
Villavägen 5, S-752 36 Uppsala, Sweden.

Table of Contents

Part III
Beyond Similarity

Part IV
Individuals Do Not Matter

CHAPTER 1

Introduction

1.1. *The Principle of Universalizability—an informal explication*

This work is concerned with the so-called Principle of Universalizability. As we shall understand it, this principle represents a claim that moral properties of things (persons, actions, state of affairs, situations) are essentially independent of their purely 'individual' or—as one often says —'numerical' aspects.[1] Thus, if a thing, x, is better than another thing, y, then this fact is not dependent on x's being x nor on y's being y. If a certain person, a, has a duty to help another person, b, then this duty does not arise as a consequence of their being a and b, respectively. And if in a certain situation, w, it ought to be the case that certain goods are transferred from one person to another, then this moral obligation does not depend on the individual identities of the persons involved.

The Universalizability Principle may also be expressed in terms of *similarities*. Instead of saying that the moral properties of x are essentially independent of the individual aspects of x, we may say that any object which is *exactly similar* to x, which is precisely like x in all non-individual, 'qualitative' respects, must exhibit exactly similar moral properties. Thus, if two persons are exactly similar to each other, (if they are placed in exactly similar circumstances, have exactly similar information, preferences, character, etc.), then they will have exactly similar rights and duties. Likewise, if two situations are exactly similar, they will exhibit exactly similar 'obligation-structures'—exactly similar things will be obligatory, permitted or forbidden in both situations.

Should we not, however, say that, according to the Universalizability Principle, exactly similar objects have the *same* moral properties? For

[1] If it is thought that talk about moral properties commits one to ethical objectivism (which we strongly doubt), and if one should wish to avoid such a commitment, then one can always choose some more neutral formulation of the Universalizability Principle, say, in terms of moral *judgments*. This principle asserts then that the status of moral judgments, their 'acceptability', is essentially independent of the 'individual' aspects of things to which these judgments refer.

instance, that exactly similar persons have the *same* rights and duties? Such a claim would be somewhat misleading. If *a* has a duty to help *b*, then this property of *a* need not apply to exactly similar persons. What does apply is that, for any such person *c*, there is some *d* exactly similar to *b* such that *c* has a duty to help *d*. Thus, according to the Universalizability Principle, *a*'s and *c*'s duties are exactly similar, but they need not be the same. To put it differently, having a duty to help *b* is a property of *a* which, in a sense, depends on *a*'s being *a*—insofar as *this* duty does not carry over to exactly similar persons. But, as we have said above, this dependence is not essential, since exactly similar persons will have exactly similar duties.[2]

The Universalizability Principles may also be formulated in terms of *relevant similarity*. Assume that all the differences between the two objects, *x* and *y*, are either purely 'individual' or morally irrelevant. That is, *x* and *y* are similar in all respects which are both morally relevant and 'non-individual'. Then, according to the Universalizability Principle, the moral properties of *x* and *y* must exhibit the same kind of similarity. For instance, if two situations, *w* and *v*, involve different individuals but otherwise are relevantly similar, then this similarity will carry over to their obligation-structures.

In this work, we shall focus on the Universalizability Principle as it applies to *situations* and their obligation-structures. And we shall start from the *similarity* versions of this principle. However, in Part III, we shall see how it is possible to move beyond the concept of similarity.

The term 'universalizability' is of a relatively recent origin. It appears for the first time in an article by R. M. Hare published in the fifties.[3] The Universalizability Principle itself has a somewhat longer history. To our knowledge, it was first formulated by Sidgwick in his *Methods of Ethics*:

---

[2] At this point, it could be asked: Is it not perfectly obvious that exactly similar objects must have exactly similar properties, whether moral or non-moral? How *could* they otherwise be exactly similar to each other? But, in such a case, the exact similarity version of the Universalizability Principle seems to be devoid of any interesting content. However, it will be seen below that this objection is erroneous. It depends, in substance, on a certain ambiguity in the notion of exact similarity—an ambiguity which will be spelled out in chapter 15 (section 15.4).

[3] Cf. R. M. Hare, 'Universalizability', *Proceedings of Aristotelian Society, 1954–5*, pp. 295–312.

"If a kind of conduct that is right (or wrong) for me is not right (or wrong) for someone else, it must be on the ground of some difference between the two cases, other than the fact that I and he are different persons."[4]

"It cannot be right for A to treat B in a manner in which it would be wrong for B to treat A, merely on the ground that they are two different individuals, and without there being any difference between the natures or circumstances of the two which can be stated as a reasonable ground for difference in treatment."[5]

But what shall we say about such classical principles as the Golden Rule[6] or Kant's Categorical Imperative?[7] Do they not already express the same idea as our universalizability thesis? As we shall argue below, this question merits a negative answer. But the fact that just such questions may be asked points to a rather serious general problem: There are many principles which are tangential to our thesis. In fact, moral philosophers who talk about 'universalizability' may often have in mind some principle which differs from the one we are concerned with here.[8] In order to prevent misunderstandings, it seems necessary, therefore, to compare our Principle of Universalizability with some other possible candidates for the name. This is what we propose to do in section 1.2.

Throughout the entire work we shall make extensive use of set-theoretical models. The first of these will be developed in section 1.3. It will be seen that the Principle of Universalizability may be represented as a certain formal condition on this model.

Finally, in section 1.4, we shall describe some of the problems which we wish to discuss in different parts of this work.

---

[4] H. Sidgwick, *Methods of Ethics*, 7th ed., London 1907, p. 379.
[5] Ibid. p. 380.
[6] For the history of the Golden Rule, see H. Reiner, 'Die Goldene Regel', *Zeitschr. für Philos. Forschung*, *3* (1948), pp. 74–105, and Marcus G. Singer, 'The Golden Rule', *Philosophy*, *38* (1963), pp. 293–314.
[7] For the different formulations of the Categorical Imperative in Kant's *Grundlegung zur Metaphysik der Sitten*, see H. J. Paton, *The Moral Law*, London 1948, pp. 22, 29–36, 67, 83–101.
[8] For the discussion of different interpretations of 'universalizability', see, for example, D. H. Monro, *Empiricism and Ethics*, Cambridge University Press, 1967; Don Locke, 'The Trivializability of Universalizability', *The Philosophical Review*, *77* (1968), pp. 25–44; B. E. Schrag, *Universalizability and the Concept of Morality*, doctoral dissertation, 1975, Xerox University Microfilms, Ann Arbor, Michigan, Order No. 76–119.

1.2. *What our Universalizability Principle is not*

(A) It should be clear from what we have said above that the Universalizability Principle, as we understand it, does *not* establish any connection between the subject's will, preference, intention or interest and his duties. In this it manifestly differs from both the Golden Rule, "Do unto others as you would have them do unto you", and from several versions of the Kantian Categorical Imperative, of which "I ought never to act except in such a way *that I can also will that my maxim should become a universal law*"[9] is perhaps best known.

According to Kant, one cannot will impossible states of affairs. Thus, his Imperative implies the following weaker thesis: I ought never to act except in such a way that my maxim could become a universal law. But even though this thesis no longer makes any reference to will, it still differs substantively from our Universalizability Principle. The latter forbids my acting on a maxim which cannot become a universal law *only if* similar agents are forbidden to act on maxims of this kind, but not otherwise. This observation leads us to our next point.

(B) Both the Golden Rule and the Kantian Imperative are, so to speak, 'categorical' in their moral content. They make a certain moral claim about a given object (in this case, the agent) without making this claim dependent on the validity of other *moral* claims. In this respect they clearly differ from our Universalizability Principle, which may be seen as a purely 'hypothetical' thesis. According to it, a certain moral claim applies to an object *only if* similar moral claims apply to similar objects.

This 'hypothetical' nature of our Universalizability Principle distinguishes it from many other related principles which appear in the literature. The following three examples illustrate this point:

(1) The Principle of Impartiality.

"One ought not to make exceptions in one's own favour."[10]

Clearly, the denial of this principle is perfectly compatible with our universalizability thesis. It is one thing to forbid partiality and quite another to claim that, if partiality is morally forbidden in one case,

---

[9] H. J. Paton, op. cit., p. 67.
[10] See, for example, D. H. Monro, op. cit., chapter 16, passim, and, by the same author, 'Impartiality and Consistency', *Philosophy, 36* (1961), p. 166.

then it is also forbidden in similar cases. It is, however, only the latter claim that follows from the Universalizability Principle.

But what if the partiality in question is of the *moral* kind? What if it consists in making *moral* exceptions in one's own (or somebody else's) favor? For instance, think of a person who claims to possess certain rights or duties while denying similar rights or duties to similar persons. Well, a person who is partial in this sense seems to come into conflict with our Principle of Universalizability (at least as long as he *recognizes* that other persons *are* similar). But the Universalizability Principle itself, in distinction from the Principle of Impartiality, does *not* imply that one is *morally forbidden* to be morally partial. To put it differently, the Universalizability Principle does not imply that anybody who rejects the Universalizability Principle does anything that he is morally forbidden to do.

(2) The Principle of Fairness.

Similars ought to be treated similarly.[11]

Our remarks regarding the Principle of Impartiality apply equally well to the Principle of Fairness. According to the universalizability thesis, the agent has a duty to be fair if, but *only* if, other, similar agents have a similar duty. This thesis does *not* imply that fairness actually is a duty of any agent. This is still true even when we consider only 'moral fairness': making similar moral judgments about similar cases.

(3) The Principle of Uniform Action.

The Principle of Fairness prescribes a similar treatment of similar 'patients'. Of course, we could have an analogous principle which prescribes that similar *agents* ought to *act* similarly. We may refer to it as the Principle of Uniform Action. Clearly, the claim made by this principle does not follow from our universalizability thesis. The latter does not demand any uniformity in acting on the part of similar agents. As long as one of them is morally permitted to choose between relevantly different actions, the same moral latitude will, by the Universalizability Principle, apply to all the others. If it is right for *a*

---

[11] The history of this principle goes back to Aristotle and his conception of distributive justice as proportionate treatment. Cf. Aristotle, *Nicomachean Ethics, Book 5*, transl. by H. Rackham, Loeb Classical Library, Cambridge, Mass., 1926.

to do X and also right to do Y, then it is right for any similar agent to do something similar to X, but it is also right to do something similar to Y. No uniformity is demanded.

However, what happens if we assume that a lacks moral latitude and that, in particular, he ought to do X but not Y? Does the Universalizability Principle entail that, at least in such situations, it ought to be the case that everybody who is similar to a, a included, does something similar to X? Clearly, this is not the case. What follows from our principle is only that every similar agent ought to do something similar to X, but not that their acting in this uniform way is anything that ought to take place. To put it somewhat differently, the universal obligation implied by the Universalizability Principle is of a *distributive*, not of a *collective*, kind. It applies to each agent similar to a and not to the whole such collection.

Of course, there is a clear difference between these two kinds of universal obligation. It may be the case that each agent in a given collection ought to act in a certain way, α, *without* it being obligatory that all of them perform α. Sometimes, in fact, such a uniform performance may even be impossible: each of the agents can, and ought, perform α, but his doing α would prevent others from acting in the same way.[12]

(C) Consider the following thesis due to Marcus Singer:

Generalization Principle: "What is right (or wrong) for one person must be right (or wrong) for any similar person in similar circumstances."[13]

The similarity referred to in this principle is to be understood as *relevant* similarity, similarity in all *relevant* respects. "The generalization principle is to be understood in the sense that what is right for one person must be right for every *relevantly* similar person in *relevantly* similar circumstances."[14]

Is this principle equivalent to our universalizability thesis? Actually, it is not. What we lack in Singer's formulation is the restriction of the respects of comparison to *non-individual* ones. To universalize moral

---

[12] On the distinction between the distributive and the collective reading of 'everyone ought' see, for instance, J. H. Sobel, "'Everyone', Consequences and Generalization Arguments", *Inquiry*, 10 (1967), pp. 373–404.
[13] M. G. Singer, *Generalization in Ethics*, New York, 1961, p. 5.
[14] Ibid. p. 20.

properties over cases which are similar in *all* relevant respects is one thing; to assume the same universalizability with respect to cases similar in all respects which are both relevant *and* non-individual is another. Thus, the Generalization Principle may be accepted even by someone who rejects our universalizability thesis and claims to possess special rights our duties simply because 'he is he', simply because he is the particular individual he is. What such a person has to do in order to avoid the conflict with Singer's principle is just to assume that purely individual characteristics constitute relevant respects of comparison.

Singer himself thinks that such a move would be logically illegitimate. According to him, it may be shown that treating purely individual properties as grounds for moral discrimination involves one in a contradiction.[15] A similar claim has also been made by Alan Gewirth.[16] If this claim were true, then our universalizability thesis would trivially follow from the Generalization Principle. However, the arguments put forward by Singer and Gewirth have already been effectively criticised by a number of commentators.[17] Therefore, it would be superfluous to discuss them here.

It should be noted that a principle similar to Singer's has been discussed by Monro under the name of 'Principle of Consistency'.[18] Contrary to Singer, Monro claims that this principle does not, by itself, exclude the possibility of treating individual properties as grounds for moral discrimination.[19]

(D) Our discussion of different 'universalizability principles' would be essentially incomplete, if we were to omit mention of the views of R. M. Hare. Unfortunately, it is not at all clear what Hare's 'thesis of universalizability' consists in. Many commentators have claimed that Hare's usage of the phrase in *Freedom and Reason* does not

---

[15] Ibid. pp. 17 f., 22 f.
[16] A. Gewirth, "The Non-Trivializability of Universalizability", *Australasian Journal of Philosophy*, *47* (1969), pp. 123–131, and *Reason and Morality*, Chicago, 1978, pp. 115–119.
[17] Cf. G. Nakhnikian, 'Generalization in Ethics', *The Review of Metaphysics*, *17* (1963–4) pp. 436–61, and B. E. Schrag, op. cit., chapter IV, esp. pp. 143–150.
[18] Op. cit., D. H. Monro, 'Impartially and Consistency', p. 164.
[19] Op. cit., D. H. Monro, *Empiricism and Ethics*, chapter 16, esp. pp. 200 ff. Compare also D. Locke, op. cit., pp. 35 ff., for the same position.

seem to be consistent and that his position is open to a number of different interpretations.[20] Therefore, instead of trying to determine Hare's 'real' position on this issue, we shall consider some of his formulations of the 'thesis of universalizability' in order to point out one important respect in which they all differ from our Universalizability Principle.

"What the thesis /of universalizability/ does forbid us to do is to make different moral judgements about actions which we admit to be exactly or relevantly similar. The thesis tells us that this is to make two logically inconsistent judgements."[21]

In distinction from our Universalizability Principle, Hare's principle refers not to the moral properties of similar actions but to the moral *judgments* which may be made about such actions. However, this difference, by itself, is not very essential. Any principle about certain properties of a given object may also be expressed as a thesis concerning the status of judgments which ascribe these properties to the object. The real difference lies elsewhere. In distinction from Hare, we do not assume that the Universalizability Principle says anything about the *logical* relations between the judgments involved. It is one thing to claim that similar moral judgments apply to similar objects, and quite another to assert that this claim is *logically* or *analytically* true. It is a controversial issue whether our Universalizability Principle is analytical or not. But even if it is, it certainly does not announce its own analyticity.[22]

This means, then, that Hare's universalizability thesis implies our Universalizability Principle, but not vice versa.

The difference between our position and Hare's becomes even more clear when we consider that he sometimes interprets his thesis of

---

[20] See, for example, D. H. Monro, *Empiricism and Ethics*, chapters 13–16, D. Locke, op. cit., and L. Bergström, "Review of R. M. Hare, 'Freedom and Reason'", *Theoria*, *30* (1964), pp. 39–49.

[21] R. M. Hare, *Freedom and Reason*, Clarendon Press, London, 1963, p. 33. That the concept of relevant similarity used by Hare takes exception to the individual respects of comparison and therefore corresponds to the one we have been using seems to follow from his comments in section 6.8. There, he asserts that a person who considers non-universal properties to be morally relevant "has not met the demands of universalizability" (p. 107).

[22] This assumption of analyticity is presumably also present, at least implicitly, in all the formulations in which Hare interprets his thesis of universalizability as a principle about the (logical?) *commitments* of the judger. Cf. R. M. Hare, *Freedom and Reason*, pp. 18, 20 and 15.

universalizability as a *linguistic* claim—as a principle about the *meanings* of moral *words*:

"The thesis of universalizability itself, however, is still a logical thesis. ... By a 'logical' thesis I mean a thesis about the meanings of words, or dependent solely upon them. I have been maintaining that the meaning of the world 'ought' and other moral words is such that a person who uses them commits himself thereby to a universal rule. This is the thesis of universalizability."[23]

Perhaps it may be claimed that the validity of our Universalizability Principle is dependent solely upon the meanings of words (though this is a controversial issue). But this principle itself is certainly not a thesis about the meanings of words.

We may conclude, then, that our Principle of Universalizability is not identical with Hare's.[24]

The list of different candidates for the 'universalizability' title, which we have presented in this section, is certainly incomplete. But the ones we considered constitute a fairly representative sample. Absence of any claim about the connection between one's wants or preferences and one's duties, 'hypothetical' character, stress on the distinction between individual and non-individual aspects of things, and neutrality with regard to the questions concerning the 'logic of morals' and the nature of moral language, seem to be the most important features which distinguish our Universalizability Principle from its different competitors.

1.3. *The Universalizability Principle as a condition on a model*

Consider a structure $\langle \mathbf{W}, \mathbf{D}, \mathbf{C} \rangle$, where $\mathbf{W}$ is a set and $\mathbf{D}, \mathbf{C}$ are dyadic relations on $\mathbf{W}$. Let $w, v, u, z, ..., w', v', ...$ be different members of $\mathbf{W}$. $\mathbf{D}$ is thought to obey the seriality condition: for every w in $\mathbf{W}$, there is some v in $\mathbf{W}$ such that $w\mathbf{D}v$. $\mathbf{C}$ is an equivalence relation. That is, for every w, v, u in $\mathbf{W}$,

---

[23] Ibid. p. 30.
[24] But this difference would not be considered as very important by Hare himself. "It does not matter very much whether we say that it [the thesis of universalizability] is a second-order statement about the logical properties of moral judgements, or that it is a first-order, but analytic, moral judgement. It could be put in either of these forms without substantially altering its character." (ibid. p. 33.)

(1) $w\mathbf{C}w$ (reflexivity)

(2) if $w\mathbf{C}v$, then $v\mathbf{C}w$ (symmetry)

and

(3) if $w\mathbf{C}v$ and $v\mathbf{C}u$, then $w\mathbf{C}u$ (transitivity).

Intuitively, **W** is to be understood as the set of *situations*, or—in somewhat different terminology—as the set of *possible worlds*. The subsets of **W** will be called *propositions* or *states of affairs*. We shall refer to them as $X, Y, ..., X', Y', ...$, etc. Thus, a proposition (a state of affairs) is a certain set of situations. For example, the proposition that John owes money to Jim is identified with the set of situations in which John owes money to Jim. Since we want our model to be 'elastic'—easily adaptable to many different purposes—we should keep it as general as possible. Therefore, it is best not to formulate any special conditions on what is to be meant by situations. In some contexts it may be reasonable to identify situations with the whole 'world-histories', with things such as 'everything that is the case'. In other contexts a more restrictive view might be more appropriate. Thus, sometimes we may want to consider different events or different cross-sections of a given world-history as different situations.

However, even though we may interpret the concept of a situation in many different ways, we shall assume that our interpretation makes it possible to talk about different states of affairs being morally obligatory, permitted, or forbidden in a given situation. Furthermore, we shall assume that, for any situation, w, it makes sense to ask about the situations in which all the obligations obtaining in w are discharged. We shall call such situations *deontic alternatives to w*.[25] The relation **D** in our model is thought to represent this concept of deontic alternative. Thus, for any w, v in **W**, $w\mathbf{D}v$ iff v is a deontic alternative to w. Note that we do *not* assume that any two situations have the same deontic alternatives. In different situations different things may be obligatory.

We have explicated the concept of deontic alternative, and thereby the relation **D**, in terms of the notion of moral obligation. However, once we have **D** in our framework, moral obligation becomes definable

---

[25] The notion of denotic alternative is a standard one in 'possible-world' semantics of deontic logic. For references, see R. Hilpinen, ed., *Deontic Logic: Introductory and Systematic Readings*, Dordrecht, 1971.

in terms of **D**. Thus, we shall say that, for any state of affairs (proposition) $X \subseteq \mathbf{W}$, and any situation (world) $w \in \mathbf{W}$, X is *obligatory in w* iff X obtains in *every* deontic alternative to w, i.e., iff, for every v in **W** such that $w\mathbf{D}v$, v belongs to X. Analogously, X is *permitted in w* iff X obtains in *some* deontic alternative to w, and *forbidden in w* iff X obtains in *no* deontic alternative to w. (These standard definitions reflect the idea that (1) X is forbidden iff its complement, $\mathbf{W}-X$, is obligatory, and (2) X is permitted iff it is not forbidden. Given these definitions, the assumption that **D** is serial amounts to the claim that X is permitted whenever it is obligatory.)

By the *obligation-structure* of w we shall understand the specification of the states of affairs which are obligatory, permitted, or forbidden in w. Since, for any state of affairs, its moral status in w may be determined by considering the set of deontic alternatives to w, it is plausible to look upon this set as a representation of w's obligation-structure.

The equivalence relation **C** on **W** is to be understood as the relation of *exact similarity*. Sometimes, we shall also call it the relation of '*copyhood*'. Thus, '$w\mathbf{C}v$' may be read as 'v is a copy of w'. Situations connected by **C** are exactly similar to each other, i.e., they are identical in all their 'non-individual', 'qualitative' aspects. To put it differently, if w and v are copies, then the only possible differences between them are of an 'individual', 'numerical' nature. Thus, for example, the individuals involved in w may be distinct from those appearing in v. Or, to take another possibility, v may result from w by a 'permutation' of individuals, by moving individuals from one position to another. To illustrate: Suppose that individuals a and b both exist in w. Imagine a situation, v, in which a and b reverse their roles, but which otherwise does not differ from w. Thus, b's circumstances in v, his behaviour, character, preferences, upbringing, etc. are exactly like the corresponding characteristics of a in w. And a in v is exactly like b in w. Then we shall say that w and v are copies. Generally speaking, two situations are copies of each other only if every individual existing in one of them has an exactly similar counterpart in the other situation.

Now, consider the following condition on our model (for convenience, universal quantifiers shall be omitted whenever possible):

(u) $w\mathbf{C}v$ & $w\mathbf{D}u$ → $\exists z(v\mathbf{D}z$ & $u\mathbf{C}z)$.

This condition asserts that, for every w, each deontic alternative to w has copies among the deontic alternatives to each copy of w. Since $\mathbf{C}$ is symmetric, (u) could also be expressed as follows: For any pair of copies, each deontic alternative to one of them is copied by some deontic alternative to the other one. Roughly speaking, if w and v are copies, then their deontic alternatives are systematically connected by the relation of copyhood.

According to the exact-similarity version of the Universalizability Principle, exactly similar situations have exactly similar obligation-structures (compare section 1.1). Since the obligation-structure of a situation may be represented by the set of deontic alternatives for that situation, we arrive at the following claim: exactly similar situations have exactly similar deontic alternatives.[26] A natural way of expressing this claim in more formal terms would be to say that, for any pair of exactly similar situations, each deontic alternative to one of them is exactly similar to some deontic alternative to the other. But this is just what the condition (u) asserts. Thus, we may conclude that (u) constitutes a fairly adequate representation of the exact-similarity variant of the Universalizability Principle (as applied to situations).

It is well known that set-theoretical models of the same kind as the one we have been using here may be applied to the interpretation of different modal languages. One could ask, therefore, whether it is possible to express the exact-similarity version of the Universalizability Principle not only as a condition on a model but also as a formula in a certain modal language which is interpreted in terms of that model. As we shall see in a moment, this question should be answered in the affirmative.

Let $\mathbf{S}$ be a language with atomic sentences A_1, A_2, ..., etc., and with the following sentence-forming operators on sentences: $\neg$, $\rightarrow$, $\mathbf{L}_1$, $\mathbf{L}_2$. $\mathbf{L}_1$ and $\mathbf{L}_2$, which are both one-place operators, may be read, respectively, as "It ought to be the case that ..." and "In all exactly similar situations it is the case that ...". Let f be a 'valuation' of $\mathbf{S}$ with respect to the model $\langle \mathbf{W}, \mathbf{D}, \mathbf{C} \rangle$. That is, f is a function which assigns subsets of $\mathbf{W}$ to sentences of $\mathbf{S}$. A sentence, A, of $\mathbf{S}$ may be said to be *true in w with respect to*

---

[26] Note that we do not assume that exactly similar situations have identical deontic alternatives. Such an interpretation of the Universalizability Principle would make it an implausible thesis. (See below, section 3.2; also, section 1.1 above.)

a valuation f iff $w \in f(A)$. A is *valid with respect to* f iff $f(A) = \mathbf{W}$. f is assumed to satisfy the following conditions:

For all sentences A, B of $\mathbf{S}$,

(1) $f(\neg A) = \mathbf{W} - f(A)$,
(2) $f(A \to B) = f(\neg A) \cup f(B)$,
(3) $f(\mathbf{L}_1 A)$ = the set of all situations w such that every deontic alternative to w belongs to $f(A)$,
(4) $f(\mathbf{L}_2 A)$ = the set of all situations w such that every copy of w belongs to $f(A)$.

Let $\mathbf{F}$ be the set of all valuations of $\mathbf{S}$ with respect to $\langle \mathbf{W}, \mathbf{D}, \mathbf{C} \rangle$. That is, $\mathbf{F}$ is the set of all functions from sentences of $\mathbf{S}$ to subsets of $\mathbf{W}$, which satisfy the conditions (1)–(4) above. A sentence of $\mathbf{S}$ shall be said to be *valid* iff it is valid with respect to every f in $\mathbf{F}$.

This concept of validity could also be applied to sentence-schemas. A sentence-schema is *valid* iff every sentence which is an instance of this schema is valid.

Now, we can formulate our question in a more formal way: Is there any sentence-schema in $\mathbf{S}$ which is valid *if*, and *only if*, $\langle \mathbf{W}, \mathbf{D}, \mathbf{C} \rangle$ satisfies the condition (u)? If such a schema exists, then we may consider it to be the equivalent of (u) in $\mathbf{S}$.

It can be shown, thought we shall not do it here, that the following schema has the desired property:

$$\mathbf{L}_1 \mathbf{L}_2 A \to \mathbf{L}_2 \mathbf{L}_1 A.$$

(This result depends on the symmetry of $\mathbf{C}$. Since $\mathbf{C}$ is symmetric, (u) is equivalent to the condition:

(u′) $w\mathbf{C}v$ & $v\mathbf{D}u \to \exists z(w\mathbf{D}z$ & $z\mathbf{C}u)$.

And it can be easily proved that (u′) corresponds precisely to the assumption that the sentence-schema above is valid.)

This means that, instead of representing the Universalizability Principle as a condition on a model, we could discuss it in the framework of a formalized modal language. Both approaches are essentially equivalent. This equivalence, however, disappears when we move to different strengthenings of (u), which shall be considered later. Some of these stronger conditions no longer have any analogues in the language **S**. What is more, it is our impression that conditions such as (u) are more readily understandable than the corresponding sentence-schemas. Therefore, the approach in terms of models seems to us much more attractive.

It could be claimed that the Universalizability Principle in its *exact-similarity* version is an extremely trivial statement. This triviality claim rests on an idea which is due to Leibniz. According to this philosopher, there are no two distinct objects which are exactly similar to each other.[27] In other words, exact similarity amounts to identity. Given this Leibnizian '*identitas indiscernibilium*'-thesis, the exact-similarity variant of the Universalizability Principle is transformed into a tautology: it is reduced to an assertion that any self-identical object exhibits self-identical moral properties.

In our model, this line of reasoning may be reconstructed as follows: If Leibniz is right, then no two distinct situations are exactly similar to each other.

Leibnizianism: For any $w, v \in \mathbf{W}$, if $w\mathbf{C}v$, then $w = v$.

Since **C** is reflexive, Leibnizianism implies that **C** coincides with the identity relation on **W**. In consequence, given Leibnizianism, the condition (u) turns out to be equivalent to a tautology:

$$w = v \ \& \ w\mathbf{D}u \ \to \ \exists z(v\mathbf{D}z \ \& \ u = z).$$

What arguments can be given in support of Leibnizianism? It may be maintained that this principle should be accepted for both epistemological and metaphysical reasons.

The Epistemological Argument. We know certain 'modal' facts about particular individuals. For instance, we know that a given person, a, could have lacked a certain property which he actually possesses. To put it differently, we know that, in some possible world (situation), a lacks a certain property which he possesses in the actual world (situation). Such a knowledge, however, presupposes that we are able to

---

[27] Cf. G. W. Leibniz, *Philosophical Papers and Letters*, transl. and ed. by L. E. Loemker, second ed., Dordrecht, 1969, pp. 286, 308, 505 f., 643, 687, 699 f.

identify individuals *across* possible worlds. Now, the only way to do this is to compare the non-individual, 'qualitative' characteristics of the individuals involved. If they share a sufficient number of such characteristics, then we are dealing with one and the same individual, and not with two distinct ones. From this it follows, in particular, that, if *w* and *v* are copies, so that any individual in one of them is exactly similar to some individual in the other one, then the individuals involved must be identical with each other. In result, *w* and *v* turn out to be one and the same world. But this means that the possibility of transworld identification presupposes Leibnizianism.

The Metaphysical Argument. One can deny Leibnizianism only if one thinks of objects as 'bare' substrata, as the propertyless 'bearers' of properties. Only then are the objects not reducible to 'bundles of qualities' and, in consequence, only then can two exactly similar, i.e., qualitatively identical, objects be numerically different. But then the absurdity of the substratum metaphysics constitutes in itself a powerful argument in support of Leibnizianism.

Both these arguments rest on some controversial assumptions which have been recently critized by Saul Kripke.[28] According to him, it is neither the case that (1) transworld identification depends on comparisons in terms of 'qualitative' characteristics, nor is it true that (2) the substratum metaphysics constitutes the only alternative to the Berkeleyan 'bundle of qualities' theory.

As for (1), Kripke claims that this assumption "depends on the wrong way of looking at what a possible world is".[29] We tend to think of it from the point of view of an observer, who is given only qualities but not the individual identities of the individuals involved. But this is simply a wrong picture. A possible world is not anything that we observe or discover. "'Possible worlds' are *stipulated*, not *discovered* by powerful telescopes."[30] In consequence, transworld identifications are done directly, by stipulation. They do not rest on any previous qualitative

---

[28] S. A. Kripke, 'Naming and Necessity', *Semantics of Natural Language*, ed. by D. Davidson and G. Harman, Dordrecht, 1972.
[29] Ibid. p. 266.
[30] Ibid. p. 267.

comparisons. "... it is *because* we can refer (rigidly) to Nixon [or any other particular individual, for that matter—W. R.], and stipulate that we are speaking of what might have happend to *him* (under certain circumstances), that 'transworld identifications' are unproblematic in such cases."[31]

As for (2), Kripke thinks that the question "are these objects *behind* the bundle of qualities, or is the object *nothing but* the bundle?" presents a 'false dilemma'. "Neither is the case; this table ... has ... properties and is not a thing without properties, behind them; but it should not therefore be identified with the set, or 'bundle', of the properties nor with the subset of its essential properties."[32] "If a quality is an abstract object, a bundle of qualities is an object of an even higher degree of abstraction, not a particular."[33]

Even though Kripke's reasoning seems rather convincing, it does not follow that Leibnizianism must be false. What we may conclude is only that this principle cannot be established with the help of the arguments which we have presented above. But it is still possible that its validity may be proved in some other way.

Because of this possibility, we should inquire whether there is a variant of the Universalizability Principle which does not rest on the concept of exact similarity, and which, therefore, does not get trivialized by the assumption of Leibnizianism. What comes to mind immediately is that we could switch from exact similarity to a 'relevant' one. As applied to situations, this new variant of the Universalizability Principle amounts to the claim that, as long as we permute or replace individuals but keep everything else in the situation if not exactly similar, then at least relevantly similar from the moral point of view, the obligation-structure will not undergo any drastic changes. In order to express this thesis in our framework, we have to switch from C to a weaker relation R. If wRv, then the individuals involved in v may be different from those in w, and, *in addition*, w and v may differ in some non-individual, qualitative respects—but *only* insofar as these qualitative differences are morally irrelevant. We shall often refer to R as 'relevant similarity', but it would be more appropriate to describe this

---

[31] Ibid. p. 270.
[32] Ibid. p. 272.
[33] Ibid. p. 272.

relation as 'relevant similarity up to (but not necessarily including) individual characteristics'. R is assumed to be an equivalence relation, just like C. However, while C-similarity entails R-similarity, the entailment does not hold in the other direction. R-similar situations need not be copies of each other. Therefore, Leibnizianism does *not* transform R into identity.

Now, consider the R-variant of (u):

(ur) wRv & $wDu \rightarrow \exists z(vDz$ & $uRz)$.

Clearly, (ur) represents the relevant-similarity version of the Universalizability Principle, just as (u) represents the same principle when formulated in terms of exact similarity.

1.4. *General outline*

Part I. We shall start by defining the concept of a *universalistic condition on* $C(R)$ *and* D. It will be shown that (u) and (ur) are only special examples of such universalistic conditions, among many others. For instance, consider the following condition on C and D:

(cu) wCv & $uDw \rightarrow \exists z(zDv$ & $uCz)$.

According to this condition, copies of deontic alternatives to any situation are themselves deontic alternatives to some copies of that situation.

(cu) is an example of a universalistic condition on C and D which would probably be accepted, along with the condition (u), by any person who subscribes to the Universalizability Principle in its informal version. We shall try to determine the *strongest* universalistic conditions on C and D and on R and D which such a person might be willing to adopt. It will be argued that, where C-conditions are concerned, one may go considerably further than in the case of their R-variants.

Different universalistic conditions on $C(R)$ and D are not only formally similar to each other. It will be seen that the similarity goes deeper: For any such condition, we shall define the set of its 'components', and we shall show that, as we move to increasingly stronger universalistic conditions, the really important components (those which express the ideas of ethical 'universalism' and 'supervenience') remain constant.

If there are so many universalistic conditions on $C(R)$ and D, how are we to account for the special position of (u) and (ur)? In order to answer this question, we shall define the concept of a *proper* universalistic condition. It will be seen that (u) and (ur) are the *simplest* conditions of this kind.

A person who does not accept Leibnizianism may feel that the formulations of the Universalizability Principle in terms of C and R are essentially equivalent. He may feel that (u) and (ur) say the same thing. We shall try to account for this feeling by showing how to derive the equivalence of the components of (u) and (ur) from a certain assumption concerning the interconnection of C and R. However, the final justification of this assumption will be deferred to Part III (section 10.2).

Part II. We shall start by introducing into our model the concept of *automorphism* (due to Kit Fine). Like C, this concept belongs to the family of exact similarity notions. Here, however, the exact similarities involved concern not just situations (as in C's case) but also *individuals* existing in these situations. To be more precise, let us say that an individual a in a situation w is *indiscernible* from an individual b in a situation v if they share all their non-individual, 'qualitative' characteristics, that is, if a in w is exactly like b in v. Thus, two situations are copies if every individual in one of them is indiscernible from some individual in the other. Now, an automorphism, p, is a permutation on individuals and situations such that, for every a and w, if a exists in w, then a in w is indiscernible from $p(a)$ in $p(w)$. (As a matter of fact, it will be seen that the notions of indiscernibility and automorphism are interdefinable. On the other hand, C is a considerably weaker concept— while it is definable in terms of automorphisms, the definition does not go the other way round.)

We shall use the concept of automorphism to present a new formulation of the exact-similarity version of the Universalizability Principle. It will turn out that this formulation, to which we shall refer as (U_A), is considerably stronger than the strongest possible universalistic condition on C and D.

Here follow some of the questions concerning the concept of automorphism which we shall try to answer: What is the connection between

Leibnizianism and the theory of automorphisms? Are there any plausible intermediate standpoints between strict Leibnizianism and the position which constitutes its extreme opposite? What permutations on individuals are extendible to automorphisms?

In connection with the last question we shall define the concept of *minimal kind* (of individuals). Another important concept which we shall consider is the notion of *purity* (due to Fine). It will turn out that (U_A) is equivalent to the claim that **D** is a pure relation.

In the last chapter of Part II, we shall use the concept of automorphism in order to define **D**-*homogeneity*. Intuitively speaking, a set of individuals is **D**-homogeneous if its members belong to the same moral category (in the sense in which all persons, for instance, might be thought to belong to the same moral category, even though, depending on circumstances, they may have very different rights and duties). It will turn out that moral theories which are incompatible with (U_A) may be represented as claims that certain minimal kinds are not **D**-homogeneous. We shall present a classification of such non-standard theories and we shall also consider certain 'normality conditions' which all moral theories should satisfy, independently of whether they are compatible with (U_A) or not.

Part III. The assumption of Leibnizianism trivializes all the formulations of the Universalizability Principle which depend on the notion of *exact* similarity. At the same time, the formulations of this principle in terms of *relevant* similarities often meet with the objection that the concept of relevance is essentially unclear or at least in need of clarification. Thus, we are presented with a dilemma: either we should prove that Leibnizianism is false, or we must produce a satisfactory analysis of relevance. Neither of these options seems to be especially attractive.

In Part III, we shall see that there is a *third* way out of this difficulty. In particular, we shall argue that, in order to understand the relation **C** as well as **R**, we need the concept of a *universal* (=non-individual) aspect of a situation. By an aspect of a situation we shall understand a proposition, i.e., a state of affairs, i.e., a set of situations (compare section 1.3 above). We shall therefore introduce a distinction between universal and individual propositions into our model. The concept of a universal proposition will be assumed as primitive, but we shall characterize it formally, by a number of axioms. As our next step, we shall use this concept in order to formulate a certain condition on the model. We shall refer to this condition as (uu). It will be seen that, from the *anti*-Leibnizian point of view, (uu) and (u) are equivalent to each other. Thus they are equally good formulations of the Universalizability Principle. On the other hand, the assumption of Leibnizianism, which trivializes (u), leaves (uu) untouched. Therefore, since (uu) does not presuppose the concept of relevance or relevant similarity (in fact, it does not depend on any concept of similarity at all), it may be argued that this condition represents a formulation of the Universalizability Principle which avoids both horns of the original dilemma.

Additional support for this claim will be given by considering the connection between (uu) and (ur). In this context, we shall formulate a number of principles which relate the concepts of universal proposition and relevance to each other. It will be seen that, given these principles, it becomes possible to derive (ur) from (uu).

Finally, we shall consider the connection between the Universalizability Principle and certain *extensions* of Leibnizianism. It will develop that these extensions entail all of our 'similarity'-formulations of the Universalizability Principle—even those in terms of **R** (although being insufficient for the derivation of (uu)). However, it will be argued that such extensions are much less plausible than Leibnizianism itself.

Part IV. While the Universalizability Principle belongs to ethics, analogous principles may be found outside the ethical domain. For instance, it is often claimed that *causal* properties—just like the moral ones—do not depend on the individual aspects of things, or, to put it differently, that (exactly or relevantly) similar things (phenomena, events, processes) exhibit similar causal characteristics.

The fact that 'universalizability principles' of this kind appear in many different areas makes one wonder whether it is possible to derive all of them from some common basic intuition. They all seem to rest on an idea that individuals (or better, the individual aspects of things) somehow do not matter, that they are unimportant, irrelevant. Obviously, however, this idea needs clarification before we may form any judgment about its value.

We shall start our discussion of this problem by defining the concept of *universalizability*, as applied to propositional operations (operations which transform propositions, or their sequences, into propositions). It will turn out that the condition (uu) amounts to the claim that a certain propositional operation, definable in terms of **D**, is *universalizable*. Analogous universalizability claims may be formulated about many other propositional operations, which fall outside the domain of ethics. (Thus, we shall consider operations such as 'causal closure', 'unavoidability closure', complement, etc.)

As our next step, we shall introduce into our model a new set of objects, which we shall call 'intensional propositions'. The propositions in our old sense (sets of situations) will be now referred to as 'extensional'. It will be seen that different intensional propositions may be true in precisely the same situations. We shall argue that even intensional propositions may be divided into universal and individual ones, though this division is not a mere replica of the corresponding division in the field of extensional propositions. Nevertheless, the two divisions may be considered to be connected with each other. We shall formulate a principle which specifies the precise nature of this connection. It will be argued that this principle constitutes a formal equivalent of the idea that 'individuals do not matter'. In particular, we shall show how to use the principle in question in derivations of (uu) and of other, non-moral universalizability claims. Thus, all such claims turn out to be reducible to a common basis.

In the context of the distinction between intensional and extensional propositions, we shall define the 'intensional' analogue, C^i, of our relation **C**. It will be argued that a certain difficulty connected with the exact similarity version of the Universalizability Principle[34] disappears when we make a clear distinction between the extensional and the intensional interpretations of exact similarity—between **C** and C^i.

Finally, we shall consider the relation between our 'Individuals-do-not-matter'-principle and Leibnizianism. Somewhat unexpectedly, it will turn out that, given certain admittedly controversial but not wholly implausible assumptions, these principles may be shown to be *incompatible* with each other. Thus, it is possible that individuals do matter from

---

[34] Cf. footnote 2 above.

the Leibnizian point of view. But then the defense of the Universalizability Principle, as represented by the condition (uu), is, in a sense, more
difficult for Leibnizians than for their opponents. While the latter can
argue for (uu) by tracing it back to a general metaphysical intuition,
this way of defense may be closed for some proponents of Leibnizianism.

PART I

Theory of Universalistic Conditions

CHAPTER 2

Questions

2.1. *The concept of universalistic condition*

Let E be any dyadic relation on **W**. By (ue) we shall understand the condition which results from (u) when all the occurrences of '**C**' in (u) have been replaced by 'E'. Consider, now, the following conditions:

(a) $wEv \ \& \ uDw \ \rightarrow \ \exists z(uEz \ \& \ zDv)^1$

(b) $wEv \ \& \ wDw \ \rightarrow \ vDv$

(c) $wEw' \ \& \ wDvDu \ \rightarrow \ \exists v', u'(vEv' \ \& \ uEu' \ \& \ w'Dv'Du')$

(d) $wEw' \ \& \ wDv \ \& \ wDu \ \& \ v \neq u \ \rightarrow \ \exists v', u'(vEv' \ \& \ uEu' \ \& \ w'Dv' \ \& \ w'Du' \ \& \ v' \neq u')$

(e) $wEw' \ \& \ wDv \ \& \ \neg(vDw) \ \rightarrow \ \exists v'(vEv' \ \& \ w'Dv' \ \& \ \neg(v'Dw'))$

All of them seem to be formally similar to (ue) and to each other. Very roughly, we could characterize this similarity as follows: Let s and s' be sequences of members of **W**. We shall say that s and s' are *E-correlated*, if s and s' are equally long and every member of s has E to the corresponding member of s'. Thus, for instance, $\langle w, v \rangle$ and $\langle w', v' \rangle$ are E-correlated if wEw' and vEv'. s shall be said to be a *w-sequence* if w is the first member of s. By a *D*-property we shall understand, roughly, any property of sequences which can be defined using '**D**' as the only extra-logical predicate (note that identity is assumed to be a logical constant). Some examples of **D**-properties are: (1) being a two-membered sequence such that the first member has **D** to the second member, (2) being a three-membered sequence such that the first member has **D** to the second and the third members and the second

---

[1] The condition (cu), which we have discussed in section 1.4, is the **C**-variant of (a).

member is distinct from the third one, etc. Let us say that an *atomic universalistic condition on E and* **D** is any condition to the effect that, for some specified **D**-property P, for every w, $w' \in$ **W** and every w-sequence s, *if* wEw' and s instantiates P, *then* there exists a w-sequence s' such that s and s' are E-correlated and s' instantiates P.

By a *universalistic condition on E and* **D** we shall understand a (finite or infinite) conjunction of one or more atomic universalistic conditions on E and **D**. This is a very sketchy characterization of the concept of a universalistic condition. A more precise definition shall be given in Chapter 4.

Now it can readily be seen that (ue) and (a)–(e) are all (atomic) universalistic conditions on E and **D**. For example, (ue) can also be expressed as follows: If P is the property of being a two-membered sequence such that the first member has **D** to the second member, then for every w, $w' \in$ **W** such that wEw' and for every w-sequence s which instantiates P, there is a v-sequence s' such that s and s' are E-correlated and s' instantiates P.

The conditions (a)–(e) can be reformulated correspondingly.

By an 'ethical universalist' (or just a 'universalist', for short) we shall mean any person who accepts the Universalizability Principle in its informal version; that is, any person who thinks that 'numerical' differences between individuals are of no consequence from the moral point of view. It seems clear that any ethical universalist will subscribe to conditions such as (u) or (ur), providing, of course, that he is prepared to discuss the matter in terms of our $\langle$**W**, **D**, **C**, **R**$\rangle$ model.

But it also seems clear that our universalist will not rest at that. He will go on and accept *other* universalistic conditions on **C** and **D** and on **R** and **D**, respectively, conditions which are not entailed by (u) and (ur), but which nonetheless 'follow' from his general universalistic position. To give just one example: **C**- and **R**-variants of a condition like (a) seem to be at least as plausible for a universalist as (u) and (ur) themselves. For instance, the **R**-variant of (a) says that, if two situations are relevantly similar to each other (up to individual identities), then, if one of them is a deontic alternative to some situation, the other one must be a deontic alternative to a relevantly similar situation.

In other words, while (ur) is a 'forward-looking' condition which goes from similarities between given situations to similarities between

their deontic alternatives, the R-variant of (a) is 'backward-looking'—
it moves backwards from similarities between the deontic alternatives
to similarities between the initial situations.

A word of caution: A universalist may agree that w and v could be
relevantly similar and still be deontic alternatives to relevantly different
situations. That is, it could be the case that $w\mathbf{R}v$, $u\mathbf{D}w$, $z\mathbf{D}v$ but $\neg(u\mathbf{R}z)$.
To put it differently, similar duties may sometimes arise in dissimilar
circumstances. However, even if this is true, it has nothing to do with
the status of the R-variant of (a). (a) should be carefully distinguished
from the following condition:

(α) $w\mathbf{E}v$ & $u\mathbf{D}w$ & $z\mathbf{D}v$ → $u\mathbf{E}z$.

And it is only the R-variant of (α), but not that of (a) which would be
falsified by cases like the one sketched above.

Analogously, we should not confuse (ue) with

(β) $w\mathbf{E}v$ & $w\mathbf{D}u$ & $v\mathbf{D}z$ → $u\mathbf{E}z$.

The R-variant of (β) entails that no situation can have relevantly
different deontic alternatives. And this seems to be a very counter-
intuitive thesis. (Note that neither (α) nor (β) are universalistic conditions in our sense of the term.)

But if, aside from (u) and (ur), there are other universalistic conditions which are plausible to a universalist, then we have a problem on
our hands: What are the strongest plausible universalistic conditions on
$\mathbf{C}$ and $\mathbf{D}$ and on $\mathbf{R}$ and $\mathbf{D}$, respectively? We shall discuss this question
in the next chapter. But already now, we can point out that $\mathbf{R}$ is a weaker
relation than $\mathbf{C}$. Therefore, it seems reasonable to expect that the
'optimal' (=the strongest plausible) universalistic condition for $\mathbf{R}$
will prove to be weaker than the corresponding condition for $\mathbf{C}$.

2.2. *Universalism and supervenience*

Let us consider another question: Suppose that 'E' stands for either
'$\mathbf{C}$' or '$\mathbf{R}$'. Imagine a person who has already accepted (ue) and now
moves on to increasingly stronger universalistic conditions. In a way, it
seems that such a movement does not represent any *normative* development. The fundamental idea of ethical universalism is already embodied
in (ue). We do not gain any new ethical insights when we go from (ue)

to, say, (ue)&(a) or to (ue)&(a)&(b). It is as if everything really important has already been said when we have taken the first step—when we have accepted (ue).

One could try to explain this, admittedly vague, intuition as follows: Let us introduce a new equivalence relation on $\mathbf{W}$ which we shall call $\mathbf{R}^+$. '$w\mathbf{R}^+v$' shall be read as "w and v are similar in *all* morally relevant respects". Note the difference between $\mathbf{R}$ and $\mathbf{R}^+$. $\mathbf{R}$ is the relation of relevant similarity *up to* individual identities. Thus, *if* numerical (individual) aspects of a situation *were* morally relevant, then two R-similar situations would *not* have to be $\mathbf{R}^+$-similar.

Clearly, $\mathbf{R}^+ \subseteq \mathbf{R}$. $\mathbf{R}^+$-similarity implies R-similarity. Consider now the following condition:

(RR⁺) $\mathbf{R} \subseteq \mathbf{R}^+$.

That is, if two situations are similar in all morally relevant 'non-individual' (= 'qualitative') respects, then they are similar in *all* respects which are morally relevant. In other words, individual aspects of a situation are irrelevant from the moral point of view.

But is this not what we mean by ethical universalism? If indeed this is so, then what is the connection between **(RR⁺)** and different universalistic conditions on $\mathbf{R}$ and $\mathbf{D}$? Consider any such condition, for instance (ur). It seems clear that, while (ur) presupposes ethical universalism, such a universalistic background is no longer present in (ur⁺)—the $\mathbf{R}^+$-variant of (ur). (ur⁺) should be acceptable even to a non-universalist.[2] By this, we do not mean to say that (ur⁺) is a wholly trivial principle. It embodies the idea that $\mathbf{D}$ is a 'grounded' relation. If (ur⁺) is true, then, for any pair $\langle w, v \rangle \in \mathbf{D}$, the $\mathbf{D}$-connection between w and v is not arbitrary. It depends on the morally relevant aspects of both situations. (Otherwise, it would be possible for two $\mathbf{R}^+$-similar situations to have $\mathbf{R}^+$-dissimilar sets of deontic alternatives. This is precisely what (ur⁺) denies.) One often hears that moral properties (or relations) are 'supervenient', i.e., that they are grounded in other, non-moral properties of objects. Perhaps we could say that conditions such as (ur⁺) express the idea that $\mathbf{D}$ *is a supervenient relation*. (The distinction between (ur) and (ur⁺) corresponds to an analogous distinc-

---

[2] (ur +) seems to be a formal equivalent of the Generalization Principle which has been formulated by Marcus Singer (cf. section 1.2 above).

tion between two different interpretations of the slogan: 'similar causes, similar effects'. If by similarity we mean here 'similarity in *all* causally relevant respects', then the resulting principle amounts to the claim that the causality relation is supervenient. But if we, from the beginning, restrict our attention to purely non-individual respects of comparison, then we get a condition which says that numerical differences between events are of no causal consequence.)

Now, note that (RR^+), together with the uncontroversial assumption that $R^+ \subseteq R$, entails that $R = R^+$. Therefore, given (RR^+), (ur) and (ur^+) become equivalent conditions. Consequently, (ur) may be thought to be a combination of two ideas: the idea of ethical universalism expressed by (RR^+) and the idea of supervenience embodied in (ur^+). More generally, if α is any universalistic condition on R and D, then (RR^+) together with the R^+-variant of α entail α.

Thus, when we move to increasingly stronger universalistic conditions on R and D, we do not develop our *universalistic* position. Instead, this process manifests our increasing demands on the connection between R^+ and D. Therefore, it is rather the *supervenience* idea which undergoes development.

2.3. *Different universalistic conditions and their interrelations*
Unfortunately, what we have said above is not the whole story.

In the first place, it seems as if the supervenience idea somehow is already fully embodied in (ur^+). *That* we accept (ur^+) depends on our belief that moral properties and relations do not hang in the air, so to speak. This belief does not become any stronger or more sophisticated as we move from (ur^+) to R^+-variants of (a) or (b).

Secondly, even if our explanation works satisfactorily for the universalistic conditions in terms of R, it loses all its appeal as soon as we move to C. Consider the condition:

(CR^+) $C \subseteq R^+$.

That is, copies are similar to each other in *all* morally relevant respects. In other words, purely individual, numerical differences between situations are morally irrelevant.

But is this not the *same* universalistic insight as that which we have expressed by (RR^+)?

As we indicated, C is included in R. Thus, (RR^+) entails (CR^+). But it is less clear whether the entailment holds in the opposite direction. In Section 1.3, we noted that the question of exact similarity which does *not* reduce to identity is a controversial metaphysical issue. If we accept Leibnizianism, then C turns out to be an identity relation. But then, since it is trivial that R^+ is reflexive, (CR^+) becomes a condition which is acceptable even to a non-universalist, even to a person who rejects (RR^+). On the other hand, if we allow that C is *not* an identity relation, then it certainly seems as if (CR^+) and (RR^+) are saying the same thing. In such a case, however, we should expect the functions of (RR^+) and (CR^+) to be exactly analogous. Thus, if our explanation above has been correct, we should be able to generate different universalistic conditions on C and D from their R^+-variants together with (CR^+), precisely as we have done with the universalistic conditions in terms of R.

Unfortunately, it does not work that way. While we could safely assume that $R^+ \subseteq R$, it is obvious that R^+ is *not* included in C. Two situations may be R^+-similar without being copies of each other. Thus, even if we accept (CR^+), we must still deny that C and R^+ coincide. Consequently, *no* universalistic condition on C and D is derivable via (CR^+) from the corresponding condition on R^+ and D. What we can derive from $(ur^+)\&(CR^+)$ is *not* (u), but only a weaker condition:

$$wCv \ \& \ wDu \ \rightarrow \ \exists z(uR^+z \ \& \ vDz).$$

In other words, (CR^+) allows us only to replace 'R^+' by 'C' in the *antecedent* of (ur^+). In order to make an analogous replacement in the *consequent* of (ur^+) we need the converse of (CR^+) and this we do not have. Thus, it seems that we have to go deeper into the whole problem, if we are to give an explanation which works for both C and R. And, as we pointed out above, such an explanation should account for our feeling that not only the universalistic idea but *also* the idea of supervenience do not undergo any changes as we move to increasingly stronger universalistic conditions on C and R, respectively.

Incidentally, the above discussion points to one more question which we should try to answer. If (RR^+) and (CR^+) make equivalent claims, then it would be interesting if we could show that this equivalence is formally derivable from some plausible condition which relates C, R and R^+ to each other. Of course, such a condition must not be question-begging. It cannot just stipulate that (RR^+) and (CR^+) are equivalent. And, clearly, its plausibility will have to be dependent on the assumption that C is *not* an identity relation, since, without this assumption, there is no equivalence to explain.

2.4. *Special status of* (u) *and* (ur)

Let 'E' stand for either 'C' or 'R'. When one looks at different possible universalistic conditions on E and D, one gets the impression that (ue) has a special position among them. One cannot account for this feeling just by referring to what we have said above. Admittedly, everything 'really important' has already been said when we have accepted (ue). But this is a property which (ue) shares with other universalistic conditions, for instance, with (ue)&(a) or with (ue)&(a)&(b). Nor is it the case that (ue) is the 'simplest' universalistic condition. According to every reasonable criterion of simplicity, conditions like (a) or (b) are at least as simple as (ue). Thus, the special status of (ue) remains to be explained.

Let us sum up our questions:

1. What are the optimal (= strongest plausible) universalistic conditions on C and D and on R and D, respectively? (By 'plausible', we mean, of course, 'plausible to an ethical universalist'.)
2. How can we express *the* universalistic idea embodied in different universalistic conditions?
3. How can we express *the* idea of supervenience embodied in different universalistic conditions?
4. How can we derive the equivalence of (CR^+) and (RR^+)?
5. What, if anything, can account for the special status of (u) and (ur)?

CHAPTER 3

Answers

3.1. *The strongest plausible universalistic condition on* **C** *and* **D**

Let E be any dyadic relation. In the next chapter, we shall prove that the following principle is the *strongest* universalistic condition on E and **D**.

(u_{ED}^i) If wEv, then there is a permutation f on **W** such that
  (1) $f(w)=v$, (2) for every $u \in$ **W**, $uEf(u)$, and
  (3) for every $u, z \in$ **W**, u**D**z iff $f(u)$**D**$f(z)$.

'i' in '(u_{ED}^i)' stands for 'isomorphy'. (u_{ED}^i) is namely a kind of isomorphy condition. In order to see that, let us introduce a number of definitions. Let f be any function and E', E'' any n-place relations. *The domain of* f, $\mathbf{d}(f)$, is the set of x such that, for some y, $f(x)=y$. *The range of* f, $\mathbf{r}(f)$, is the set of y such that, for some x, $f(x)=y$. f is a function *from X into Y*, if $\mathbf{d}(f)=X$ and $\mathbf{r}(f) \subseteq Y$. f is *onto* Y if $\mathbf{r}(f)=Y$. f is *one–one* if, for every x, x' in the domain of f, if $f(x)=f(x')$, then $x=x'$. f is a *permutation on X* if f is a one–one function from X onto X. Define $f(E')$ as the set of n-tuples $y_1, ..., y_n$ such that, for some $x_1, ..., x_n \in \mathbf{d}(f)$, $\langle x_1, ..., x_n \rangle \in E'$ and $\langle y_1, ..., y_n \rangle = \langle f(x_1), ..., f(x_n) \rangle$.

Let us say that f is an *isomorphy between* $\langle X, E' \rangle$ *and* $\langle Y, E'' \rangle$ if f is a one–one function from X onto Y such that $f(E')=E''$. If, in addition, $X=Y$ and $E'=E''$, then we shall say that f is an *E'-isomorphous permutation on X*. If E is any 2-place relation, then f shall be said to be an *E-function* if $f \subseteq E$ (i.e., if, for every x in $\mathbf{d}(f)$, $xEf(x)$).

(u_{ED}^i) can now be expressed as follows:

If wEv, then there is a **D**-isomorphous E-permutation on **W** which assigns v to w.

Let (u_{CD}^i) be the **C**-variant of (u_{ED}^i). Is (u_{CD}^i) plausible to an ethical universalist? If the answer is affirmative, then we have found the strongest plausible condition on **C** and **D**.

How can a universalist argue for (u_{CD}^i)? He can reason as follows:

According to the Universalizability Principle in its informal version, exactly similar objects have exactly similar moral characteristics. Thus, in particular, for any two exactly similar situations, w and v, and for any moral characteristic α of w, v must exhibit some exactly similar moral characteristic, β. Now, assume that this feature α of w consists in w's being the first member of a certain sequence s of situations such that s instantiates a certain D-property P. Then it seems that β will consist in v's being the first member of a certain sequence s' which also instantiates P and which is exactly similar to s. Now, if s and s' are exactly similar, then this must mean at least that s and s' are equally long and that their corresponding members are exactly similar to each other. That is, s and s' are C-correlated. Thus, the Universalizability Principle seems to commit us to the following condition on C and D:

For any w, $v \in$ W, for any w-sequence s of situations, and for any D-property P such that s instantiates P, if wCv, then there is a v-sequence s' of situations such that s and s' are C-correlated and s' instantiates P.

In the next chapter, we shall prove that this condition is just another formulation of the condition (u^1_{CD}). Thus, insofar as the former would be acceptable to an ethical universalist, the same must apply to the latter.

3.2. Segerberg's proposal and the concept of alternative

Even if (u^1_{CD}) is the strongest universalistic condition on C and D, one may still wonder whether it is not possible to make the connection between C and D even stronger. Let E and E' be any relations on W such that E is dyadic and E' is n-place. We shall say that E' is *superuniversalizable over E* iff, for all n-tuples s and s', if s and s' are E-correlated and $s \in E'$, then $s' \in E'$. To put it differently, E' is superuniversalizable over E iff, for any E-permutation on W, $f(E') = E'$. In particular, E' shall be said to be *strictly pure* iff E' is superuniversalizable over C.

In a paper on deontic logic, Krister Segerberg proposes the following two conditions on R$^+$ and D:

(S1) wDv & vR^+u $\rightarrow$ wDu

(S2) wDv & wR^+u $\rightarrow$ uDv[3]

---

[3] Krister Segerberg, "Some Logics of Commitment and Obligation", *Deontic Logic: Introductory and Systematic Readings*, ed. by R. Hilpinen, Dordrecht 1971. Actually, Segerberg uses a symbol 'S' instead of 'R$^+$', but his explication of S coincides exactly with our explication of R$^+$.

Now, since R^+ is reflexive, it is easy to prove that (S1) and (S2) taken together are equivalent to:

(S3) **D** is superuniversalizable over R^+.

If we are universalists, then we must claim that $C \subseteq R^+$. But then, if (S3) is correct, there is no reason not to accept a similar condition for **C** and **D**:

(S4) **D** is superuniversalizable over **C**.

That is, **D** is strictly pure.

It can be proved that conditions like (S1)–(S4) are *not* universalistic, in our sense of the term. Thus, in particular, (S4) entails the strongest universalistic condition on **C** and **D**, (u_{CD}^1), but *not* vice versa. According to (u_{CD}^1), we can find, for every pair of copies $\langle w, v \rangle$, *some* **D**-isomorphous **C**-permutation on **W** which assigns v to w. But (S4) makes a much stronger claim: if wCv, then *every* **C**-permutation on **W** which assigns v to w is **D**-isomorphous.

Thus we have shown that (S4) is stronger than the strongest universalistic condition on **C** and **D**. But is (S4) an acceptable condition? It can hardly be considered as such, at least not as long as **D** is the relation which connects members of **W** with their deontic *alternatives*.

Let us introduce a new symbol, '**A**', in order to represent the general concept of *alternative*. We shall say that wAv if v is an alternative to w in the sense that v constitutes some possibility which is *open* from the point of view of w. For instance, if, in w, John makes a promise, then there is no such alternative to w in which John has *not* made any promise. On the other hand, it may well be that John fulfills his promise in some of the alternatives to w, but not in others.

Generally speaking, the obligations obtaining in a situation are discharged in some of its alternatives but not necessarily in all of them. Thus, **D** is included in **A** but not vice versa. Now, consider the **A**-variant of (u_{CD}^1)—the condition which results from (u_{CD}^1) when we replace **D** with **A**. We shall refer to this condition as (u_{CA}^1). According to it, for every pair of copies, w and v, there exists an **A**-isomorphous **C**-permutation on **W** which assigns v to w. In other words, there exists a **C**-permutation f on **W** which assigns v to w and which does not disturb any **A**-connections: for every $v, u \in W$, vAu iff $f(v)Af(u)$. (u_{CA}^1) seems to be a very intuitive principle. As a matter of fact, it is not necessary to be an ethical universalist in order to accept this. Even if (u^1_{CD}) is denied, it is still possible to subscribe to its A-variant. Analogously, it seems indisputable that the A-variant of (u) will be accepted even by a person who rejects (u). On the other hand, one can easily show that **A** is not strictly pure and that this is the reason why **D** cannot be strictly pure either.

Suppose that w is a situation in which John makes some promise to Jim (but not vice versa—Jim makes no promises at all) and assume that w has an alternative, v, in which John fulfills his promise. Assume that u is a copy of v. The only difference between u and v consists in that John's position in v is, in u, occupied by Jim, and vice versa. John 'moves' in u to the position which, in v, belonged to Jim. Clearly, in u, it is *Jim* who fulfills his promise to *John*. But then u cannot be among w's alternatives since, in w, Jim has not made any promises at all! Thus, while wAv and vCu, it is *not* the case that wAu.

Since **A** is not strictly pure, the same applies to **D**. In the above example, we could have stipulated that the alternative v, in which John discharges his promise, is a *deontic* alternative to w. At the same time, u is not among w's deontic alternatives, simply because u does not constitute any alternative for w at all!

What we have just said applies equally well to conditions such as (S1)–(S3). **D** does not satisfy any of them, *because* **A** is not super-universalizable over R^+. In particular, relevantly similar situations do not have to have *identical* alternatives. It is quite enough if their alternatives are *relevantly similar* to each other. And vice versa: Relevantly similar members of **W** do not have to be alternatives to the *same* situation. It is fully sufficient if they are alternatives to *relevantly similar* situations.

3.3. *The strongest plausible universalistic condition on* **R** *and* **D**

We proceed now to the second part of our first question: What is the strongest plausible universalistic condition on **R** and **D**?

We can approach this problem by looking at one of the conditions entailed by (u^1_{CD}):

(f) If wCv, then there is a one–one C-function from **D**(w) onto **D**(v).

(By $D(w)$ we understand the set of deontic alternatives to w. $D(v)$ is the analogous set for v.)

(f) entails, in particular, that $D(w)$ and $D(v)$ have the same cardinality.

By (f_R) we shall mean the R-variant of (f) and we shall denote the A-variant of (f_R) by (f_{RA}). That is, we get (f_R) from (f) by substituting R for C. And if we also replace D with A, we get (f_{RA}).

Now, it seems that (f_R) is not a very plausible condition. We encounter here a situation with which we are already familiar. The implausibility of (f_R) *depends* on the implausibility of its A-variant, (f_{RA}).

To illustrate what we have just been talking about, let us suppose that, in w, we can do something in two different ways. For instance, we can repay some debt of ours either in cash or with a cheque. Assume that the difference in question is quite trivial and wholly *irrelevant* from the moral point of view. Suppose also that the number of w's alternatives is finite. Now, consider a situation, v, which is quite similar to w. Specifically, we have in v a debt hanging over us, our financial resources are the same as in w, etc. However, for some trivial reason, we do not have any cash available. Thus, in v, we must repay our debt with a cheque, if at all. Now, we would argue that w and v are R+-similar and therefore even R-similar to each other. If a difference between two possible ways of doing things is morally irrelevant, then even the fact *that* there are such different possible ways of acting seems morally irrelevant (if not always, then at least at times). Nevertheless, the number of alternatives open in v is *less* than that in w. Thus, we have found a case in which (f_{RA}) is invalid. While w and v are R-similar to each other, $A(v)$, i.e., the set of alternatives to v, is smaller than $A(w)$. Therefore, there is no one–one function from $A(w)$ onto $A(v)$.

Or course, the same example can be used in order to show the implausibility of (f_R)—just suppose that, in both w and v, it is obligatory that we repay our debt. Then $D(v)$ will turn out to be smaller than $D(w)$. In other words, (f_R) is unacceptable *because* (f_{RA}) is unacceptable.

All this suggests that plausible universalistic conditions on R and D (and on R and A) should be free from any *cardinality considerations*.

To put it differently, but still somewhat vaguely:

We know that a universalistic condition on E and $\mathbf{D}$ is any condition to the effect that, for some specified set Γ of $\mathbf{D}$-properties, for every $P \in \Gamma$, for every w, v and every w-sequence s, if w and v are E-similar and s instantiates P, then there is an E-correlated v-sequence s' which also instantiates P.

Now, we shall say that, for every universalistic condition α, α is a *homomorphy condition* (or just *h-condition*, for short) if the $\mathbf{D}$-properties specified in α are definable without the use of the identity predicate. It is well known that the concept of cardinality presupposes the notion of identity. Thus, h-conditions will, of necessity, be cardinality-neutral.

Although it may not be obvious at first glance, neither $(u^i_{E\mathbf{D}})$ nor (f) are h-conditions. On the other hand, if we look at the list of universalistic conditions presented in section 2.1, we can see that all of them, with the exception of (d), are h-conditions.

A much more precise characterization of h-conditions will be given in Chapter 4. There, we shall also explain why we call them *homomorphy* conditions in the first place. Also, we shall prove that the following formula represents the *strongest h-condition* (on E and $\mathbf{D}$):

($u^h_{E\mathbf{D}}$) If wEv, then there is an E-function f from $\mathbf{W}$ into $\mathbf{W}$ such that (1) $f(w) = v$, and (2) for every u, $z \in \mathbf{W}$, $u\mathbf{D}z$ iff $f(u)\mathbf{D}f(z)$.

The difference between ($u^h_{E\mathbf{D}}$) and ($u^i_{E\mathbf{D}}$) should be duly noted. While the latter demands that f shall be a permutation on $\mathbf{W}$, i.e., a one–one function from $\mathbf{W}$ *onto* $\mathbf{W}$, the former stipulates only that f is a (possibly many–one) function from $\mathbf{W}$ *into* $\mathbf{W}$.

If we are correct, plausible conditions on $\mathbf{R}$ and $\mathbf{D}$ should be cardinality-neutral. That is, they should all be h-conditions. And perhaps this is the *only* restriction that has to be made. In other words, it is a fair guess that the $\mathbf{R}$-variant of ($u^h_{E\mathbf{D}}$) is the strongest *plausible* universalistic condition on $\mathbf{R}$ and $\mathbf{D}$.

However, we do not wish to press this point. Perhaps we ought to be more cautious and choose some condition weaker than ($u^h_{\mathbf{R}\mathbf{D}}$). In any case, however, it seems that our final choice will depend not on any 'moral' considerations but on our beliefs concerning the connection between $\mathbf{R}$ and $\mathbf{A}$. We shall choose ($u^h_{\mathbf{R}\mathbf{D}}$) *if* we think that ($u^h_{\mathbf{R}\mathbf{A}}$) is a plausible principle. Of course, this applies to other cases as well. If we believe that the connection between **R** and **A** is strong, then we shall opt for a strong connection between **R** and **D**. If, on the other hand, we feel that **R** and **A** are rather weakly connected, then the same will apply to **R** and **D**.

As we already know, we have the same sort of dependence in the case of **C**. (u_{CD}^1) is plausible only under the assumption that its **A**-variant is satisfactory. Thus, all universalistic conditions on **D** are grounded in the corresponding universalistic conditions on **A**.

3.4. *Components of universalistic conditions*

What we have said above suggests an answer to our second and third questions. It seems that now we can identify both the universalistic and the supervenience idea present in different universalistic conditions on **D** and also give an account of what happens when we proceed from one such condition to another.

We shall start with an example. Consider a universalistic condition such as (u). If what we have said above is correct, then (u) is acceptable only if its **A**-variant, (u_A), is acceptable. ((u_A) says that, for any two **C**-similar situations, any alternative to one of them is **C**-similar to some alternative to the other.) But how can we *derive* (u) from (u_A)? Clearly, for such a derivation, we need additional premises. We have said previously that *the* universalistic component common to the different universalistic conditions on **C** and **D** seems to be embodied in the principle (**CR**$^+$), according to which **C** is included in **R**$^+$. If (**CR**$^+$) is true, then the numerical, individual differences between situations are morally irrelevant. Thus, the whole problem reduces to the following question: If we already have (**CR**$^+$) and (u_A), what *more* do we need in order to derive (u)? Well, (**CR**$^+$) connects **C** with **R**$^+$, and (u_A) connects **C** with **A**. Thus, in order to derive the corresponding connection between **C** and **D**, we need some principle which relates **R**$^+$ and **A** to **D**. A very natural proposal would be:

The Bridging Condition (B): wDv & wR^+u & vR^+z & $uAz \rightarrow uDz$.

Informally: If z is an *alternative* to u and if z is **R**$^+$-similar to some deontic alternative to a situation which is **R**$^+$-similar to u, then z is a *deontic* alternative to u.

Thus, according to (B), R^+ functions as a 'bridge' between D and A: for any two situation-pairs, s and s', if s belongs to D, s is R^+-correlated with s' and s' belongs to A, then s' must belong to D.

This seems to be a very reasonable demand.

We have said before, in connection with Segerberg's proposal, that D is not superuniversalizable over R^+. In other words, if $\langle w, v \rangle \in D$ (which implies that $\langle w, v \rangle \in A$) and if $\langle w, v \rangle$ is R^+-correlated with $\langle u, z \rangle$, then it need not be the case that $\langle u, z \rangle \in D$. This is so simply because it may happen that $\langle u, z \rangle \notin A$!

It is just this possibility that the Bridging Condition excludes. Thus, we may say that this condition replaces the implausibly strong principle put forward by Segerberg.

Can we now derive (u)? Actually, this is quite simple. Observe that (CR^+)&(B) entails the C-variant of (B):

$$wDv \ \& \ wCu \ \& \ vCz \ \& \ uAz \ \rightarrow \ uDz.$$

Suppose, now, that (1) wDv and (2) wCu. We have to show that (3) there is such z that vCz and uDz. Since $D \subseteq A$, (1) entails that (4) wAv. By (u_A), (2) and (4) imply that there is z such that (5) uAz and (6) vCz. And it follows from (1), (2), (5) and (6), via the C-variant of the Bridging Condition, that (7) uDz. (7) and (6) give us (3). Q.E.D.

The same type of reasoning applies to other universalistic conditions on C and D which we have been discussing. For instance, (u_{CD}^i) follows from (u_{CA}^i)&(CR^+)&(B). Also, when we change from C to R, we only have to replace (CR^+) by (RR^+). Thus, to give just one example, (u_{RD}^h) follows from (u_{RD}^h)&(RR^+)&(B).

While (CR^+) and (RR^+), respectively, represent the unchanging universalistic component common to different universalistic conditions on C and D and on R and D, (B) seems to embody the supervenience idea common to all such conditions. Let us elaborate on this thought a little.

A moral property, P, is supervenient if the morally relevant aspects of an object determine univocally whether the object in question instantiates P or not. In other words, P is supervenient if, for any objects x and y, if x and y are similar in *all* morally relevant respects, then Px iff Py. Now, we can treat D as a property of situation-pairs.

Instead of saying that $w\mathbf{D}v$, we shall say that $\langle w, v\rangle$ has the property $\mathbf{D}$. The question arises: when are two situation-pairs, say $\langle w, v\rangle$ and $\langle u, z\rangle$, similar to each other in all morally relevant respects? Clearly, such a similarity presupposes that $w\mathbf{R}^+u$ and $v\mathbf{R}^+z$. But this is not fully sufficient. Suppose that $w\mathbf{A}v$. Of course, we can treat $\mathbf{A}$ as a property of situation-pairs, exactly as we have done with $\mathbf{D}$. Now, it seems indisputable that $\mathbf{A}$ is a morally relevant property of $\langle w, v\rangle$—since, without having $\mathbf{A}$, $\langle w, v\rangle$ cannot have $\mathbf{D}$ either. At the same time, we already know that $\mathbf{A}$ is not superuniversalizable over $\mathbf{R}^+$. Thus, it seems that $\mathbf{A}$ is a morally relevant aspect of $\langle w, v\rangle$ which is *not* reducible to the morally relevant aspects of w and v, taken in isolation. Consequently, relevant similarity between $\langle w, v\rangle$ and $\langle u, z\rangle$ presupposes not only that (1) $w\mathbf{R}^+u$ and (2) $v\mathbf{R}^+z$, but also that (3) $w\mathbf{A}v$ iff $u\mathbf{A}z$. And perhaps this is all that we need as far as $\mathbf{D}$ is concerned. Perhaps, if (1)–(3) are satisfied, then $\langle w, v\rangle$ instantiates $\mathbf{D}$ iff $\langle u, z\rangle$ does. The Bridging Condition rests on this assumption. In fact, it is easy to ascertain that the following holds: The Bridging Condition is true iff (1)–(3) imply that $w\mathbf{D}v$ iff $u\mathbf{D}z$. (This equivalence depends on the symmetry of $\mathbf{R}^+$ and the fact that $\mathbf{D}\subseteq\mathbf{A}$.)

If we are correct, then, the Bridging Condition is the nearest thing to the supervenience principle for $\mathbf{D}$ that we can obtain in our framework. In the same way as $(\mathbf{RR}^+)$ and $(\mathbf{CR}^+)$, respectively, constitute the universalistic component of different universalistic conditions on $\mathbf{R}$ and $\mathbf{D}$ and on $\mathbf{C}$ and $\mathbf{D}$, the Bridging Condition may be said to be the supervenience component common to all of them.

We would like to make one additional point here. It could be said that some moral relations are more supervenient than others. A (moral) relation shall be said to be *strictly supervenient* if it depends *only* on the (morally) relevant aspects of the relata, taken in isolation. Thus, it does not depend on the *connections* between the relata, as far as these connections themselves are not strictly supervenient.

In particular, a (moral) relation on $\mathbf{W}$ is *strictly supervenient* iff it is superuniversalizable over $\mathbf{R}^+$.

We already know that $\mathbf{D}$ is *not* strictly supervenient. On the other hand, in terms of $\mathbf{D}$ and $\mathbf{R}^+$ it is easy to define at least one strictly supervenient relation: $\{\langle w, v\rangle : \exists u, z(u\mathbf{R}^+w \ \& \ z\mathbf{R}^+v \ \& \ u\mathbf{D}z)\}$. Given that $\mathbf{R}^+$ is transitive, it is easy to show that this relation is superuniversalizable over R^+. As a matter of fact, R^+ itself is strictly supervenient. Another, and more interesting example of a strictly supervenient relation will be given below.

Incidentally, note that (CR^+) entails that every strictly supervenient relation is strictly pure (but not vice versa).

Let us return, however, to our main problem. It seems as if we have found a general way of looking at universalistic conditions on **D**. Such a condition, α, can be, so to speak, 'divided' into three independent components: the universalistic component $((CR^+)$ or (RR^+), depending on whether α is formulated in terms of **C** or **R**), the supervenience component = the Bridging Condition, and the A-variant of α.

Of course, these components are not literally *parts* of α, since none of them is derivable from α. The derivation goes instead in the opposite direction—*from* the components of α *to* α itself. However, if we are correct, the following seems to be the case:

Let **Comp**(α) be the conjunction of the components of α. From the logical point of view, α is weaker than **Comp**(α). But, at the same time, it seems as if the plausibility of the former presupposes the plausibility of the latter.

What happens when we move from α to another universalistic condition on **D**, say α'? The first two components of α do not change. What *does* change is the A-variant of α. It gets replaced by the A-variant of α'. Thus, when we move to new, increasingly stronger universalistic conditions, the universalistic and supervenience components remain constant. The whole process reflects only our increasing understanding of the connection between **A** and **C** (or **R**).

3.5. *Normal universalistic conditions*

At this point we must make an important qualification. Let E stand for **C** or **R** and consider the condition (e) from section 2.1:

(e) wEw' & wDv & $\neg(vDw) \rightarrow \exists v'(vEv'$ & $w'Dv'$ & $\neg(v'Dw'))$.

Let (e_A) stand for the A-variant of (e). That is, (e_A) is exactly like (e) but with **A** substituted for **D**.

Now, it is easy to prove that (e) does *not* follow from **Comp**(e). In other words, it may be the case that $E \subseteq R^+$, (e_A) is true, the Bridging Condition is valid and still there are w, w' and v such that w and w'

are E-similar, v is a deontic alternative to w but not vice versa, and there is *no v'* such that v' satisfies the consequent of (e). To illustrate: Let $E = \mathbf{R}^+ = \{\langle w, w'\rangle, \langle w', w\rangle\} \cup \{\langle u, u\rangle : u \in W\}$. Define $\mathbf{A}$ as $\{\langle w, v\rangle, \langle v, w\rangle\} \cup \{\langle u, u\rangle : u \in W\}$ and assume that $\mathbf{D} = \mathbf{A} - \{\langle v, w\rangle\}$. One can easily check that, in such a model, all the components of (e) turn out to be true without (e) being true.

Let us say that a universalistic condition α on E and $\mathbf{D}$ is *normal* iff α follows logically from $\mathbf{Comp}(\alpha)$, together with the assumptions that $\mathbf{D} \subseteq \mathbf{A}$, that $\mathbf{D}$ is serial and that E is an equivalence relation.

We have just seen that some universalistic conditions on E and $\mathbf{D}$ are *not* normal.

(As a matter of fact, our definition of normality may be simplified somewhat. When we prove that a given condition α is normal, we always use (B) and the universalistic component of α ($E \subseteq \mathbf{R}^+$) *only* to derive the E-variant of (B):

(BE) $w\mathbf{D}v \ \& \ wEu \ \& \ vEz \ \& \ u\mathbf{A}z \ \rightarrow \ u\mathbf{D}z.$

Thus, we do not have to refer to these two components at all in our definition of normality. We can replace both of them by (BE):

(α_{ED}) is *normal* iff it follows logically from (α_{EA}) and (BE), together with the assumptions that $\mathbf{D} \subseteq \mathbf{A}$, that $\mathbf{D}$ is serial and that E is an equivalence relation.)

Now, what shall we say about this problem? At first sight, it seems as if our approach is not as general as we have thought it to be. If α is 'abnormal' then it cannot be generated from its own components. But then we have no explanation of what happens when we accept such an α.

On the other hand, this difficulty is perhaps only spurious. If we take a second look at the condition (e), then we see that it would be wholly arbitrary to accept it as our *optimal* universalistic condition on E and $\mathbf{D}$. Conditions like (e) are too 'particular', so to speak, to be accepted *in isolation*. They always appear as parts of more 'general' universalistic conditions, which are no longer abnormal. For instance, it would be very unnatural to accept (e) without at the same time accepting its 'positive' analogue:

(e′) *wEw′* & *wDv* & *vDw* → ∃*v′*(*vEv′* & *w′Dv′* & *v′Dw′*).

And the conjunction of (e) and (e′) is no longer abnormal.

Thus, we have no real difficulty here. Our approach allows us to divide universalistic conditions into normal and abnormal. At the same time, when we look for the optimal universalistic condition on *E* and **D**, the abnormal conditions seem to be unworthy of consideration. Therefore, the normality-abnormality distinction, instead of creating difficulties, proves to be of some value.

Actually, what troubles us is *not* that some conditions are abnormal, but rather that there are too *few* of them! One of the questions we wanted to answer concerned the supposed special status of (u). Now, we have already seen that (u) is *not* the simplest universalistic condition on **C** and **D**. Thus, simplicity alone is not sufficient to explain the special position of (u). But perhaps something weaker is true: perhaps (u) is at least the simplest *normal* condition on **C** and **D**? Unfortunately, the C-variants of (a) and (b), which are at least as simple as (u), are both normal.

What we need, therefore, is to find some important characteristic of (u) which would be even more restrictive than normality. Then we could combine that characteristic with simplicity in order to explain the special status of (u).

We think that this can be done. But, to achieve this, we have to go a little deeper in our analysis.

3.6. *Deep components of universalistic conditions*

As we know, **D** is included in **A**. But what, precisely, is the connection between these two relations? It seems that the concept of *deontic alternative* must be somehow definable in terms of the notion of *alternative*. The simplest proposal would be to treat deontic alternatives as those alternatives which are at least as good as any other alternative to a given situation. Thus, **D** is definable in terms of **A** and some *preference order* **B** on situations. ('**B**' stands for 'better than'.) Can we take it that **B** is a *dyadic* preference order? In other words, is it reasonable to think that there is some 'absolute' criterion for value-comparisons between situations, quite independent from the situation in which the comparison is made? Perhaps, or perhaps not. Perhaps preference

structure changes as we move from one situation to another. A *triadic* **B** will therefore be a safer choice. In what follows, '$\mathbf{B}_w(v, u)$' shall stand for 'v is better than u, with respect to w'. We shall assume that **B** is a *strict partial order:* irreflexive and transitive. That is,

(1) for *no* w, v, $\mathbf{B}_w(v, v)$,

and

(2) if $\mathbf{B}_w(v, u)$ and $\mathbf{B}_w(u, z)$, then $\mathbf{B}_w(v, z)$.

Anybody who thinks that a dyadic **B** would be better may simply assume that, for any w, w', $\mathbf{B}_w = \mathbf{B}_{w'}$ (i.e., that for any u, z, $\mathbf{B}_w(u, z)$ iff $\mathbf{B}_{w'}(u, z)$).

Note that we do *not* assume that **B** is a *weak* order. That is, we do not assume that it is never the case that, for some w, v, u and z, $\neg\mathbf{B}_w(v, u)$ and $\neg\mathbf{B}_w(u, z)$, but still $\mathbf{B}_w(v, z)$. One could argue, perhaps, that such cases are impossible. But this is a controversial issue.

For instance, some persons may think that value-comparisons between situations are not always meaningful. Two wholly 'disparate' situations may prove to be incomparable with each other (with respect to a given w). But, if they are incomparable, then neither is better than the other. At the same time, incomparability is not a 'connected' relation. A situation, u, may be incomparable with both v and z, even though v and z are comparable with each other. If we now suppose that v, as a matter of fact, is better than z (with respect to w), then we have found what we sought: a case where $\neg\mathbf{B}_w(v, u) \& \neg\mathbf{B}_w(u, z)$ is compatible with $\mathbf{B}_w(v, z)$.

Such considerations show that it is better not to assume that **B** is (or is not) a weak order, especially since this issue has no bearing on our present problem.

We can now define **D** in terms of **A** and **B**:

(D) $wDv \leftrightarrow wAv \ \& \ \forall u(wAu \rightarrow \neg\mathbf{B}_w(u, v))$.

That is, v is a deontic alternative to w iff v is an alternative to w and no alternative to w is better than v, with respect to w.

Is such a definition wholly trivial? Some philosophers would disagree. In our model, **D** constitutes a formal representation of the concept of obligation. Therefore, (**D**)—when taken as a definition—embodies the idea that the concept of Obligation is *secondary* to the concept of Value. Of course, such an idea is repulsive to some people. (Kant would be an apt example here.[4]) But even they could perhaps accept (D), not as a definition, but at least as a true equivalence.[5] This is all that we need for our purpose.

Consider now the following condition on **B**:

(SB) **B** is strictly supervenient (= **B** is superuniversalizable over **R**+).

In order to get a better understanding of the claim made by (SB), let us divide it into two parts:

(SB1) If $w\mathbf{R}^+w'$, then $\mathbf{B}_w = \mathbf{B}_{w'}$;
(SB2) If $v\mathbf{R}^+v'$ and $u\mathbf{R}^+u'$, then $\mathbf{B}_w(v, u)$ iff $\mathbf{B}_w(v', u')$.

Providing that **R**+ is reflexive and transitive, (SB) is equivalent to the conjunction of (SB1) and (SB2).

According to (SB2), the preference-order among situations can be determined without looking at the connections between them. For instance, in order to known whether v is better than u (with respect to w), we do not have to find out whether v is an alternative to u or not. The only thing that matters in such value-comparisons are the morally relevant aspects of each of the situations, nothing more. It should be noted that if we make an assumption that **B** is a weak order, then (SB2) reduces to the following simple condition:

For any w, v, and v', if $\mathbf{B}_w(v, v')$, then $\neg (v\mathbf{R}^+v')$.

In other words, if one situation is better than another (with respect to some w), then there must be some morally relevant differences between them.

(SB1) says that relevantly similar situations generate the same preference-orders on **W**. In other words, it is sufficient to know all the morally relevant features of a situation, w, in order to decide what

---

[4] Cf. I. Kant, *Critique of Practical Reason*, translated by L. W. Beck, Indianapolis–New York, 1958, Book I, Chapter II, esp. pp. 65 f.
[5] Providing, of course, that they fix the 'goodness' of a situation, its position in the ordering **B**, by reference to the moral obligations which are discharged in that situation. Thus, according to Kant, the 'supreme' good (in distinction from the 'perfect' good) consists in moral virtue (ibidem, Book I, Chapter II, pp. 114–117)—and the latter concept is definable in terms of the concept of duty.

is good from w's point of view. Of course, if we think that there is no need for a triadic **B**, because he preference-order is the same for *all* situations, then (SB1) becomes redundant.

In what follows, we shall assume that (SB) is a true principle.

What is the relation between (SB)&(D) and the Bridging Condition? Can we derive the latter from the former? At this point, we cannot. However, such a derivation goes through if we add one additional premiss: (u_{R^+A}), i.e., the condition which results from (u) when we, in (u), replace **C** by **R⁺** and **D** by **A**.

As a matter of fact, it can be shown that (u_{R^+A}) is the simplest universalistic condition on **R⁺** and **A** which has that effect. (For our simplicity criteria, see Chapter 4.) Thus, we begin at last to get some support for our feeling that there is something special about conditions such as (u) and its different variants. But more is to come.

It could be said that, if we already have (SB) and (D) at our disposal, then there is no longer any need for the Bridging Condition. Let us say that, for any universalistic condition α on **C(R)** and **D**, the *deep components of α* (**DeepComp(α)**, for short) are:

(1) the universalistic component: (CR⁺) or (RR⁺),
(2) the supervenience component: (SB),
(3) (D),

and

(4) the **A**-variant of α.

The first three components are constant, while the fourth varies in different universalistic conditions.

Now, it is often the case that α is logically derivable from the set of its deep components (without use of the Bridging Condition). Let us see how such a derivation goes through in the case of (u):

It should be noted that (CR⁺)&(SB) entail the **C**-variant of (SB):

(SBC) **B** is superuniversalizable over **C**(= **B** is strictly pure).

Now, suppose that (1) w**D**v and (2) w**C**u. We have to show that (3) there is a z such that u**D**z and v**C**z. By (D), (1) entails that (4) w**A**v. From (2) and (4) it follows, by the **A**-variant of (u), that there is a z such that (5) uAz and (6) vCz. Suppose that (7) $\neg(u$D$z)$. From (5) and (7) it follows, by (D), that, for some z', (8) uAz' and (9) $\mathbf{B}_u(z', z)$. Since **C** is symmetric, (2) and (8), together with the A-variant of (u), imply that there is v' such that (10) wAv' and (11) z'Cv'. Given (SBC), (3), (2), (6) and (11) entail that (12) $\mathbf{B}_w(v', v)$. But, according to (D), (1) is incompatible with (10)&(12). Thus, our hypothesis that $\neg(u$D$z)$ leads to a contradiction. This fact, together with (6), entails (3). Q.E.D.

3.7. *Proper universalistic conditions and the special status of* (u) *and* (ur)

If E is some equivalence relation (like **C** or **R**), then we shall say that a universalistic condition α on E and **D** is *proper* iff α logically follows from **DeepComp**(α), together with the assumptions that **D** is serial and that E is an equivalence relation.

(This definition can be simplified in exactly the same way as the definition of normality. When we prove that α is proper, we always use (SB) and the universalistic component ($E \subseteq \mathbf{R}^+$) *only* in order to derive the E-variant of (SB):

(SBE) **B** is superuniversalizable over E.

Thus, a simpler definition would look as follows: (α_{ED}) is *proper* iff it follows logically from (SBE), (D) and (α_{EA}), together with the assumptions that **D** is serial and that E is an equivalence relation.)

In the next chapter, we shall prove that *every proper condition is normal.* However, there are normal conditions which are *not* proper. In particular, we shall prove that, for any E, (ue)—the E-variant of (u)—is the *simplest proper* universalistic condition on E and **D**.

Thus, propriety is the characteristic of (u) and (ur) we have been looking for. This characteristic seems to be rather important. We have said above that, when we look for the optimal universalistic condition on E and **D**, we should, from the beginning, exclude all abnormal candidates. It seems that we shall do even better if we restrict ourselves to *proper* conditions. It should be noted, in particular, that conditions (u^l_{CD}) and (u^h_{RD}) are both proper.

We have said that (ue) is the simplest proper condition on E and **D**. But perhaps we should go further and claim that (ue) is the *weakest* such condition (i.e., that every proper (α_{ED}) entails (ue))? Unfortunately, this is not the case. Condition (d) from section 2.1 is both proper and independent from (ue):

(d) wEw' & wDv & wDu & $v \neq u$ → $\exists v'$, $u'(vEv'$ & uEu' & $w'Du'$ & $w'Dv'$ & $v' \neq u')$.

But what shall we say about the following possibility? (ue), but not (d), is a *homomorphy* condition. Perhaps, then, (ue) *is the weakest proper homomorphy condition on E and* **D**? We do not pretend to know the answer. This problem, therefore, remains open.

3.8. *The relation between* (**CR**⁺) *and* (**RR**⁺)

We have one question left. Providing that **C** is not an identity relation, how can we show that

(**CR**⁺) $C \subseteq R^+$

and

(**RR**⁺) $R \subseteq R^+$

say the same thing?

Consider the following condition:

(**CRR**⁺) wRv → $\exists u(wR^+u$ & $uCv)$.

(**CRR**⁺) says that **R** is the relative product of **R**⁺ and **C**. If v is **R**-similar to w, then there is a situation which, so to speak, intervenes between v and w: v has a copy which is similar to w in *all* relevant respects.

Since **R**⁺ is reflexive and transitive, (**CRR**⁺) entails that (**CR**⁺) and (**RR**⁺) are equivalent, just as we wished them to be. ((**CR**⁺) follows from (**RR**⁺), given that **R**⁺ is reflexive and that (**CRR**⁺) holds from right to left. And if (**CRR**⁺) holds from left to right and **R**⁺ is transitive, (**CR**⁺) entails (**RR**⁺)). But what is the status of (**CRR**⁺) itself?

(**CR**⁺) and (**RR**⁺) taken together entail (**CRR**⁺). (The proof assumes that **C** is reflexive and **R** is transitive.) Thus, you *must* accept the latter condition, *if* you already are an ethical universalist. At the same time, if you *both* reject universalism *and* accept Leibnizianism,[6] then (**CRR**⁺)

---

[6] As we remember, Leibnizianism consists in the claim that copyhood implies identity (section 1.3 above).

turns out to be an unacceptable condition: it reduces to the claim that R coincides with R^+, and this is, of course, repulsive to any non-universalist.

(**CRR$^+$**) is therefore really interesting only from the point of view of someone who rejects Leibnizianism and, simultaneously, either rejects or, at least, does not yet subscribe to ethical universalism.[7]

How can we persuade such a person that (**CRR$^+$**) should be accepted? We shall defer our answer to this question to Part III (section 10.2). There, we shall see that, for the opponents of Leibnizianism, (**CRR$^+$**) follows from the analysis of the relation R.

3.9. *Conclusions*

Let us sum up our main results:

(1) We have argued that (u_{CD}^i) is the optimal universalistic condition on C and D. As for R, it seems that only (proper) homomorphy conditions on R and D are plausible candidates. Among these, (u_{RD}^h) is the strongest and therefore, perhaps, it is the one that lies best in the optimality contest.

(2)–(3) Every universalistic condition α on E and D, where E stands for either C or R, can be 'divided' into four deep components:

(a) the universalistic component: $E \subseteq R^+$,
(b) the definition of D in terms of the alternative-relation A and the preference order B,
(c) the supervenience component: B is superuniversalizable over E, and
(d) the A-variant of α.

It is only the last component that varies when we move to increasingly stronger universalistic conditions on E and D. The first three components are constant.

(4) The equivalence of different universalistic components—(**CR$^+$**) and (**RR$^+$**)—is derivable from the principle according to which R is the relative product of R^+ and C. However, the status of this principle is, as yet, unclear. We shall return to this problem in section 10.2.

---

[7] Note that (**CRR$^+$**) from right to left is quite trivial—it follows from three assumptions which we have already accepted: (a) $C \subseteq R$, (b) $R^+ \subseteq R$, and (c) R is transitive. Thus, the real issue is whether (**CRR$^+$**) holds from left to right.

(5) A universalistic condition on E and **D** is proper if it is derivable from the set of its own deep components. It seems that only proper conditions are plausible candidates for the optimality title. (ue) turns out to be the simplest proper condition on E and **D**. Possibly, one can also prove that (ue) is the weakest proper homomorphy condition on E and **D**.

CHAPTER 4

Formalities

We assume that **W** can be *well-ordered*. That is, there exists a dyadic relation S on **W** such that S is transitive, anti-symmetric and connected, and, for every non-empty $X \subseteq$ **W**, X contains some w such that, for every $v \in X$, wSv.

Note that it follows from the Axiom of Choice that *every* set can be well-ordered.

Let $\mathbf{O_W}$ be the *lowest* ordinal number such that, for some well-ordering S of **W**, $\mathbf{O_W}$ is the order type of $\langle \mathbf{W}, S \rangle$. (The existence of such $\mathbf{O_W}$ is guaranteed by the fact that **W** can be well-ordered.) To put it differently: We shall think of every ordinal number, x, as the set of all ordinal numbers lower than x. Thus 0 is the empty set, $1 = \{0\}$, $2 = \{0, 1\}$, etc. Now, since **W** can be well-ordered we can choose some such well-ordering S of **W** which is the 'shortest' possible. We can then assign 0 to the first element in such an ordering, 1 to the second and so on. By $\mathbf{O_W}$ we shall then understand that ordinal number which is the set of all ordinal numbers which we have assigned to different members of **W**. Thus, if **W** has n elements, where n is some finite number, $\mathbf{O_W}$ will simply equal n. And if **W** is infinite but denumerable, $\mathbf{O_W}$ will be identical with the set of all natural numbers, etc. Below, we shall refer to members of $\mathbf{O_W}$ as $x, y, ..., x', x'', ..., x_1, x_2, ...,$ etc.

We define now the notion of a sequence. s is a *sequence* iff s is a function from some $x \in \mathbf{O_W}$ higher than zero into **W**. It should be noted that sequences may be infinite and even non-denumerable (providing that $\mathbf{O_W}$ is non-denumerable). Let $\mathbf{l}(s)$ be the domain of s (i.e., the length of s) and define $\mathbf{r}(s)$ as the range of s. To illustrate: the sequence $\langle w, v \rangle$ is a function from 2 into **W**. $\mathbf{l}(\langle w, v \rangle) = 2 = \{0, 1\}$ and $\mathbf{r}(\langle w, v \rangle) = \{w, v\}$. We shall say that s is a *w-sequence* if $s(0) = w$. Thus, a *w*-sequence is a sequence which begins with w.

A sequence s is *exhaustive* if $\mathbf{r}(s) = \mathbf{W}$. An exhaustive sequence contains all the elements of **W**. Obviously, its length equals $\mathbf{O_W}$. If E is a dyadic relation on W and s, s' are sequences of the same length, then we shall say that s is *E-correlated* with s' iff, for every $x \in I(s)$, $s(x) E s'(x)$.

In what follows, we shall use the symbols E, E', E'', ... in order to refer to relations on W. If E is n-place, then we may express it by indexing E with n.

If f is a function with W as domain and E is an n-place relation on W, then $f(E)$ shall stand for the set of n-tuples $\langle v_1, ..., v_n \rangle$ such that for some $w_1, ..., w_n \in W$, $E(w_1, ..., w_n)$ and $\langle v_1, ..., v_n \rangle = \langle f(w_1), ..., f(w_n) \rangle$. If X is a subset of W, then $E | X$, *the restriction of E to X*, shall be the set of n-tuples $\langle w_1, ..., w_n \rangle$ such that $E(w_1, ..., w_n)$ *and* $w_1, ..., w_n \in X$.

Now consider two pairs, $\langle s, E \rangle$ and $\langle s', E' \rangle$, where s, s' are sequences and E, E' are relations on W.

We shall say that $\langle s, E \rangle$ and $\langle s', E' \rangle$ are *isomorphous* iff

(a) E and E' have the same number of places,
(b) $I(s) = I(s')$, and
(c) there is a permutation f on W such that (1) $f(E | r(s)) = E' | r(s')$, and
(2) for every $x \in I(s)$, $f(s(x)) = s'(x)$.

Informally speaking, $\langle s, E \rangle$ and $\langle s', E' \rangle$ are isomorphous if s and s' are equally long and there is a one–one mapping f of W onto itself such that f assigns to every member of s the corresponding member of s' *and*, for every $w_1, ..., w_n$ in the range of s, $E(w_1, ..., w_n)$ iff $E'(f(w_1), ..., f(w_n))$. Note that isomorphy, defined as above, is a very strong notion. In particular, it is stronger than a relation which we could call *internal* isomorphy. $\langle s, E \rangle$ and $\langle s', E' \rangle$ are *internally isomorphous* iff E and E' have the same number of places, $I(s) = I(s')$, and there is a one–one function f from $r(s)$ onto $r(s')$ such that f satisfies the clauses (1) and (2) above. Now, think of W as the set of natural numbers and let $E = E'$ be the relation $\leqslant$ on W. Let s be the sequence: $0, 1, 2, ...$ and define s' as the series of odd numbers: $1, 3, 5, ...$ Then, obviously, $\langle s, \leqslant \rangle$ and $\langle s', \leqslant \rangle$ are internally isomorphous without being isomorphous, since there is no *permutation* on W which to every member of $r(s) = W$ assigns some member of $r(s')$.

We move now to a relation between pairs $\langle s, E \rangle$ and $\langle s', E' \rangle$ which is even weaker than internal isomorphy. $\langle s, E \rangle$ and $\langle s', E' \rangle$ are *homomorphous* iff

(a) E and E' have the same number of places, say n,

(b) $l(s) = l(s')$, and

(c) for any $x_1, ..., x_n \in l(s)$, $E(s(x_1), ..., s(x_n))$ iff $E'(s'(x_1), ..., s'(x_n))$.

Note that s and s' may have the same length without having the same number of distinct members. To illustrate: $s = \langle w, v, u \rangle$ and $s' = \langle w, v, v \rangle$. This means that the homomorphy of $\langle s, E \rangle$ and $\langle s', E' \rangle$ is compatible with the possibility that $r(s)$ and $r(s')$ have different cardinalities.

Some terminological conventions:

An *sr-pair* (sequence-relation pair) is a pair which consists of a sequence and a relation.

Let K be any set of sr-pairs.

K is *canonical* iff, for every $\langle s, E \rangle$, $\langle s', E' \rangle \in K$, E and E' have the same number of places and $l(s) = l(s')$.

The notation '$K_{n,x}$' shall be used in order to refer to a canonical set such that for every $\langle s, E \rangle$ in $K_{n,x}$, E is n-place and $l(s) = x$. We shall also say of such a $K_{n,x}$ that it is *n-place* and *of the length x*.

K is *closed under isomorphy* (*homomorphy*) if, for every $\langle s, E \rangle$, $\langle s', E' \rangle$, if $\langle s, E \rangle \in K$ and $\langle s, E \rangle$ is isomorphous (homomorphous) with $\langle s', E' \rangle$, then $\langle s', E' \rangle \in K$.

If K is n-place and of the length x, then:

Pos(K) is the set of $\langle y_1, ..., y_n \rangle$ such that $y_1, ..., y_n \in x$ and, for *every* $\langle s, E \rangle \in K$, $E(s(y_1), ..., s(y_n))$;

Neg(K) is the set of $\langle y_1, ..., y_n \rangle$ such that $y_1, ..., y_n \in x$ and, for *every* $\langle s, E \rangle \in K$, $\neg E(s(y_1), ..., s(y_n))$;

Id(K) is the set of number-pairs $\langle y_1, y_2 \rangle$ such that $y_1, y_2 \in x$, $y_1 \neq y_2$ and, for *every* $\langle s, E \rangle \in K$, $s(y_1) = s(y_2)$;

NonId(K) is the set of number-pairs $\langle y_1, y_2 \rangle$ such that $y_1, y_2 \in x$ and, for *every* $\langle s, E \rangle \in K$, $s(y_1) \neq s(y_2)$.

$K_{n,x}$ is *non-trivial* iff there is some $\langle y_1, ..., y_n \rangle \in$ **Pos**$(K) \cup$ **Neg**(K) such that, for some y_i $(1 \leqslant i \leqslant n)$, $y_i = 0$.

Now, we shall say that P is an *sr-property* iff P is a non-empty canonical non-trivial set of sr-pairs such that P is closed under isomorphy.[8]

If P is n-place and of the length x, then we may refer to it as '$P_{n,x}$'. By $l(P)$ and $pl(P)$, we shall understand the length of P and its number of places, respectively.

We shall use symbols P, P', ..., P_1, P_2, ... in order to refer to different sr-properties.

If P is an sr-property closed under homomorphy then we shall say that P is a *homomorphous* sr-property.

By P^u we shall understand the set of all sr-pairs $\langle s, E \rangle$ such that s is a 2-membered sequence, E is dyadic and the first member of s has E to the second member. Thus,

$$P^u = \{\langle\langle w, v\rangle, E_2\}: wE_2v\}$$

It is clear that P^u is a 2-place homomorphous property of the length 2. Let us indicate some other examples of sr-properties:

$$P^a = \{\langle\langle w, v\rangle, E_2\rangle: vE_2w\}$$
$$P^b = \{\langle\langle w\rangle, E_2\rangle: wE_2w\}$$
$$P^c = \{\langle\langle w, v, u\rangle, E_2\rangle: wE_2vE_2u\}$$
$$P^d = \{\langle\langle w, v, u\rangle, E_2\rangle: wE_2v \ \& \ wE_2u \ \& \ v \neq u\}$$
$$P^e = \{\langle\langle w, v\rangle, E_2\rangle: wE_2v \ \& \ \neg(vE_2w)\}$$

All of these are 2-place but of varying lengths: $l(P^b)=1$, $l(P^a)=2$, $l(P^c)=l(P^d)=3$. And all, with the exception of P^d, are homomorphous.

Note that every sr-property P can be uniquely represented by the following structure:

$$\langle l(P), pl(P), \mathbf{Pos}(P), \mathbf{Neg}(P), \mathbf{Id}(P), \mathbf{NonId}(P)\rangle.$$

One can prove that, if P is a homomorphous sr-property, then $\mathbf{Id}(P) = \mathbf{NonId}(P) = \varnothing$. In other words, homomorphous sr-properties ignore identity and non-identity relations between members of sequences.

As an example, consider P^u. P^u is uniquely determined by the following description:

---

[8] Instead of talking about **D**-properties of sequences, as we did in the preceding chapters, we may talk about sr-properties of sr-pairs which consist of a sequence and the relation **D**.

$l(P^u) = 2$, $pl(P^u) = 2$, $Pos(P^u) = \{\langle 0, 1 \rangle\}$, $Neg(P^u) = Id(P^u)$
$= NonId(P^u) = \emptyset$.

Descriptions of other sr-properties are analogous.

Γ shall be said to be an *n-place sr-property set* iff Γ is a non-empty set of sr-properties such that, for any $P \in \Gamma$, P is n-place.

If Γ is n-place, then let $pl(\Gamma) = n$. We shall sometimes refer to such Γ as 'Γ_n'. Symbols $\Gamma, \Gamma', \ldots$ shall be used in order to refer to sr-property sets.

Note that sr-properties which belong to the same Γ may *differ in length*. Thus, for instance, $\{P^u, P^b\}$ is an sr-property set, even though $l(P^u) \neq l(P^b)$.

The next definition is crucial:

For any relations E, E' on W such that E is dyadic and E' is n-place, and for any n-place Γ,

E' is *Γ-universalizable over* E iff, for every $P \in \Gamma$, for every $w, v \in W$ and every w-sequence s, *if* wEv and $\langle s, E' \rangle \in P$, then there is such a v-sequence s' that

(1) s is E-correlated with s' and
(2) $\langle s', E' \rangle \in P$.

E' shall be said to be *P-universalizable over* E if E' is $\{P\}$-universalizable over E.

A *universalistic condition on* E_2 *and* E'_n is any condition to the effect that, for some specified Γ_n, E'_n is Γ_n-universalizable over E_2.

Thus, every such condition can be represented by a structure (E, E', Γ').[9] In particular, such a condition is *atomic*, if Γ is a unit-set. If $\Gamma = \{P\}$, then, instead of $(E, E', \{P\})$, we shall simply write (E, E', P). Thus:

(u) $= (\mathbf{C}, \mathbf{D}, P^u)$
(ur) $= (\mathbf{R}, \mathbf{D}, P^u)$
(a) $= (E, \mathbf{D}, P^a)$
(b) $= (E, \mathbf{D}, P^b)$
etc.

If Γ contains only homomorphous sr-properties, then we shall say that Γ is *homomorphous*.

---

[9] Note that, in such a structure, $\mathbf{E'}$ and Γ are supposed to have the same number of places, while $\mathbf{E}$ is dyadic.

(E, E', Γ) shall be said to be a *homomorphy condition on E and E'*, if Γ is homomorphous.

Thus, (u), for instance, is an (atomic) homomorphy condition on **C** and **D**.

Let Γ_n^i be the set of *all n*-place sr-properties, while Γ_n^h shall stand for the set of *all homomorphous n*-place sr-properties.

Clearly, $(E_2 E_n, \Gamma_n^i)$ is the *strongest* universalistic condition on E_2 and E_n' and (E_2, E_n, Γ_n') is the *strongest homomorphy* condition on E_2 and E_n^h.

Consider now the following principles:

$(u_{E_2 E_n}^i)$ If wE_2v, then there is a permutation f on **W** such that (1) $f(w) = v$, (2) for every $u \in \mathbf{W}$, $uE_2f(u)$, and (3) $f(E_n) = E_n$.

$(u_{E_2 E_n}^h)$ If wE_2v, then there is a function f from **W** into **W** such that (1) $f(w) = v$, (2) for every $u \in \mathbf{W}$, $uE_2f(u)$, and (3) for every $u_1, ..., u_n \in \mathbf{W}$, $E_n(u_1, ..., u_n)$ iff $E_n(f(u_1), ..., f(u_n))$.

We shall prove two theorems:

T4.1 $(u_{E_2 E_n}^i)$ is logically equivalent to (E_2, E_n, Γ_n^i),[10]
T4.2 $(u_{E_2 E_n}^h)$ is logically equivalent to (E_2, E_n, Γ_n^h).

T4.1 entails that (u_{CD}^i) is the strongest universalistic condition on **C** and **D**. At the same time, given T4.2, (u_{RD}^h) is the strongest homomorphy condition on **R** and **D**.

Proof of T4.1:

From left to right. Suppose that $P \in \Gamma_n^i$, wE_2v and s is a w-sequence such that $\langle s, E_n \rangle \in P$. By $(u_{E_2 E_n}^i)$, there is a permutation f on **W** such that (1) $f(w) = v$, (2) for every $u \in \mathbf{W}$, $uE_2f(u)$, and (3) $f(E_n) = E_n$. Define s' as the relative product of s and f. That is, s' is the function from $l(s)$ into **W** which to every $x \in l(s)$ assigns $f(s(x))$. Clearly, $l(s) = l(s')$. By (3) it follows that $f(E_n|r(s)) = E_n|r(s')$. And, for every $x \in l(s)$, $f(s(x)) = s'(x)$. Thus $\langle s, E_n \rangle$ and $\langle s', E_n \rangle$ are isomorphous. Therefore, since $\langle s, E_n \rangle \in P$, $\langle s', E_n \rangle$ must also belong to P. And, by (1) and (2), it follows that s' is a v-sequence and that s is E_2-correlated with s'. Q.E.D.

---

[10] 'T4.1' stands for 'the first theorem in Chapter 4'. A similar convention shall be used with respect to definitions. Thus, for example, 'D10.2' should be read as 'the second definition in Chapter 10'.

From right to left. Suppose that wE_2v. Let s be any exhaustive w-sequence. The existence of such s is guaranteed by the fact that W can be well-ordered. Define P as the set of all sr-pairs isomorphous to $\langle s, E_n \rangle$. Since isomorphy is transitive and reflexive, $P \in \Gamma_n^i$ and $\langle s, E_n \rangle \in P$. Therefore, by (E_2, E_n, Γ_n^i), there is a v-sequence s' such that s is E_2-correlated with s' and $\langle s', E_n \rangle \in P$. Thus, $\langle s, E_n \rangle$ and $\langle s', E_n \rangle$ are isomorphous. Since s is exhaustive, it follows from the definition of isomorphy that there is such a permutation f on W that (1) $f(w)=v$, (2) $f(E_n)=f(E_n|\mathbf{r}(s))=E_n|\mathbf{r}(s')=E_n$, and (3) for every $u \in W$, $uE_2f(u)$. Q.E.D.

Proof of T 4.2:

From left to right. Suppose that $P \in \Gamma_n^h$, wE_2v and that s is a w-sequence such that $\langle s, E_n \rangle \in P$. If wE_2v, then, by $(u_{E_2 E_n}^h)$, there is a function f from W into W such that (1) $f(w)=v$, (2) for every $u \in W$, $uE_2f(u)$, and (3) for every $u_1 \dots, u_n \in W$, $E_n(u_1, \dots, u_n)$ iff $E_n(f(u_1), \dots, f(u_n))$. Define s' as the relative product of s and f. Clearly, $\mathbf{l}(s)=\mathbf{l}(s')$. And, by (3), for every $x_1, \dots, x_n \in \mathbf{l}(s)$, $E_n(s(x_1), \dots, s(x_n))$ iff $E_n(s'(x_1), \dots, s'(x_n))$. Thus, $\langle s, E_n \rangle$ and $\langle s', E_n \rangle$ are homomorphous. Therefore, since P is homomorphous and $\langle s, E_n \rangle \in P$, $\langle s', E_n \rangle$ must belong to P as well. From (1) and (2) it follows that s is E_2-correlated with s' and that s' is a v-sequence. Q.E.D.

From right to left. Suppose that wE_2v. Let s be an exhaustive w-sequence without repetitions (i.e., such that for any $x, y \in \mathbf{l}(s)$, if $x \neq y$, then $s(x) \neq s(y)$.). Define P as the set of sr-pairs homomorphous with $\langle s, E_n \rangle$. Since homomorphy is transitive and reflexive, $P \in \Gamma_n^h$ and $\langle s, E_n \rangle \in P$. Thus, according to (E_2, E_n, Γ_u^h), there is a v-sequence s' such that s is E_2-correlated with s' and $\langle s', E_n \rangle \in P$. By the definition of P, $\langle s, E_n \rangle$ and $\langle s', E_n \rangle$ are homomorphous. Consequently, (1) $\mathbf{l}(s)=\mathbf{l}(s')$, (2) for every $x_1, \dots, x_n \in \mathbf{l}(s)$, $E_n(s(x_1), \dots, s(x_n))$ iff $E_n(s'(x_1), \dots, s'(x_n))$. Define f as the set $\{\langle u, z \rangle: \exists x \in \mathbf{l}(s)(s(x)=u \& s'(x)=z)\}$. Since s is exhaustive and without repetitions, f is a function from W into W. Clearly, $f(w)=v$ and, for every $u \in \mathbf{r}(s)=W$, $uE_2f(u)$. And, by (2), we get the consequence that, for every $u_1, \dots, u_n \in \mathbf{r}(s)=W$, $E_n(u_1, \dots, u_n)$ iff $E_n(f(u_1), \dots, f(u_n))$. Q.E.D.

We shall now define the concepts of normality and propriety. But, first, we need some preparatory definitions:

Let E, E', E'' be any dyadic relations on **W**. And let E''' be some triadic relation on **W**.

We shall say that *there is an E-bridge from E' to E''* iff, for every w, v, u, $z \in \mathbf{W}$, *if* $\langle w, v \rangle \in E'$, $\langle w, v \rangle$ *is E-correlated with* $\langle u, z \rangle$ *and* $\langle u, z \rangle \in E''$, *then* $\langle u, z \rangle \in E'$.

E' *is E'''-included in E''* iff

$$E' = \{\langle w, v \rangle : wE''v \ \& \ \forall u(wE''u \ \rightarrow \ \neg E'''(w, u, v))\}.$$

E''' is a *strict partial order* iff, for every w, v, u, $z \in \mathbf{W}$, (1) $\neg E'''(w, v, v)$, and (2) if $E'''(w, v, u)$ and $E'''(w, u, z)$, then $E'''(w, v, z)$. In what follows, we shall write '$E'''_w(v, u)$' instead of '$E'''(w, v, u)$'.

E_n is *superuniversalizable over E* iff, for every $w_1, ..., w_n, v_1, ..., v_n \in \mathbf{W}$, if $\langle w_1, ..., w_n \rangle \in E_n$ and $\langle w_1, ..., w_n \rangle$ is E-correlated with $\langle v_1, ..., v_n \rangle$, then $\langle v_1, ..., v_n \rangle \in E_n$.

E_n is *serial*, if, for every $w \in \mathbf{W}$, there are $v_1, ..., v_{n-1}$ such that $E_n(w, v_1, ..., v_{n-1})$.

Γ is *normal* iff, for every dyadic E, $E' E''$,
if (1) E is an equivalence relation,
   (2) E' is serial,
   (3) $E' \subseteq E''$,
   (4) there is an E-bridge from E' to E'',
   and
   (5) E'' is Γ-universalizable over E,
then E' is Γ-universalizable over E.

Γ is *proper* iff, for every dyadic E, E', E'' and triadic E''',
if (1) E is an equivalence relation,
   (2) E' is serial,
   (3) E''' is a strict partial order,
   (4) E''' is superuniversalizable over E,
   (5) E' is E'''-included in E'',
   and
   (6) E'' is Γ-universalizable over E,
then E' is Γ-universalizable over E.

If $\{P\}$ is normal (proper), then we shall say that P is *normal (proper)*. A universalistic condition (E, E', Γ) is *normal (proper)*, if Γ is normal (proper), E is an equivalence relation and E' is serial.

T4.3 Every proper Γ is normal.

(Consequently, every proper universalistic condition is normal.)

Proof: Suppose that Γ is proper. And let E, E', E'' be any dyadic relations such that (1) E is an equivalence relation, (2) E' is serial, (3) $E' \subseteq E''$, (4) there is an E-bridge from E' to E'', and (5) E'' is Γ-universalizable over E.

We have to prove that (6) E' is Γ-universalizable over E. Define E''' as $\{\langle w, v, u\rangle: \exists w', w'', v', u' \ (w'Ew \ \& \ w''Ew \ \& \ v'Ev \ \& \ u'Eu \ \& \ w'E'v' \ \& \ w''E''u' \ \& \ \neg(w''E'u'))\}$.

We have to show that

(A) E''' is a strict partial order,
(B) E''' is superuniversalizable over E,
and
(C) E' is E'''-included in E''.

Since Γ is proper, (A)–(C), together with (1) and (5), entail (6).

Let us take (A) first. We have to show that (α) E'''_w is irreflexive, and (β) E'''_w is transitive.

Proof of (α): Suppose that $E'''_w(v, v)$. Then, by definition of E''', $\langle w, v\rangle$ is E-correlated with some pairs $\langle w', v'\rangle$ and $\langle w'', v''\rangle$ such that $\langle w', v'\rangle$ but not $\langle w'', v''\rangle$ belongs to E' and $\langle w'', v''\rangle \in E''$. This, however, is impossible, given (1) and (4).

Proof of (β): Suppose that $E'''_w(v, u)$ and $E'''_w(u, z)$. Then, by definition of E''', $\langle w, u\rangle$ is E-correlated with some pairs $\langle w', u'\rangle$ and $\langle w'', u''\rangle$ such that $w'E''u'$, $w''E'u''$ but not $w'E'u'$. But this is impossible, given (1) and (4). Thus E'''_w is *trivially* transitive.

As for (B), the superuniversalizability of E''' over E immediately follows from the fact that E is transitive. It remains to show that (C) is true. In particular, we have to show that, for every $w, v \in \mathbf{W}$,

(C1) If $wE'v$, then (i) $wE''v$ and (ii) $\forall u(wE''u \ \rightarrow \ \neg E'''_w(u, v))$
(C2) If (i) $wE''v$ and (ii) $\forall u(wE''u \ \rightarrow \ \neg E'''_w(u, v))$, then $wE'v$.

Proof of (C1): Suppose that $wE'v$. Then (3) implies that (i) $wE''v$. Suppose that (ii) is false, i.e., that, for some u, (a) $wE''u$ and (b) $E'''_w(u, v)$.

From (b), by definition of E''', it follows that there is some pair $\langle w', v \rangle$ E-correlated with $\langle w, v \rangle$ and such that $w'E''v'$ but $\neg(w'E'v')$. This, however, is impossible, given (1) and (4).

Proof of (C2): Suppose that (i) $wE''v$ and (ii) $\forall u(wE''u \rightarrow \neg E_w'''(u, v))$. It follows from (2), (3) and (ii) that there is some u such that (a) $wE'u$ and (b) $E_w'''(u, v)$. But, by definition of E''', and by the reflexivity of E, (i) together with (a) and (b) entail that $wE'v$. Q.E.D.

We move now to a different problem. In section 3.6, we have shown that (u) is proper. Of course, the propriety of (u) follows from the propriety of P^u:

T4.4 P^u is proper.

Now, we want to prove a stronger result:

T4.5 P^u is the simplest proper sr-property-set.

But before we can do this, we must first say something about our criteria of simplicity.

For any set, X, let $c(X)$ stand for the cardinality of X. If P is an sr-property, then by *the factors of* P we shall understand the following numbers: $l(P)$, $pl(P)$, $c(Pos(P) \cup Neg(P))$ and $c(Id(P) \cup NonId(P))$. $l(P)$ and $l(P')$ shall be said to be *corresponding* factors of P and P'. Analogously for other factors: $pl(P)$ corresponds to $pl(P')$, and so on.
We shall make the following three assumptions:

A1. For any two sr-properties P and P', if *no* factor of P is *higher* than the corresponding factor of P', and if *some* factor of P is *lower* than the corresponding factor of P', then P is *simpler than* P'.

A2. For any two sr-properties P and P', if every factor of P equals the corresponding factor of P', then P and P' are *equally simple*.

A3. For any sr-properties P and P', and for any sr-property set Γ such that Γ contains P' together with some *other* sr-properties, if P is *at least as simple as* P', then P is *simpler* than Γ.

From the definition of propriety, it follows that every proper Γ consists of 2-place sr-properties. Now, it follows from A1, that P^u is simpler than all 2-place sr-properties which are not on the following list:

$P1 = \{\langle\langle w\rangle, E_2\rangle: wE_2w\rangle$

$P2 = \{\langle\langle w\rangle, E_2\rangle: \neg(wE_2w)\}$

$P3 = \{\langle\langle w, v\rangle, E_2\rangle: vE_2w\}$

$P4 = \{\langle\langle w, v\rangle, E_2\rangle: \neg(wE_2v)\}$

$P5 = \{\langle\langle w, v\rangle, E_2\rangle: \neg(vE_2w)\}$

In particular, $P1$ and $P2$ are simpler than P^u, while, according to A2, $P3$–$P5$ have the same degree of simplicity as P^u itself. Therefore A3 entails that P^u is simpler than all 2-place Γ's that are not on the following list:

$\Gamma_1 = \{P1\}, \Gamma2 = \{P2\}, \Gamma3 = \{P3\}, \Gamma4 = \{P4\}, \Gamma5 = \{P5\},$
$\Gamma6 = \{P1, P2\}.$

Now, it is easy but tedious to prove that no Γ on this list is proper. But then T4.5 follows.

PART II

Universalizability and Automorphisms

CHAPTER 5

Introductory Remarks

5.1. *The concept of automorphism*

In this part, we shall be concerned with the *exact-similarity* version of the Universalizability Principle, the one which we have previously been representing in terms of the relation **C** on worlds (situations).

Clearly, **C** is only one exact-similarity relation among many others. We can talk not only about similar worlds, but also about similar sets or worlds, about similar individuals or sets or individuals (in a given world), about similar properties, relations, etc.

One especially interesting type of exact-similarity relation involves *both* worlds *and* individuals. Consider two individuals, *a* and *b*, and two worlds, *w* and *v*, such that *a* exists in *w*, while *b* exists in *v*. We shall say that *a in w is indiscernible from b in v* (in symbols, $\mathbf{Ind}(a_w, b_v)$), whenever *w* and *v* are copies and *a*'s position in *w* is exactly the same as *b*'s position in *v*. In other words, $\mathbf{Ind}(a_w, b_v)$ whenever *a* in *w* is exactly similar to *b* in *v*. That is, whenever the only differences between *a* and *b* in *v* (if there are any) are purely 'individual', and not 'qualitative'.

This notion of indiscernibility is closely related to the concept of *automorphism*, due to Kit Fine.[1]

Informally speaking, "an automorphism is a permutation of individuals and worlds that respects the structure of each world. It sends each world into one that is isomorphic to it under the permutation of individuals. Intuitively speaking, two worlds are isomorphic if they are qualitatively the same, i.e., if they are the same but for the identity of

---

[1] Cf. Kit Fine, 'Properties, Propositions and Sets', *Journal of Philosophical Logic*, *6* (1977), pp. 135–191.

the individuals in the worlds. Thus an automorphism systematically correlates each world with a qualitative counterpart."[2]

If we want to express Fine's idea in terms of **Ind**, we can say that an automorphism, p, is a permutation on individuals and worlds which assigns worlds to worlds and individuals to individuals and is such that, for every individual a and every world w, a in w is indiscernible from $p(a)$ in $p(w)$.

(Obviously, this implies that w and $p(w)$ are copies of each other or, to use Fine's terminology, that they are 'isomorphic', 'qualitatively the same'.)

Thus, the concept of automorphism is definable in terms of our notion of indiscernibility. It also seems that we could have a definition which goes in the opposite direction: to say that a in w is indiscernible from b in v amounts to saying that a exists in w, b exists in v, and there is an automorphism which assigns b to a and v to w.

Therefore, if we want to talk about exact similarities which involve both individuals and worlds, it does not matter very much whether we choose the relation of indiscernibility or the concept of automorphism as our point of departure. However, we shall follow Fine and take automorphism as the primitive concept.

Note that many other types of exact-similarity relations are easily definable in terms of the concept of automorphism. Two worlds are exactly similar (i.e., they are copies) if there is an automorphism which assigns one of them to the other. Two sets of worlds, X and Y, are exactly similar if there is a one–one mapping of X onto Y which is embeddable in some automorphism. Two individuals, a and b, are exactly similar (in a given world, w) if there is an automorphism which assigns a to b (and w to w). And so on. Thus, it seems that, given the concept of automorphism, we are able to deal with varied contexts which demand the use of the exact-similarity idiom.

In Chapter 6, we shall discuss the notion of automorphism in greater detail. Some of the questions we will then consider are:

What permutations on individuals are extendible to automorphisms?

What is the connection between Leibnizianism and the theory of automorphisms?

---

[2] Ibid. p. 136.

Are there any plausible intermediate standpoints between Leibniz' thesis and its outright rejection?

Fine argues that, given the concept of automorphism, we are able to answer a number of notoriously difficult ontological questions: When is it proper to say that an entity such as proposition, property, or relation *exists in* a given possible world? What does it mean that a proposition or a property is '*non-individual*', 'qualitative'? How can we distinguish between *logical* and non-logical entities, and between those entities which are (essentially) *modal* and those which are not? Finally, what does it mean to say that one entity is a *constituent of* another entity?

We shall examine only one of Fine's questions more closely: the distinction between 'individual' and 'non-individual' entities. Clearly, this distinction must be important for anybody who is interested in universalizability. One could perhaps say that the universalist standpoint in ethics amounts to treating the 'individual' aspects of things as morally irrelevant.

5.2. *The Universalizability Principle as a condition on automorphisms*

According to the exact-similarity version of the Universalizability Principle, exactly similar objects exhibit exactly similar moral properties. How can we express this idea in terms of **D** and the concept of automorphism?

Consider two pairs of worlds, $\langle w, v \rangle$ and $\langle w', v' \rangle$. The pairs in question are exactly similar iff there is an automorphism, p, such that p assigns w' to w and v' to v. At the same time, they exhibit exactly similar moral properties only if they are indistinguishable in terms of **D**, that is, only if $w\mathbf{D}v$ iff $w'\mathbf{D}v'$.

In consequence, we get the following formulation of the Universalizability Principle:

(U_A) **D** stays invariant under automorphisms.

Or, to put it more elaborately,

> for all worlds w and v, and for every automorphism p, $w\mathbf{D}v$ iff $p(w)\mathbf{D}p(v)$.

It is easy to verify that (U_A) entails (u^1_{CD}). We have said above that two worlds are copies iff there is an automorphism which assigns one of them to the other. Therefore, (U_A) implies that, if wCv, then there is an automorphism, p, such that $p(w) = v$ and $\mathbf{D}$ is invariant under p. But then (u^1_{CD}) follows: if wCv, then there is a permutation f on worlds (namely, the restriction of p to $\mathbf{W}$) such that (1) f assigns v to w, (2) for every $u \in \mathbf{W}$, $uCf(u)$ and (3) $\mathbf{D}$ is invariant under f (i.e., $f(\mathbf{D}) = \mathbf{D}$).

Note that (U_A) is much stronger than (u^1_{CD}). Not only because the copy-hood relation used in the latter principle is a less powerful notion than the concept of automorphism, but also because the following weakening of (U_A) would be quite sufficient for the derivation of (u^1_{CD}):

For any pair of copies, w and v, there is *some* automorphism p such that $p(w) = v$ and $\mathbf{D}$ stays invariant under p.

But perhaps (U_A) is *too* strong? Does it not imply that, contrary to what we have said in section 3.2 above, $\mathbf{D}$ is invariant under *every* permutation on W which assigns copies to copies?[3]

In fact, it does not, for the simple reason that such a permutation on W does not have to be embeddable in any automorphism.

To see this, it is sufficient to consider the following example:

Suppose that w, v, $u \in \mathbf{W}$, a and b are the only individuals that exist in w, v and u, a in w is discernible from b in w, and the same applies to v and u, a in v is indiscernible from b in u, and b in v is indiscernible from a in u.

Note that v and u are copies (by our explication of the notion of indiscernibility) and, of course, w is a copy of itself. Consider any permutation f on $\mathbf{W}$ which assigns copies to copies and which, in particular, assigns w to itself and u to v. Suppose that f is embeddable in some automorphism, p. What assignment does p make to a? By our explication of the concept of automorphism, (1) $\mathbf{Ind}(a_w, p(a)_{p(w)})$ and (2) $\mathbf{Ind}(a_v, p(a)_{p(v)})$. Since $p(w) = f(w) = w$, and, in w, no individual distinct from a is indiscernible from a, (1) implies that (3) $p(a) = a$. And since $p(v) = f(v) = u$, and, in u, b is the only individual indiscernible from a in v, (2) implies that (4) $p(a) = b$. But since a and b are distinct

---

[3] Note that the assumption of the invariance of $\mathbf{D}$ under *all* C-permutations is equivalent to the claim that $\mathbf{D}$ is strictly pure, i.e., superuniversalizable over C.

individuals, (3) and (4) cannot both be true. Thus, we have shown that f is not embeddable in any automorphism.

We could also express the same idea as follows:

In our example, the pairs $\langle w, v \rangle$ and $\langle w, u \rangle$ are *not* exactly similar to each other, even though their members are correlated by copyhood ($w\mathbf{C}w$ and $v\mathbf{C}u$). They are not exactly similar since no automorphism simultaneously assigns w to w and u to v. Therefore, there is no reason to believe that the pairs in question are indistinguishable in terms of $\mathbf{D}$. In particular, it may well be the case that $w\mathbf{D}v$ but $\neg(w\mathbf{D}u)$, even though v and u are copies of each other.

It may be argued that the relation $\mathbf{D}$ is a rather crude moral concept. w has $\mathbf{D}$ to v iff v is optimal (good, permitted) with respect to w. One way of understanding this would be to say that $w\mathbf{D}v$ iff v is an alternative to w such that no other alternatives to w are better than v. Now, in many contexts, our interests seem to be more selective. Instead of asking what are the best alternatives to a given w, we consider questions of a different order: What would be the best thing for an individual (or a set of individuals) to do, given that all other individuals act as they do? This suggests that, in many contexts, it may be appropriate to replace the dyadic $\mathbf{D}$ by its triadic variant, which involves both worlds and individuals. Let us say that a world, v, is a *deontic alternative to* a world, w, *with respect to* a set of individuals, X, (in symbols, $\mathbf{d}(X, w, v)$) iff (i) the set, $\mathbf{I}_w$, of individuals existing in w includes X, and (ii) v is a best alternative to w among those in which the behavior of all the members of $\mathbf{I}_w-X$ is kept fixed. In terms of this concept others may be easily defined:

$\mathbf{d}(a, w, v) = \mathrm{df}\ \mathbf{d}(\{a\}, w, v),$
$\mathbf{D}(w, v) = \mathrm{df}\ \mathbf{d}(\mathbf{I}_w, w, v).$

How shall we formulate the Universalizability Principle in terms of $\mathbf{d}$? The answer is obvious:

($\mathrm{U}^{\mathbf{d}}_A$) $\mathbf{d}$ stays invariant under automorphisms.

In other words, for every set X of individuals, for all worlds w and v, and for every automorphism p, $\mathbf{d}(X, w, v)$ iff $\mathbf{d}(p(X), p(w), p(v))$, where $p(X)$ is the set of all individuals assigned by p to the members of X.

Given our definition of $\mathbf{D}$ in terms of $\mathbf{d}$, it is easy to prove that (U_A) is just a special instance of (U_A^d).

We shall not pursue this line of reasoning any further. The relation $\mathbf{d}$ has been introduced here only because we wished to show that our present approach can be easily generalized. Consider any moral concept, e, which can be identified with some set-theoretical construction on individuals and worlds. For any such e, we have the corresponding 'universalizability principle' which simply says that e stays invariant under automorphisms.

However, in this work we shall confine our attention to $\mathbf{D}$. In particular, in Chapter 7, we shall discuss ethical theories which *reject* (U_A). We shall refer to them as *non-universalistic*. In this connection, we shall then consider the following two questions:

Are there any non-trivial conditions on $\mathbf{D}$ and the concept of automorphism which follow from (U_A) but which ought to be accepted even by non-universalists?

Providing that such 'normality conditions' can be found, how are we to distinguish between different possible types of 'normal' non-universalistic theories?

CHAPTER 6

Theory of Automorphisms[4]

6.1. *General axioms*

We shall introduce two new elements into our model: the 'existence'-function **I** which assigns to every world w in **W** the set of all individuals that exist in w, and the set $\mathcal{A}$ of automorphisms. We shall write '$\mathbf{I}_w$' instead of '$\mathbf{I}(w)$' and we shall often use the symbol '**I**' in order to refer to the set of all individuals which exist in one world or another. Thus, '**I**' shall frequently represent the union of all values of the existence-function. If a is an individual, then by $\mathbf{W}_a$ we shall understand the set of all worlds in which a exists, i.e., $\{w \in \mathbf{W}: a \in \mathbf{I}_w\}$. Letters $a, b, c, d, \ldots$ shall stand for individuals (= members of **I**), and we shall refer to the members of $\mathcal{A}$ as $p, p', p'', \ldots$.

At this point it is convenient to introduce some terminological conventions:

If f is a function and X is a subset of f's domain, then $f \,|\, X$ (the *restriction* of f to X) $= \{\langle x, y \rangle: x \in X \,\&\, f(x) = y\}$, $f(X)$ (the f-*image* of X) $= \{y: \exists x \in X(f(x) = y)\}$, and f is *fixed* on X iff, for every $x \in X$, $f(x) = x$. (If f is fixed on $\{x\}$, then we shall also say that f is fixed on x.)

$\breve{f}$ (the *inverse* of f) $= \{\langle y, x \rangle: f(x) = y\}$.

If f and g are functions, then f/g (the *relative product* of f and g) $= \{\langle x, y \rangle: g(f(x)) = y\}$.

If f is one–one and E is an n-place relation on the domain of f, then $f(E)$, the f-*image* of E, is $\{\langle y_1, \ldots, y_n \rangle: \langle \breve{f}(y_1), \ldots, \breve{f}(y_n) \rangle \in E\}$.

Every $p \in \mathcal{A}$ is a permutation on $\mathbf{I} \cup \mathbf{W}$ such that $p(\mathbf{I}) = \mathbf{I}$, $p(\mathbf{W}) = \mathbf{W}$ and $p \,|\, \mathbf{W} \subseteq \mathbf{C}$. Informally speaking, every automorphism permutes individuals into other individuals and worlds into their copies. If we also

---

[4] Below, we shall mark with an asterisk all important principles and definitions which we have appropriated from Fine's paper (cf. footnote 1 above).

assume that every pair of copies is embeddable in some automorphism, then the relation **C** becomes definable in terms of $\mathcal{A}$:

D6.1 $\mathbf{C}(w, v) = \exists p \in \mathcal{A}(p(w) = v)$.

To assume that every instance of **C** is embeddable in some automorphism is to regard **W** as being *complete* in an important sense. We can perhaps explain this by means of an example: Assume that w and v are copies, a in w is indiscernible from b in v, and, for every $c \in \mathbf{I}_v$ distinct from b, a in w is discernible from c in v. Then it follows from our informal explication of the concept of automorphism in terms of indiscernibility that $\langle w, v \rangle$ is embeddable in some automorphism only if, for *every* world $u \in \mathbf{W}$ in which a exists, **W** contains some copy z of u such that a in u is indiscernible from b in z. In other words, D6.1 works satisfactorily only if, for every instance of **C**, **W** contains enough 'corresponding' instances of **C**.

As we may remember, the concept of automorphism is sufficient for the definition of indiscernibility:

D6.2 $\mathbf{Ind}(a_w, b_v) = a \in \mathbf{I}_w \ \& \ b \in \mathbf{I}_v \ \& \ \exists p \in \mathcal{A}(p(w) = v \ \& \ p(a) = b)$.

Below, we shall prove that, given some reasonable assumptions, we could choose **Ind** as our primitive concept and then define $\mathcal{A}$ in terms of **Ind**: $p \in \mathcal{A}$ iff p is a permutation on $\mathbf{I} \cup \mathbf{W}$ such that $p(\mathbf{I}) = \mathbf{I}$, $p(\mathbf{W}) = \mathbf{W}$ and, for every $a \in \mathbf{I}$ and $w \in \mathbf{W}$, (1) if $a \in \mathbf{I}_w$, then $\mathbf{Ind}(a_w, p(a)_{p(w)})$, and (2) if $\mathbf{I}_w = \varnothing$, then $p(w) = w$.

Thus, $\mathcal{A}$ and **Ind** are interdefinable.

We shall stipulate that $\mathcal{A}$ is (a) *non-empty*, (b) *closed under inverses*, and (c) *closed under relative products*.

Non-emptiness of **A** follows from the reflexitivity of **C**. Let p_i be *the identity permutation* on $\mathbf{I} \cup \mathbf{W}$, i.e., the permutation such that, for every $x \in \mathbf{I} \cup \mathbf{W}$, $p_i(x) = x$. Since **C** is thought to be reflexive, p_i satisfies our intuitive description of an automorphism. Thus, $\mathcal{A}$ has at least one member. Analogously, symmetry and transitivity of **C** correspond, respectively, to the closure of $\mathcal{A}$ under inverses and relative products.

It follows from our informal explication of the concept of automorphism that, if $p \in \mathcal{A}$ and $a \in \mathbf{I}_w$, then a in w must be indiscernible from

$p(a)$ in $p(w)$, and, in consequence, $p(a)$ must exist in $p(w)$. We can now formulate this requirement as a condition on $\mathcal{A}$:

Existents–into Existents (EE):

$\forall p \in \mathcal{A} \; \forall w \in \mathbf{W} \; \forall a \in I_w \; (p(a) \in \mathbf{I}_{p(w)})$.

Can there be an automorphism p *distinct* from p_1 but such that $p|\mathbf{I} = p_1|\mathbf{I}$? In other words, can we keep all the individuals fixed and still vary world-assignments? Obviously, it is impossible. Any automorphism which is fixed on individuals must be fixed on worlds as well. Thus:

*Sufficiency of Individuals (SI):

$\forall p \in \mathcal{A} \; (p \text{ is fixed on } \mathbf{I} \to p = p_1)$.

Actually, it seems that we can go even further. Consider any automorphism p and any world w such that p is fixed on all the individuals which *exist* in w. It seems that any such automorphism must be fixed on w as well. In other words, assignments to the individuals which do *not* exist in w cannot influence our assignment to w. Thus:

*Sufficiency of Existents (SE):

$\forall p \in \mathcal{A} \; \forall w \in \mathbf{W} \; (p \text{ is fixed on } \mathbf{I}_w \to p(w) = w)$.

Clearly, (SE) is a strengthening of (SI).

It may seem that principles such as (SI) and (SE) are not sufficiently general. For instance, according to (SI), the identity permutation on $\mathbf{I}$ is embeddable in p_1 but not in any other automorphism. Why not generalize this intuition and say that *no* permutation on individuals is embeddable in two *distinct* automorphisms? Or, what amounts to the same, that

T6.1 $\forall p, p' \in \mathcal{A} \; (p|\mathbf{I} = p'|\mathbf{I} \to p = p')$?

Analogously, (SE) invites the following, seemingly more general principle:

T6.2 $\forall p, p' \in \mathcal{A} \; \forall w \in \mathbf{W} \; (p|\mathbf{I}_w = p'|\mathbf{I}_w \to p(w) = p'(w))$.

However, appearances are misleading. In fact, T6.1 and T6.2 are deducible from (SI) and (SE), respectively.

Proof of T6.1. Suppose that (1) $p, p' \in A$, and (2) $p|\mathbf{I} = p'|\mathbf{I}$. Since A is closed under inverses and relative products, (1) entails that (3) $\breve{p}/p' \in A$. And (2) implies that (4) $\breve{p}/p'$ is fixed on $\mathbf{I}$. Given (SI), it follows from (3) and (4) that (5) $\forall w \in \mathbf{W}(\breve{p}/p'(w) = w)$. Therefore, (6) $\forall w \in \mathbf{W}(\breve{p}/p'(p(w)) = p(w))$. Since $\breve{p}/p'(p(w)) = p'(w)$, (6) implies that (7) $p'|\mathbf{W} = p|\mathbf{W}$. And (7) together with (2) imply that $p = p'$.   Q.E.D.

Proof of T6.2 If $p, p' \in A$ and $p|\mathbf{I}_w = p'|\mathbf{I}_w$, then $\breve{p}/p'$ is fixed on $\mathbf{I}_{p(w)}$ and belongs to A. In consequence, given (SI), $\breve{p}/p'(p(w)) = p(w)$. But then, since $\breve{p}/p'(p(w)) = p'(w)$, $p'(w) = p(w)$.   Q.E.D.

6.2. *Indiscernibility and identity*

According to (SI), an automorphism fixed on individuals must be fixed on worlds. But what about the principle which goes in the opposite direction? Should we stipulate that

Sufficiency of Worlds (SW):
$\forall p \in A$ (p is fixed on $\mathbf{W} \to p = p_1$)?

We can think of the following objection against (SW): Suppose that there are two distinct individuals, a and b, such that, whenever one of them exists, the other one exists as well, and, whenever they exist in a world, w, a in w is indiscernible from b in w. Let p be the permutation on $\mathbf{I} \cup \mathbf{W}$ such that p is fixed on $(\mathbf{I} \cup \mathbf{W}) - \{a, b\}$ and $p(a) = b$. From our informal explication of the concept of automorphism in terms of indiscernibility, it follows that, in the situation described, $p \in A$, even though p is fixed on $\mathbf{W}$ and distinct from p_1.

However, this argument rests on an unreasonable assumption. It seems that there can be *no* such two individuals that are indiscernible from each other in every world in which at least one of them exists. That is, the argument fails if the following is true:

Weak Identity of Indiscernibles (WII):
$\forall a, b \in \mathbf{I}$ ($\forall w \in \mathbf{W}((a \in \mathbf{I}_w \vee b \in \mathbf{I}_w) \to \mathbf{Ind}(a_w, b_w)) \to a = b$).

Informally: If a and b are indiscernible from each other in every world in which at least one of them exists, then a is the same individual as b. It can be shown that (WII) entails (SW). Indeed, it also entails the following strengthening of (SW):

Existential Sufficiency of Worlds (ESW):

$\forall p \in \mathcal{A} \; \forall a \in I$ (p is fixed on $\mathbf{W}_a \to p(a) = a$).

Informally: If an automorphism is fixed on every world in which a exists, then it is also fixed on a.

Note that the relation between (ESW) and (SE) is the same as that between (SW) and (SI). (ESW) and (SW) result from (SE) and (SI), respectively, if we in the latter principles replace all references to individuals by references to worlds and vice versa.

Proof of (ESW) *from* (WII): If $p \in \mathcal{A}$ is fixed on $\mathbf{W}_a$, then, by (EE) and the closure of $\mathcal{A}$ under inverses, (1) for every $w \in \mathbf{W}_a$, $\mathbf{Ind}(a_w, p(a)_w)$, and (2) $\mathbf{W}_a = \mathbf{W}_{p(a)}$. From (1) and (2) it follows that, for every world w, if $a \in \mathbf{I}_w$ or $p(a) \in \mathbf{I}_w$, then $\mathbf{Ind}(a_w, p(a)_w)$. But then (WII) implies that $a = p(a)$.   Q.E.D.

Conditions such as (WII), (ESW) or (SW) are very weak variants of the Leibnizian *identitas indiscernibilium*. If we define Leibnizianism as we have done in section 1.3 above ('copyhood amounts to identity'), then it is easy to prove that Leibnizianism is equivalent to a principle which is considerably stronger than (WII):

Identity of Indiscernibles (II):

$\forall a, b \in I \; \forall w, v \in \mathbf{W} \; (\mathbf{Ind}(a_w, b_v) \to a = b)$.

In other worlds, indiscernible individuals are never distinct from each other.

Proof: By (SW) and D6.1, Leibnizianism is equivalent to the claim that

(a) There are no automorphisms aside from p_1.

Given D6.2, (II) immediately follows from (a). At the same time, D6.2 and (EE) imply that the following condition

(b) Every automorphism is fixed on $\mathbf{I}$

is equivalent to (II). And the equivalence of (a) and (b) follows from (SI).   Q.E.D.

Obviously, (II) trivializes the whole theory of automorphisms since it reduces A to the identity permutation on $I \cup W$ (cf. the condition (a) above).

There is, however, a moderate version of *identitas indiscernibilium* which does not have such shattering consequences. We may agree with Leibniz that, *within a given world*, indiscernibilities amount to identities. At the same time, we can still claim that, as far as the comparisons *across the worlds* are concerned, indiscernible individuals may well be distinct. If this is correct, then we should replace (II) by a substantially weaker principle:

Local Identity of Indiscernibles (LII):
$$\forall a, b \in I \ \forall w \in W \ (\mathbf{Ind}(a_w, b_w) \to a = b).$$

This condition can also be formulated as follows:

T6.3 $\forall p \in A \ \forall w \in W \ (p(w) = w \to p \,|\, \mathbf{I}_w = p_i \,|\, \mathbf{I}_w)$,
T6.4 $\forall p, p' \in A \ \forall w \in W \ (p(w) = p'(w) \to p \,|\, \mathbf{I}_w = p' \,|\, \mathbf{I}_w)$.

T6.4 follows from (LII) by (EE) and the closure of A under inverses and relative products. T6.3 is just a special instance of T6.4 and, of course, T6.3 trivially entails (LII). (LII) is clearly stronger than (WII). While (WII) forbids distinct individuals to be *constantly* 'locally' indiscernible from each other, (LII) treats *every* case of local indiscernibility as a case of identity.

Thus, we have at least four different options with regard to the Problem of Indiscernibles. These are, in the order of strength:

(1) Leibnizianism   = acceptance of (II)
(2) local Leibnizianism = acceptance of (LII) and rejection of (II)
(3) weak Leibnizianism = acceptance of (WII) and rejection of (LI)
(4) 'everything goes'   = rejection of (SW)

The last position is clearly implausible. As for the remaining ones, local Leibnizianism seems to be an attractive compromise between (1) and (3).

6.3. *Automorphous permutations on individuals and minimal kinds*
We proceed now to a different problem. Let f be any function from some $X \subseteq I \cup W$ into $I \cup W$. We shall say that f is *automorphous* iff f is

extendible to an automorphism, i.e., iff there is some $p \in \mathcal{A}$ such that $f \subseteq p$. In particular, a permutation f on I is automorphous iff there is some permutation f' on W such that $f \cup f' \in \mathcal{A}$. The question arises: *What permutations on I are automorphous?*

Strict Leibnizians have their answer ready: according to (II), the identity permutation on I is the only automorphous assignment to I. On the other end of the scale, we find the following, radically liberal, principle:

Homogeneity of Individuals (HI):

> *Every* permutation on I is automorphous.

While (HI) is obviously incompatible with Leibnizianism (if only I contains at least two members), local Leibnizians can accept (HI) without being inconsistent.

It follows from (HI) that, for *every* two individuals a and b, there are such worlds, w and v, that a in w is indiscernible from b in v. Suppose, however, that our set I of individuals includes very different types of objects: persons, animals, inanimate objects. etc. Assume that, in a world w, a is a person, while b is an inanimate object, say, a stone. It follows then from (HI) that there must be some world w such that b in v is indiscernible from a in w. That is, an object which is a stone in one world has to be a person in another world. It is rather difficult to swallow such a result.

Can we find some compromise between (II) and (HI)? That is, can we find some (non-trivial) necessary and sufficient condition of automorphy which avoids both Leibnizianism and the homogeneity assumption? In fact, we can. Consider the following definition:

D6.3 $X \subseteq I$ is a *minimal kind* $= \exists a \in I \ \forall b \in I \ (b \in X \leftrightarrow \exists p \in \mathcal{A} \ (p(a) = b))$.

Informally: a minimal kind is the set of all individuals which different automorphisms assign to some given individual.

T6.5 Every individual belongs to exactly one minimal kind.

Proof: It follows immediately from D6.3 that every individual belongs to some minimal kind. Suppose now that $a \in I$ belongs to two distinct minimal kinds. Then D6.3 implies that there are $b, c, d \in I$ and

$p, p', p'' \in A$ such that (1) $p(b) = a$, (2) $p'(c) = a$, (3) $p''(c) = d$, and (4) for no $p \in A$, $p(b) = d$. (1) & (2) & (3) entail that (5) $p/\breve{p}'/p''(b) = d$. Since p, p', $p'' \in A$ and A is closed under inverses and relative products, $p/\breve{p}'/p'' \in A$. But then (5) contradicts (4). Q.E.D.

Clearly, T6.5 implies that belonging to the same minimal kind is an equivalence relation on **I**. Note also that the following holds:

T6.6 Two individuals, a and b, belong to the same minimal kind iff there is some $p \in A$ such that $p(a) = b$.

Proof: If a and b belong to the same minimal kind, then, by D6.3, there are some $c \in \mathbf{I}$ and $p, p' \in A$ such that $p(c) = a$ and $p'(c) = b$. But then $\breve{p}/p'(a) = b$ and, by the closure of A under inverses and relative products, $\breve{p}/p' \in A$. Q.E.D.

The notion of minimal kind corresponds, roughly, to the Aristotelian concept of *infima species* (lowest species).[5] Two individuals belong to the same lowest species iff they share all their essential properties.[6] But what is an essential property? Perhaps it can be said that essential properties of an individual, a, are necessary properties of a, in the following sense:

P is a *necessary* property *of a* iff a instantiates P in *every* world in which a exists.

However, it seems obvious that necessity is insufficient for essentiality. Essential properties should not only be necessary but also 'non-individual'. They should not depend on the individual identity of objects which instantiate them. For instance, if we want to claim, as Aristotelians certainly would have wanted to, that Socrates and Plato belong to the same lowest species, then we must deny essentiality to such 'individual' necessary properties of Socrates as 'being Socrates', 'being distinct from

---

[5] Cf. especially Aristotle, *Posterior Analytics*, book II, chapter XIII (96a20–97b40), transl. by H. Tredennick, The Loeb Classical Library, Harvard & London, 1960. For other references, see T. W. Organ, *An Index to Aristotle in English*, Princeton 1940, under '*infimae species (atoma eide)*'.

[6] "... not every differentia entails a specific distinction; many differences are attributable (but neither essentially nor *per se*) to things which are specifically the same." (*Posterior Analytics*, loc. cit., 97a13–15.)

Plato', etc. Below we shall suggest an explication of the concept of individual property in terms of $\mathcal{A}$. It will then be seen that, given this explication, our definition of minimal kind works satisfactorily. A minimal kind will turn out to be a maximal set of individuals such that every two members of it have all their non-individual necessary properties in common.

Which sets of individuals constitute minimal kinds? For instance, can we say that there exists a minimal kind of *persons*? Or should we be more generous and count, say, all the sentient beings as belonging to the same minimal kind? Or perhaps, instead, we should be more restrictive and divide the set of persons into different minimal kinds? It is difficult to answer such questions. According to T6.6 two individuals belong to the same minimal kind iff there is an automorphism which binds them together. In other words, a and b belong to the same minimal kind iff there are *possible* worlds, w and v, such that a in w is indiscernible from b in v. But this means that our answer to particular questions concerning extensions of minimal kinds must depend on our conception of *possibility*. We cannot determine what minimal kinds there are unless we know what worlds are possible.

Let f be a function from some $X \subseteq \mathbf{I}$ into $\mathbf{I}$. We shall say that f is *minimal-kind preserving* iff, for every $a \in X$, a and $f(a)$ belong to the same minimal kind. We shall accept the following principle:

Extendibility (E):

> Every minimal-kind preserving permutation on $\mathbf{I}$ is extendible to an automorphism.

Note that (E) follows from both (HI) and (II) but implies neither. In fact, (II) is equivalent to the condition that there are as many minimal kinds as there are individuals, while (HI), given (E), reduces to the claim that all individuals belong to the same minimal kind.

6.4. *Extendibility and complex individuals*

However, even (E) seems to be a controversial principle. One could argue that (E) is correct only if *no individuals are combinations of other individuals*. In order to see this more clearly, let us consider the following example: Suppose that individuals a, b, c and d all belong to the same minimal kind. Assume now that the sets $\{a, b\}$ and $\{c, d\}$ also are individuals. In such a case, it is natural to accept the following condition on automorphisms:

(α) Every automorphism which assigns c to a and d to b must assign $\{c, d\}$ to $\{a, b\}$.

However, (α) is incompatible with (E). Define g as $\{\langle a, c \rangle,\ \langle b, d \rangle,\ \langle \{a, b\}, \{a, b\} \rangle\}$. Since a, b, c and d all belong to the same minimal kind, (E) implies that g is an automorphous function. This, however, contradicts (α).

Thus, (E) is acceptable only if we do not allow members of **I** to be sets, or groups, or wholes, composed of other members of **I**. This is a rather severe restriction, since, in many contexts, it is convenient to ignore the distinction between collections and their members and to treat them all on par, as individuals. However, as we shall see below (section 7.3), having (E) at our disposal allows us to make considerable simplifications in our theory. Therefore, we shall accept this principle but, at the same time, we shall try not to use it whenever other, less controversial, conditions may be used instead. A list of such conditions follows below. Each of the conditions on this list is weaker than (E) in this sense: It is entailed by (E) but, unlike (E), it allows for the possibility that some individuals are constructible from other individuals.

(E1) If $X \subseteq \mathbf{I}$ is a minimal kind, then every permutation on X is automorphous.

(E2) If f is a permutation on **I** such that, for every $w \in \mathbf{W}$, $f|\mathbf{I}_w$ is automorphous, then f is automorphous.

(E3) If f is a permutation on **I** such that, for every $X \subseteq \mathbf{I}$, there is some $p \in \mathcal{A}$ such that $p(X) = f(X)$, then f is automorphous.

Comments. We shall consider (E1) first. Recall our argument against (E). There, we assumed that a, b, c and d belong to the same minimal kind, and that $\{a, b\}$ and $\{c, d\}$ are individuals. And we argued that the function g, which assigns c to a, d to b and $\{a, b\}$ to $\{a, b\}$, is not automorphous. Now, it is very natural to assume that, if $\{a, b\}$ and $\{c, d\}$ belong to **I** at all, then they cannot belong to the same minimal kind as a, b, c and d. Otherwise, we would have to assume that, for instance, there is an automorphism which assigns $\{a, b\}$ to a. This is, surely, a rather absurd position. But if $\{a, b\}$ and $\{c, d)$ belong to a different

minimal kind than a, b, c and d, then there is *no* minimal kind X
and *no* permutation f on X such that $g \subseteq f$. Thus, there is nothing in
(E1) that would commit us to the position that g is automorphous.
Consequently, our argument against (E) is quite irrelevant as far as (E1)
is concerned.

Let us now turn to (E2). Our argument against (E) would be relevant
to (E2) only if there is a permutation f on $\mathbf{I}$ such that (1) $g \subseteq f$ and (2)
for every $w \in \mathbf{W}$, $f | \mathbf{I}_w$ is automorphous. Note that, if $\{a, b\} \in \mathbf{I}$, then, for
some world w, $\{a, b\} \in \mathbf{I}_w$. Now, Fine has formulated the following, very
intuitive existence criterion for sets:

"a set exists in a world iff all its members do."[7]

If we accept this criterion, then the existence of $\{a, b\}$ in w entails
that $a, b \in \mathbf{I}_w$. Therefore, for every permutation f on $\mathbf{I}$ such that $g \subseteq f$,
$g \subseteq f | \mathbf{I}_w$. Since we already know that g is not automorphous, $f | \mathbf{I}_w$
cannot be automorphous either (if f includes g). Thus, we see that no
permutation f on $\mathbf{I}$ can simultaneously satisfy the conditions (1) and
(2) above.

As for (E3), let us note that $g(\{a, b, \{a, b\}\}) = \{c, d, \{a, b\}\}$. Recall
that in our argument against (E) we have assumed that (α) holds,
i.e., that every automorphism which assigns c to a and b to d must
assign $\{c, d\}$ to $\{a, b\}$. If we also assume that the minimal kind
$\{a, b\}$ is different from the minimal kinds of a and b (as we have done
in our comment on (E1)), then it follows that, for *no* automorphism
$p, p\,(\{a, b, \{a, b\}\}) = g(\{a, b, \{a, b\}\})$. But this means that no extension
of g satisfies the antecedent of (E3).

6.5. *Indiscernibility and automorphisms*

We have promised to show that $\mathcal{A}$ is definable in terms of **Ind**, or, more
precisely, that the following equivalence holds:

T6.7 For any permutation p on $\mathbf{I} \cup \mathbf{W}$ such that $p(\mathbf{I}) = \mathbf{I}$ and $p(\mathbf{W}) = \mathbf{W}$,
$p \in \mathcal{A}$ iff, for every $a \in \mathbf{I}$ and $w \in \mathbf{W}$,
  (1) if $a \in \mathbf{I}_w$, then $\mathbf{Ind}(a_w, p(a)_{p(w)})$,
and
  (2) if $\mathbf{I}_w = \varnothing$, then $p(w) = w$.

___
[7] K. Fine, op. cit., p. 136.

Now, given (E) and (LII), T6.7 is easily provable. But both these principles are rather controversial. Therefore, it may be interesting to ask whether we can use some weaker principles for the derivation of T6.7. As a matter of fact, it can be done. Instead of (E), we may use (E2) and we may replace (LII) by the following principle:

Embeddability of Systematic Indiscernibilities (ESI):

> For every $w, v \in W$ and every one–one mapping f of I_w onto I_v, if I_w is non-empty and, for every $a \in I_w$, **Ind**$(a_w, f(a)_v)$, then there is some automorphism p such that $f \subseteq p$ and $p(w) = v$.

In other words, if I_w and I_v can be correlated with each other by means of **Ind**, then this correlation is embeddable in an automorphism which assigns v to w.

Proof of (ESI) *from* (LII): Suppose that w, v and f satisfy the antecedent of (ESI). Then, by the definition of **Ind**, there is $p \in A$ such that $p(w) = v$. We shall show that $f \subseteq p$. Suppose that $f \nsubseteq p$, i.e., that there is some $a \in I_w$ such that $f(a) \neq p(a)$. Then, by (EE), a in w is indiscernible from both $f(a)$ and $p(a)$ in v. This entails (by closure of A under inverses and relative products) that $f(a)$ in v is indiscernible from $p(a)$ in v, despite the fact that $f(a) \neq p(a)$. But this is impossible, given (LII).   Q.E.D.

We see, then, that (ESI) follows from (LII). At the same time, it is a much weaker condition.

In particular, (ESI) seems to be perfectly plausible even from the point of view of someone who lacks any Leibnizian inclinations.

Proof of T6.7 *from* (E2) *and* (ESI):

From left to right. Suppose that $p \in A$. Let a be any member of I_w. By (EE), $p(a) \in I_{p(w)}$. Therefore, by D6.3, **Ind**$(a_w, p(a)_{p(w)})$. Suppose that $I_w = \varnothing$. Then p is fixed on I_w and (SE) entails that $p(w) = w$.   Q.E.D.

From right to left. Suppose that (1) for every a and w such that $a \in I_w$, **Ind**$(a_w, p(a)_{p(w)})$, and (2) if $I_w = \varnothing$, $p(w) = w$, but (3) $p \notin A$.

Case 1: $p|I$ is not automorphous. Therefore, by (E2), there is such $w \in W$ that $p|I_w$ is not automorphous. This is, however, excluded by

(ESI), since, according to (1), $p|I_w$ is a one–one mapping of I_w onto $I_{p(w)}$ such that, for every $a \in I_w$, $\mathbf{Ind}(a_w, p(a)_{p(w)})$.

Case 2: $p|I$ is automorphous, but every automorphism p' which includes $p|I$ is distinct from p. Consider any such automorphism p'. Since $p|I = p'|I$ but $p \neq p'$, there must be some w such that $p(w) \neq p'(w)$. By (ESI), (1) and (2) imply that there is some $p'' \in \mathcal{A}$ such that $p|I_w \subseteq p''$ and $p''(w) = p(w)$. Note that $p'|I_w = p''|I_w$. Therefore, it follows by T6.2 that $p'(w) = p''(w) = p(w)$, contrary to the hypothesis.   Q.E.D.

6.6. *Entities*

We shall now introduce some new definitions. Let us say that all individuals and worlds are (*basic*) *entities*. Further, for any $n \geqslant 1$, if e is a set of n-tuples $\langle e_1, ..., e_n \rangle$ such that $e_1, ..., e_n$ are entities, then e itself is a (*compound*) *entity*. (We assume that, for every entity e, $\langle e \rangle = e$.)

Examples of entities: *propositions* = sets of worlds; *properties* (of individuals) = sets of pairs $\langle a, w \rangle$ such that $a \in I_w$;[8] *relations between worlds* = sets of pairs $\langle w, v \rangle$, where $w, v \in \mathbf{W}$, etc.

It should be noted that, if we allow that some individuals are combinations of other individuals, the division of entities into basic and compound will *not* be dichotomous. For instance, if a, b and $\{a, b\}$ all belong to I, then $\{a, b\}$ is both basic and compound.

If p is an automorphism and e an entity, then we shall define the functions p^0 and p^1 on entities as follows:

(1^0) If e is basic and not compound, then $p^0(e) = p(e)$

(2^0) If e is a set of n-tuples of entities, then $p^0(e) = \{\langle e_1, ..., e_n \rangle: \exists e_1', ..., e_n'$ ($\langle e_1', ..., e_n' \rangle \in e$ & $p^0(e_1') = e_1$ & ... & $p^0(e_n') = e_n$)}.

(1^1) If e is basic, then $p^1(e) = p(e)$.

(2^1) If e is a non-basic set of n-tuples of entities, then $p^1(e) = \{\langle e_1, ..., e_n \rangle:$ $\exists e_1', ..., e_n'$ ($\langle e_1', ..., e_n' \rangle \in e$ & $p^1(e_1') = e_1$ & ... & $p^1(e_n') = e_n$)}.

This distinction can be illustrated as follows: If $a, b, \{a, b\} \in I$, then, since $\{a, b\} = \{\langle a \rangle, \langle b \rangle\}$, $p^0(\{a, b\}) = \{p(a), p(b)\}$, while $p^1(\{a, b\}) = p(\{a, b\})$.

But is there any substantial difference between p^0 and p^1? That is, is there any entity e such that $p^0(e) \neq p^1(e)$? Clearly, such an e would have

---

[8] We presuppose that individuals have properties only in those worlds in which they *exist*.

to be both basic and compound, or it would have to be constructible in terms of entities which are both basic and compound. Thus p^0 and p^1 coincide if our model satisfies the following condition:

Simplicity (S): No entity is both basic and compound.

However, instead of assuming (S), we may simply stipulate that p^0 and p^1 are identical:

Uniqueness (UN): For every $p \in \mathcal{A}$ and every entity e, $p^0(e)=p^1(e)$.

(UN) follows from (S) but not vice versa. In our argument against (E) we have been assuming that (S) is false but that something like (UN) is true. We have presupposed, namely, that, if a, b, c, d, $\{a, b\}$, $\{c, d\}$ all belong to **I**, then:

(α) Every automorphism which assigns c to a and d to b must assign $\{c, d\}$ to $\{a, b\}$.

It is easy to ascertain that (α) is just a consequence of (UN). If (α) were false, then there would be some p such that $p(\{a, b\}) \neq \{p(a), p(b)\}$. But this means that $p^1(\{a, b\}) \neq p^0(\{a, b\})$, contrary to what (UN) demands.

In what follows, we shall presuppose the validity of (UN). Since, given this presupposition, there is no reason to distinguish between p^0 and p^1, we shall use the neutral sign 'p' instead. Thus, if e is an entity, $p(e)=p^0(e)=p^1(e)$.

6.7. *Pure entities*

Let us say that an entity e is *invariant under* an automorphism p iff $p(e)=e$.

D6.4 An entity e is *pure* = e is invariant under automorphisms, i.e., for every $p \in \mathcal{A}$, $p(e)=e$.

We shall say that e is *impure* iff e is not pure.

As a matter of fact, purity may be reduced to something simpler. Let us say that a *non-compound* entity e is *closed under* an automorphism p if $p(e)=e$. And, if e is *compound*, i.e., if e is a set of n-tuples of entities, then e is *closed under* p iff $p(e) \subseteq e$. Clearly, purity entails closure under automorphisms. But the opposite entailment also holds:

T6.8 Entities closed under automorphisms are pure.

Proof: If e is not compound, T6.8 is trivially true. Consider, therefore, an entity e which is a set of n-tuples of entities. Suppose that e is closed under automorphisms but impure. That is, there is some $p \in \mathcal{A}$ such that $e \not\subseteq p(e)$. This means that there is some $\langle e_1, ..., e_n \rangle \in e$ such that $\langle \breve{p}(e_1), ..., \breve{p}(e_n) \rangle \not\in e$. But since $\breve{p}$ is an automorphism (by the closure of $\mathcal{A}$ under inverses) and e is closed under automorphisms, $\langle \breve{p}(e_1), ..., \breve{p}(e_n) \rangle$ must belong to e, contrary to the hypothesis. Q.E.D.

Thus, purity and closure under automophisms are equivalent properties.

Some examples of pure entities:

An individual, a, is pure iff $p(a) = a$, for all $p \in \mathcal{A}$. That is, a is pure iff $\{a\}$ is a minimal kind. More generally, we can prove that

T6.9 Minimal kinds are the smallest non-empty pure sets of individuals.

In other words, X is a minimal kind iff X is a non-empty pure subset of **I** and every non-empty proper subset of X is impure.

Proof: It is enough to show that the following lemmas hold:

L1. Every minimal kind is pure.
L2. Every set of individuals which overlaps, but does not include, some minimal kind is impure.

First, we prove that L1&L2 $\Rightarrow$ T6.9.

If X is a minimal kind, then X is pure by L1, non-empty by definition, and lacks pure non-empty proper subsets by L2.

Suppose now, that X satisfies the right-hand side of T6.9. Since X is a non-empty set of individuals and we know that every individual belongs to some minimal kind, X overlaps some minimal kind, Y. Note that X must include Y, since, otherwise, X would be impure according to L2. Now, Y cannot be a *proper* subset of X, since the purity of Y is implied by L1 and we know that X does not contain any (non-empty) pure proper subsets. Thus $X = Y$. Consequently, X is a minimal kind. Q.E.D.

Proof of L1. Suppose that X is impure. Then, by T6.8, there is some $p \in A$ such that $p(X) \not\subseteq X$. That is, for some $a \in X$ and $b \in I$, $p(a) = b$ and $b \notin X$. According to T6.6, however, the existence of an automorphism which assigns b to a entails that a and b belong to the same minimal kind. Therefore, X is not a minimal kind.   Q.E.D.

Proof of L2: Suppose that X overlaps, but does not include, some minimal kind. Then there are $a, b \in I$ such that $a \in X$, $b \notin X$ and b belongs to the same minimal kind as a. Thus, by T6.6, there is $p \in A$ such that $p(a) = b$. Consequently, $p(X) \not\subseteq X$, that is, X is impure.   Q.E.D.

A *world* is pure iff it does not have any copies. $X \subseteq W$ shall be said to be a *copy-set* iff there is a world w such that X is the set of all copies of w. It is easy to see that minimal kinds and copy-sets are analogous entities. Just as each individual belongs to exactly one minimal kind, each world belongs to exactly one copy-set. The following analogue of T6.9 can be shown to be valid:

T6.10 Copy-sets are the smallest non-empty pure sets of worlds.

A *property*, P, is pure iff, for every $\langle a, w \rangle \in P$ and every automorphism p, $\langle p(a), p(w) \rangle \in P$.

A *proposition* $X \subseteq W$ is pure iff X is closed under copyhood.

6.8. *Purity and universal properties*

Above, we have promised to explicate the distinction between *individual* and *non-individual* (*universal*) properties. Now, it seems clear that every impure property is individual, or, what amounts to the same:

(A) Every universal property is pure.

A property is universal whenever it does not depend on the identity of objects that instantiate it. Thus, if two objects are only *numerically* distinct but otherwise exactly similar and one of them instantiates a universal property P, then the other one must instantiate P as well. But this means that universal properties are closed under indiscernibilities, i.e., that

(1) If P is a universal property, $\langle a, w \rangle \in P$ and $\mathbf{Ind}(a_w, b_v)$, then $\langle b, v \rangle \in P$.

Now, it is easy to see that (1) is equivalent to the following condition:

(2) If P is a universal property, $\langle a, w \rangle \in P$, and $p \in A$, then $\langle p(a), p(w) \rangle \in P$.

And (2) is equivalent to (A) (cf. T6.8).
What should we say about the converse of (A)?

(B) Every pure property is universal.

Clearly, this assumption is unacceptable to (strict) Leibnizians, since Leibnizianism is equivalent to the claim that all entities, and, in particular, all properties, are pure. Thus, according to Leibnizians, even such paradigmatically individual properties as 'being Socrates' or 'being Plato' satisfy the condition of purity. However, (B) seems to be a very attractive option for anybody who rejects Leibnizianism. (This applies even to local Leibnizians.) The assumptions (A) and (B), taken together, allow one to identify universality with purity (and individuality with impurity). As we remember, the distinction between universal and individual properties was used in our informal explication of the concept of indiscernibility,[9] and thereby of the concept of automorphism. Now we can go the other way round—we can use the concept of automorphism (or indiscernibility) in order to define the distinction in question.[10] It should be remembered, however, that this option is open only as long as Leibnizianism is rejected. Leibnizians must find some other way of analyzing the notions of universality and individuality.[11]

Given the assumptions (A) and (B), it becomes possible to define the notion of essentiality. A property P is *essential* for a iff P is a necessary property of a and P is pure ($=$universal). We can now prove that our definition of minimal kind satisfies the condition which we have placed on it in section 6.3:

T6.11 X is a minimal kind iff X is a maximal set of individuals such that, for every $a, b \in X$, a and b share all their essential properties.

----

[9] a in w is indiscernible from b in v iff the only differences between them are purely 'individual' (cf. section 5.1 above).
[10] P is universal iff P is pure iff P is invariant under automorphisms iff P is closed under indiscernibilities. Otherwise, P is individual.
[11] We shall examine the universality-individuality distinction in much greater detail in Parts III and IV.

Proof: Let X be a minimal kind. Suppose that a, $b \in X$ and $c \notin X$. Let P be any essential property of a. We have to show that (1) P is an essential property of b, and (2) there is some essential property Q of a such that Q is *not* an essential property of c. As for (2), it is enough to consider $Q = \{\langle b, v \rangle : b \in I_v \ \& \ b \in X\}$. Clearly, Q is a necessary property of a, while c never instantiates Q. At the same time, the purity of X (guaranteed by T6.9) entails that Q is pure.

As for (1), it should be observed that, since a and b belong to the same minimal kind, there is some $p \in A$ such that $p(a) = b$ (by T6.9). Consider any w such that $b \in I_w$. Since $\breve{p}(b) = a$, $\langle \breve{p}(b), \breve{p}(w) \rangle \in P$. Clearly, if $p \in A$, $\breve{p} \in A$. Essential properties are pure and, therefore, $\langle p(\breve{p}(b)), p(\breve{p}(w)) \rangle = \langle b, w \rangle \in P$. But this means that P is an essential property of b. Q.E.D.

The notion of a pure property is a very powerful one. As a matter of fact, we could choose it as our *primitive* concept and then introduce the notion of automorphism *by definition*:

T6.12 A permutation p on $\mathbf{I} \cup \mathbf{W}$ such that $p(\mathbf{I}) = \mathbf{I}$ and $p(\mathbf{W}) = \mathbf{W}$ is an automorphism iff
(1) every pure property is invariant under p, and
(2) for every $w \in \mathbf{W}$, if $I_w = \varnothing$, then $p(w) = w$.

Proof:

From left to right. (1) follows trivially from the definition of purity. As for (2), compare the proof of T6.9.

From right to left. It follows from T6.9 that p is an automorphism if p satisfies (2) and

(1′) $\forall w \in \mathbf{W} \ \forall a \in I_w \ \mathbf{Ind}(a_w, p(a)_{p(w)})$.

Thus, it is sufficient to show that (1) entails (1′). Consider any a and w such that $a \in I_w$ and define P as $\{\langle b, v \rangle : \mathbf{Ind}(a_w, b_v)\}$. Clearly, P is closed under automorphisms, and therefore pure (by T6.8). Thus, by (1), P is invariant under p. But then $\mathbf{Ind}(a_w, p(a)_{p(w)})$.   Q.E.D.

CHAPTER 7

Morality Without Purity

7.1. *Non-universalistic theories*

Let us recall our formulation of the Principle of Universalizability in terms of the concept of automorphism and the relation **D**:

D stays invariant under automorphisms.

(section 5.2)

In other words,

(U_A) **D** is a pure entity.

In this chapter we shall discuss *non-universalistic* moral theories, or, to be more precise, theories which reject the purity of **D**.

Before we begin, a word of caution is in order. By a 'universalist' we mean a person who thinks that individual properties of objects do not influence their moral status. Now, it is clear that non-universalism does not automatically imply the rejection of (U_A). In particular, for a Leibnizian, the acceptance of (U_A) is mandatory. (From the Leibnizian point of view, *all* entities are pure.) Thus, our discussion in this chapter will only be interesting for those who are not already committed to Leibnizianism.

Furthermore, some non-universalists may want to withhold judgment on such metaphysical issues as the Problem of Indiscernibles. They would reason as follows: *If* Leibniz was wrong, that is, if some entities are impure, then **D** will be among them. But *if* he was right, then **D** is pure, as is any other entity. Such persons will, of course, reserve their judgement as far as the status of (U_A) is concerned. Here, however, we shall concentrate on non-universalistic theories which explicitly reject (U_A).

7.2. **D**-*homogeneous sets of individuals*

One way to characterize the universalistic standpoint would be to say that it consists in a certain assumption of homogeneity. According to a universalist, minimal kinds constitute *morally homogeneous* sets. That is, individuals belonging to the same minimal kind are homogeneous from the moral point of view, belong to the same 'moral category'. In each situation we can replace one such individual by another without changing the moral structure of the situation in question.

The non-universalistic theories, on the other hand, deny this homogeneity assumption. According to them, there exist minimal kinds that contain morally heterogeneous individuals. For instance, a non-universalist may claim that different persons belong to different moral categories. Some of us deserve quite a different treatment than ordinary human beings.

The question arises: How are we to define this concept of moral homogeneity? Or rather, since morality in our model is represented by the relation **D**, how are we to define the notion of **D**-homogeneity (=homogeneity with respect to **D**)?

The following proposal seems rather attractive: Moral homogeneity presupposes belonging to the same minimal kind. Individuals are morally homogeneous if they can be replaced by one another in different situations (=worlds) without changing the moral status of the situation in question. But this implies that morally homogeneous individuals must be freely replaceable. This is to say that they must belong to the same minimal kind. Now, consider any set X of individuals such that X is wholly included in some minimal kind. If X is **D**-homogeneous, then no permutation on X should influence the relation **D**. That is, **D** should stay invariant under every automorphism p which permutes members of X, providing, of course, that p is fixed on the individuals which do *not* belong to X. Clearly, if I–X contains some pair a, b of individuals which are not **D**-homogeneous, then **D** may not be invariant under an automorphism which assigns a to b, despite the fact that individuals in X *are* **D**-homogeneous. This explains our demand that the relevant automorphism should be *fixed* on I–X. We can now formulate our proposal in a more precise way:

D7.1 $X \subseteq \mathbf{I}$ is a **D**-*homogeneous* set =
    (1) X is included in some minimal kind, and
    (2) for every $p \in \mathcal{A}$ fixed on I–X, $p(\mathbf{D}) = \mathbf{D}$.

Note that, given D7.1, we can immediately prove the following result:

T7.1 If **D** is pure, then every minimal kind is **D**-homogeneous.

In other words, given D7.1, (U_A) entails the universalistic homogeneity assumption, just as we expected. We also expected the *converse* of T7.1 to hold: if every minimal kind is **D**-homogeneous, then **D** is pure. Or, to put it differently,

T7.2 If **D** is impure, then some minimal kind is not **D**-homogeneous.

However, the proof of T7.2 is not as simple as it may seem at first glance. In fact, this theorem rests on an important assumption which we shall introduce later in this chapter (cf. section 7.4).

7.3. **D**-*homogeneity and complex individuals*

Is D7.1 a correct definition of **D**-homogeneity? To answer this question we must go back to our Principle of Extendibility, (E). (As we remember, according to (E), every minimal-kind preserving permutation on **I** is extendible to an automorphism.) We shall argue that D7.1 is acceptable *only if* (E) is acceptable. That is, anyone who assumes that some individuals in **I** are combinations of other individuals, and therefore rejects (E), must reject D7.1 as well.

We shall use the following adequacy criterion which has to be satisfied by any correct definition of **D**-homogeneity:

Let X be a set of individuals and let f be any automorphous permutation on X. Suppose now that f, though automorphous, *cannot* be extended to an automorphism which keeps **D** invariant. That is, for every $p \in A$ such that f is included in p, $p(\mathbf{D}) \neq \mathbf{D}$. In such a case, it seems, we should conclude that X is *not* a **D**-homogeneous set. To put it formally,

T7.3 If $X \subseteq \mathbf{I}$ is **D**-homogeneous, then, for every automorphous permutation f on X, there is some $p \in A$ such that $f \subseteq p$ and $p(\mathbf{D}) = \mathbf{D}$.

Now, *given* (E), T7.3 follows from D7.1.

Proof: Let X be **D**-homogeneous and let f be an automorphous permutation on X. Since f is automorphous, (E) entails that f is extendible to an automorphism, p, fixed on $\mathbf{I}$–X. And since X is **D**-homogeneous, D7.1 implies that $p(\mathbf{D}) = \mathbf{D}$.   Q.E.D.

7 – 792479 *Rabinowicz*

On the other hand, if we *reject* (E), then it is easy to construct a case in which D7.2 and T7.3 are incompatible with each other. Suppose that $X = \{a, b\}$ and $f = \{\langle a, b \rangle, \langle b, a \rangle\}$. Let $I = \{a, b, \{a\}, \{b\}\}$ and $W = \{w, v\}$. Suppose that $D = \{\langle w, v \rangle\}$ and that $\mathcal{A}$ consists of two members: the identity automorphism p_i and the automorphism p^*, which assigns b to a, $\{b\}$ to $\{a\}$, v to w, and vice versa.

(Our conditions on the concept of automorphism guarantee that p_i and p are the only automorphisms available in the described situation. In particular, T6.1 entails that there is no such automorphism which coincides with p^* on I but is fixed on W. And (UN) guarantees that no automorphism coincides with p^* on X but is fixed on I–X.)

Now, it is easy to ascertain that *no* automorphism which includes f keeps D invariant. The only such automorphism is p^*, and p^* transforms the pair $\langle w, v \rangle$, which belongs to D, into $\langle p^*(w), p^*(v) \rangle = \langle v, w \rangle$, which is *not* a member of D. Thus, since f is an automorphous permutation on X, T7.3 implies that X is not D-homogeneous. D7.1, on the other hand, leads to the opposite result. p_i is the *only* automorphism fixed on I–X. Of course, $p_i(D) = D$. Thus, by D7.1, X is a D-homogeneous set.

Less formally, we could rephrase this whole argument as follows:

Suppose that some individuals in I are combinations of other individuals, so that (E) does not hold. And suppose that I contains two morally heterogeneous individuals, a and b, that belong to the same minimal kind. As a result, no automorphism which assigns a to b and b to a keeps D invariant. Suppose, however, that I also contains members which are constructed in terms of a and b: $\{a\}$, $\{b\}$, $\{a, b\}$, $\{a, \{a, b\}\}$, etc. Then (UN) guarantees that *every* automorphism which is fixed on all individuals other than a and b must be fixed on a and b as well! Thus, every such automorphism keeps D invariant. But then D7.1 implies that the set $\{a, b\}$ is D-homogeneous, contrary to our intuitions.

To summarize: D7.1 is acceptable only if the principle (E) holds.

But can we give a definition of D-homogeneity which does *not* presuppose the validity of (E)? We believe this is possible, but such a definition will turn out to be rather complicated. Consider the following proposal:

According to D7.1, X is D-homogeneous only if D stays invariant under every automorphism fixed on I–X. But what if we relax our fixity condition? Perhaps the relevant automorphisms do not have to be literally fixed on I–X. It may be enough if they are 'sufficiently' fixed —more fixed than the automorphisms under which **D** does *not* stay invariant. The following definition is intended to express this idea:

D7.2 $X \subseteq I$ is a **D**-*homogeneous*$^+$ set =
   (1) X is included in some minimal kind,
   and
   (2) for every permutation f on X and every subset Y of I–X such that $f \cup p_i | Y$ is automorphous, there is some set Z such that (a) $Y \subseteq Z \subseteq I–X$, (b) $f \cup p_i | Z$ is automorphous, and (c) for every $p \in \mathcal{A}$, if p includes $f \cup p_i | Z$, then $p(\mathbf{D}) = \mathbf{D}$.

The second clause in this definition could also be expressed as follows: If X is **D**-homogeneous$^+$, then, for every automorphism p which permutes X onto itself, but which does not keep **D** invariant, we can find some automorphism p' which coincides with p on X and is fixed on all individuals on which p is fixed, but which, in distinction from p, does keep **D** invariant. Furthermore, every automorphism which coincides with p and p' on X and is fixed on all individuals on which p' is fixed, also keeps **D** invariant.

D-homogeneity$^+$ is meant to replace **D**-homogeneity in those models in which the principle (E) does not hold. The following variant of T7.3 can be easily proved:

T7.4 If X is **D**-homogeneous$^+$, then, for every automorphous permutation f on X, there is some $p \in \mathcal{A}$ such that $f \subseteq p$ and $p(\mathbf{D}) = \mathbf{D}$.

Thus, **D**-homogeneity$^+$ satisfies our adequacy condition.

Obviously, **D**-homogeneous$^+$ sets always are **D**-homogeneous. (If $p \in \mathcal{A}$ is fixed on I–X and $p(\mathbf{D}) \neq \mathbf{D}$, then the second clause of D7.2 is not satisfied when $f = p | X$ and $Y = I–X$.) But some **D**-homogeneous sets lack **D**-homogeneity$^+$. For instance, in our example above, the set $\{a, b\}$ is **D**-homogeneous (according to D7..1) but not **D**-homogeneous$^+$. There is no automorphism p such that $p | \{a, b\} = p^* | \{a, b\}$ and $p(\mathbf{D}) = \mathbf{D}$. However, **D**-homogeneity and **D**-homogeneity$^+$ coincide in the presence of (E).

Proof: Assume that $X \subseteq I$ is **D**-homogeneous. Consider any permutation f on X and any set $Y \subseteq I–X$ such that $f \cup p_i | Y$ is automorphous. By (E), there exists some $p \in \mathcal{A}$ such that $f \subseteq p$ and p is fixed on I–X. By **D**-homogeneity of X, $p(\mathbf{D}) = \mathbf{D}$. But then the second clause of D7.1 is satisfied when $Z = $ I–X. Q.E.D.

T7.5 (E) $\Rightarrow$ For every $X \subseteq$ I, X is **D**-homogeneous[+] iff X is **D**-homogeneous.

Therefore, in the presence of (E), the need for a separate concept of **D**-homogeneity[+] disappears.

When we do not have (E) at our disposal, working with **D**-homogeneity[+] proves to be a rather complicated affair. To illustrate: If p is fixed on I–X and X is a subset of Y, then p must be fixed on Y as well. Consequently:

T7.6 Subsets of **D**-homogeneous sets are themselves **D**-homogeneous.

But what about **D**-homogeneity[+]? Is this property also closed under subsets? Perhaps, but how are we prove it? What is more, it could be argued that our intuitive notion of moral homogeneity certainly *is* closed under subsets. Thus, if it would turn out that the +-variant of T7.6 is invalid, we would have to modify our definition of **D**-homogeneity[+] in order to keep it in agreement with our intuitions:

D7.3 $X \subseteq$ I is a **D**-*homogeneous*[+] set =
   (1) X is included in some minimal kind,
   and
   (2) for every $X' \subseteq X$, for every permutation f on X' and for every $Y \subseteq$ I–X' such that $f \cup p_i \,|\, Y$ is automorphous, there is some set Z such that (a) $Y \subseteq Z \subseteq$ I–X', (b) $f \cup p_i \,|\, Z$ is automorphous, and (c) for every $p \in \mathcal{A}$, if p includes $f \cup p_i \,|\, Z$, then $p(\mathbf{D}) = \mathbf{D}$.

Now the +-variant of T7.6 follows trivially. But, at the same time, the concept of **D**-homogeneity[+] becomes even more complicated and difficult to work with.

This should explain why we have incorporated the principle (E) into our model. Given (E), all difficulties conveniently disappear. **D**-homogeneity[+] reduces to a simple and easy manageable concept of **D**-homogeneity.

Up to now, we have been talking about **D**-homogeneous *sets*. But we can also define the corresponding *relation* of **D**-homogeneity:

D7.4 *a* is **D**-*homogeneous with b* $(a\mathbf{H_D}b) =$
{*a, b*} is a **D**-homogeneous set.

Let us say that an automorphism *p* is *ab-determined* iff *p* assigns *a*
to *b* and *b* to *a*, and is fixed on all the individuals distinct from *a* and *b*.
(SI) guarantees that, for every *a* and *b*, there exists *at most one ab*-deter-
mined automorphism. And (E) implies that, for any *a* and *b* which
belong to the same minimal kind, there exists *at least one ab*-determined
automorphism.

Thus, for any **D**-homogeneous {*a, b*}, there exist exactly two automorphisms fixed on **I**–{*a, b*}: the *ab*-determined automorphism and p_1.
Since $p_1(\mathbf{D}) = \mathbf{D}$, we get the following simplification of D7.4:

T7.7 $a\mathbf{H_D}b$ iff **D** is invariant under the *ab*-determined automorphism.

That is, *a* is **D**-homogeneous with *b* iff there is $p \in \mathcal{A}$ such that *p* is *ab*-
determined and $p(\mathbf{D}) = \mathbf{D}$.

Clearly, $\mathbf{H_D}$ is reflexive and symmetric. In fact it is also transitive. Thus:

T7.8 $\mathbf{H_D}$ is an equivalence relation.

Proof: We shall show only that $\mathbf{H_D}$ is transitive. Suppose that (1) $a\mathbf{H_D}b$
and (2) $b\mathbf{H_D}c$. We have to prove that (3) $a\mathbf{H_D}c$. Given T7.7, (1) and (2)
imply that there are automorphisms *p* and *p*′ such that

(1a) *p* is *ab*-determined, and (1b) $p(\mathbf{D}) = \mathbf{D}$,

while

(2a) *p*′ is *bc*-determined, and (2b) $p'(\mathbf{D}) = \mathbf{D}$.

Define *p*″ as $p/p'/p$. (1a) & (2a) entail that (3a) *p*″ is *ac*-determined.

(*p*″ is fixed on every individual distinct from *a, b* and *c*. As for *b*, $p''(b) =$
$p'/p(a) = p(a) = b$. Thus, *p*″ is fixed on **I**–{*a, c*}. At the same time,
$p''(a) = p'/p(b) = p(c) = c$ and $p''(c) = p'/p(c) = p(b) = a$.)

(1b) and (2b) entail that (3b) $p''(\mathbf{D}) = \mathbf{D}$.

(Proof: Consider any $w, v \in \mathbf{W}$. By (1b), $w\mathbf{D}v$ iff $p(w)\mathbf{D}p(v)$. By (2b),
$p(w)\mathbf{D}p(w)$ iff $p/p'(w)\mathbf{D}p/p'(v)$. By (1b), $p/p'(w)\mathbf{D}$ $p/p'(v)$ iff $p/p'/p(w)\mathbf{D}$
$p/p'/p(v)$, that is, iff $p''(w)\mathbf{D}p''(v)$.)

Given T7.7, the conjunction of (3a) and (3b) entails (3). Q.E.D.

7.4. *A normality condition on moral theories*

We proceed now to a different problem. The principle (U_A) is an example of a non-trivial condition which connects the concept of automorphism with the relation **D**. By 'non-trivial', we mean here a condition which does not follow from the theory of automorphisms alone. (U_A) is non-trivial and, correspondingly, purity is a non-trivial property of **D**, since there are many *impure* relations on **W**. We can now formulate our problem: Are there any *non-trivial* conditions on **D** and the concept of automorphism, conditions which *follow from* (U_A) but, at the same time, are so 'innocent' that even *non-universalistic* theories ought to obey them?

Before we attempt to answer this question, we must introduce some additional definitions.

We have already discussed **D**-homogeneous sets and the relation of **D**-homogeneity. Now we shall consider a new concept which belongs to the same family:

D7.5 $p \in \mathcal{A}$ is **D**-*homogeneous in* $X \subseteq I =$
   for every $a \in X$, $a\mathbf{H}_\mathbf{D}p(a)$.

D7.6 $p \in \mathcal{A}$ is **D**-*homogeneous* $= p$ is **D**-homogeneous in **I**.

That is, an *automorphism* is **D**-homogeneous if it couples every individual with a **D**-homogeneous partner. p_1 is a trivial example of a **D**-homogeneous automorphism. If (U_A) is true, then every automorphism is **D**-homogeneous. But even non-universalistic theories may well admit the existence of **D**-homogeneous automorphisms (distinct from p_1).

Now, consider the following principle:

(N1) **D** stays invariant under all **D**-homogeneous automorphisms.

Clearly, (N1) is considerably weaker than (U_A). While the latter condition demands the invariance of **D** under every automorphism, (N1) restricts this demand to those in the **D**-homogeneous category.

It can be argued, that any moral theory, universalistic or not, ought to obey (N1). The non-universalistic thesis that **D** varies under *some* automorphisms seems to rest on an assumption that such automorphisms involve coupling of (some) individuals with **D**-heterogeneous partners. It is only when we replace some a in **I** with an individual from a different 'moral category' that we can get an automorphism which transforms **D** into a different relation.

But is (N1) a non-trivial condition? Is it independent of our general theory of automorphisms? In other words: Is there *any* dyadic relation E on **W** such that, for some E-homogeneous automorphism p, $p(E) \neq E$?

Unfortunately, we must admit that we do not know the answer to this question. We have not found any such relation E which would disprove the universal validity of (N1), but perhaps it is simply because we have not been looking hard enough.

What we certainly can derive from the general theory of automorphisms is a 'finite' variant of (N1):

T7.9 Let p be a **D**-homogeneous automorphism such that the number of $a \in \mathbf{I}$ for which $a \neq p(a)$ is *finite*. Then $p(\mathbf{D}) = \mathbf{D}$.

Corollary: If **I** is finite, then **D** stays invariant under all **D**-homogeneous automorphisms.

Outline of the proof: Suppose that $p \in \mathcal{A}$ is **D**-homogeneous and let X be the set of all $a \in \mathbf{I}$ for which $a \neq p(a)$. Suppose that X is finite. Let f^* be that permutation on X which is included in p. By a *transposition* on X we shall understand any permutation g on X such that, for some a, $b \in X$, g assigns a to b, b to a, and is fixed on all other members of X. Now, it is well known that, for *any* permutation f on a finite X, there is such a finite sequence $\langle g_1, ..., g_k \rangle$ of transpositions on X that (i) $f = g_1/g_2 .../g_k$, and (ii) for every g_i $(1 \leqslant i \leqslant k)$, if $g_i(a) = b$ and $a \neq b$, then there is a sequence $\langle c_1, ..., c_n \rangle$ such that $a = c_1$, $b = c_n$, and, for every c_j $(1 \leqslant j \leqslant n)$, $f(c_j) = c_{j+1}$ or $\tilde{f}(c_j) = c_{j+1}$.[12]

Consequently, there is also such a sequence $\langle g_1^*, ..., g_k^* \rangle$, which corresponds to our permutation f^*. Define p_1 as that automorphism which includes g_1^* and is fixed on $\mathbf{I} - X$, p_2 as that automorphism which includes g_2^* and is fixed on $\mathbf{I} - X$, and so on up to p_k. (The existence of $p_1, ..., p_k$ is entailed by (E).) It is easy to verify that (1) $p = p_1/.../p_k$ (which follows from (i) above), and that (2) for every p_i $(1 \leqslant i \leqslant k)$, there are $a, b \in \mathbf{I}$ such

---

[12] Cf. I. N. Herstein, *Topics in Algebra*, Blaisdell Intern. Textbook Series, Waltham, Mass., 1964, Chapter 2, section 10.

that $a\mathbf{H_D}b$ and p_i is ab-determined (which follows from (ii), given that $f\subseteq p$, p is **D**-homogeneous and $\mathbf{H_D}$ is an equivalence relation).

By T7.7, (2) implies that **D** stays invariant under every p_i. But then it follows from (1) that $p(\mathbf{D})=\mathbf{D}$. Q.E.D.

Thus, (N1) is trivial for the finite case. But it may still be non-trivial for an infinite **I**.

To summarize: *If* (N1) is non-trivial, then it constitutes an example of a non-trivial condition on **D** and $\mathcal{A}$, which follows from $(\mathbf{U}_{\mathcal{A}})$ but which still ought to be obeyed by every moral theory, universalistic or not.

Given (N1), we are able to prove a number of important and useful theorems. In particular, we can now derive our theorem T7.2, according to which the impurity of **D** implies that some minimal kind is not **D**-homogeneous.

Proof: If **D** is impure, then, for some $p\in\mathcal{A}$, $p(\mathbf{D})\neq\mathbf{D}$. By (N1), p is not **D**-homogeneous. That is, for some $a\in\mathbf{I}$, $\neg\,a\mathbf{H_D}p(a)$. In consequence, $\{a,p(a)\}$ is not **D**-homogeneous. Since, by T7.6, every subset of a **D**-homogeneous set must be **D**-homogeneous, the minimal kind which includes a and $p(a)$ cannot be **D**-homogeneous. Q.E.D.

Another important theorem which is provable with the help of (N1):

T7.10 If $X\subseteq\mathbf{I}$ and, for every a, $b\in X$, $a\mathbf{H_D}b$, then X is **D**-homogeneous.

Proof. If X is not **D**-homogeneous, then there exists some automorphism p fixed on $\mathbf{I}$–X and such that $p(\mathbf{D})\neq\mathbf{D}$. But then, by (N1), there are a and $p(a)$ such that $\neg\,a\mathbf{H_D}p(a)$. Since p is fixed on $\mathbf{I}$–X, both a and $p(a)$ must belong to X. Q.E.D.

T7.10 allows drawing 'collective' conclusions from pairwise comparisons. In order to determine whether a given collection X is or is not **D**-homogeneous, we do not have to look at the collection as a whole. It is fully sufficient to compare the members of the collection with each other. As a matter of fact, we can prove a somewhat stronger theorem: It is not necessary to compare each member of X with every other member. We have only to choose some a in X and then compare every other member of X with a. Accordingly:

T7.11 If $X \in I$, $a \in X$ and, for every $b \in X$, $a\mathbf{H_D}b$, then X is $\mathbf{D}$-homogeneous.

T7.11 follows from T7.10 given the fact that $\mathbf{H_D}$ is an equivalence relation.

Our next theorem incorporates a similar idea.

Let us say that $p \in \mathcal{A}$ is a *transposition* iff there are a, $b \in I$ such that p is ab-determined.

T7.12 If $\mathbf{D}$ stays invariant under all transpositions in $\mathcal{A}$, then $\mathbf{D}$ is pure.

Proof. If $\mathbf{D}$ stays invariant under all transpositions, then, by T7.7, every automorphism in $\mathcal{A}$ is $\mathbf{D}$-homogeneous. But then, by (N1), $\mathbf{D}$ is pure. Q.E.D.

According to T7.12, we do not have to consider all automorphisms in order to determine whether $\mathbf{D}$ is pure. It is enough to examine 'simple' permutations which replace one individual with another and keep the rest of I fixed.

7.5. *Maximal* $\mathbf{D}$-*homogeneous sets*

Consider the definition:

D7.7 $X \subseteq I$ is a *maximal* $\mathbf{D}$-*homogeneous* set $= X$ is $\mathbf{D}$-homogeneous and no proper superset of X is $\mathbf{D}$-homogeneous.

The question arises: Can we partition I into maximal $\mathbf{D}$-homogeneous sets? Obviously, if (U_A) is true, then such a partition simply coincides with the set of minimal kinds. But what if (U_A) does not hold? In particular, we are interested in the following theorem:

T7.13 Every $a \in I$ belongs to exactly one maximal $\mathbf{D}$-homogeneous set, namely, to the set of all $b \in I$ such that $a\mathbf{H_D}b$.

If we want to treat maximal $\mathbf{D}$-homogeneous sets as 'moral minimal kinds' and if we interpret $\mathbf{H_D}$ as the relation of moral homogeneity, then it seems clear that T7.13 should hold. In fact, T7.13 is derivable from (N1).

Proof: First we shall prove the following theorem:

T7.14 If X and Y are overlapping **D**-homogeneous sets, then their union, $X \cup Y$, is **D**-homogeneous.

Proof of T7.14: Since X and Y overlap, there is some a such that $a \in X \cap Y$. If $X \cup Y$ is not **D**-homogeneous, then, by T7.11, $X \cup Y$ contains some b such that $\neg a\mathbf{H_D}b$. Suppose that $b \in X$. Since $a \in X$, X contains some non-**D**-homogeneous subset. But then T7.6 implies that X cannot be **D**-homogeneous, contrary to hypothesis. By the same reasoning, b cannot belong to Y. Thus, the assumption that $X \cup Y$ is not **D**-homogeneous leads to a contradiction.   Q.E.D.

Now, we can return to the proof of T7.13.
Consider any $a \in \mathbf{I}$. Let X be the set of all $b \in \mathbf{I}$ such that $a\mathbf{H_D}b$. Obviously $a \in X$. By T7.11, X is **D**-homogeneous. Consider any $c \in \mathbf{I}$ such that $c \notin X$. $X \cup \{c\}$ contains a subset, $\{a, c\}$, which is not **D**-homogeneous. Thus, by T7.6, $X \cup \{c\}$ is not **D**-homogeneous. But then X is a maximal **D**-homogeneous set. Suppose, now, that a belongs to *distinct* maximal **D**-homogeneous sets, X and Y. Since X and Y overlap, T7.14 implies that $X \cup Y$, which is a proper superset of both X and Y, must be **D**-homogeneous. But then X and Y cannot both be maximal **D**-homogeneous sets, contrary to the hypothesis. T7.13 follows.   Q.E.D.

As we have already said, T7.13 allows us to treat maximal **D**-homogeneous sets as formal equivalents of 'moral minimal kinds' (or, to use another expression, 'minimal moral categories of individuals'). As a result, we are now able to construct a classification of different possible non-universalistic theories in terms of our model.

7.6. *Classification of non-universalistic theories*

Let us start with a number of definitions. Let E be any dyadic relation on **W** which satisfies the E-variant of T7.13. That is, for every $a \in \mathbf{I}$, a belongs to exactly one maximal E-homogeneous set, namely, to the set of all $b \in \mathbf{I}$ such that $a\mathbf{H}_E b$. We shall now define different types of such relations.

D 7.8 E is *restricted* = I contains at most one minimal kind which is not a maximal E-homogeneous set.

D 7.9 E is *finite* = Every minimal kind in I includes a finite number of maximal E-homogeneous sets.

D 7.10 E is *dichotomous* = some minimal kind in I includes two maximal E-homogeneous sets, and no minimal kind in I includes more than two such sets.

D 7.11 E is *individualistic* = For some impure $a \in I$, $\{a\}$ is a maximal E-homogeneous set.

D 7.12 E is *collectivistic* = E is not individualistic.

D 7.13 E is *strongly individualistic* = I contains some minimal kind X with more than one member such that, for every a in X, $\{a\}$ is a maximal E-homogeneous set.

D 7.14 E is *centered* = E is individualistic and no minimal kind in I includes more than one unit-set which is a maximal E-homogeneous set.

A *moral theory* shall be said to be restricted iff it assumes that **D** is restricted, finite iff it assumes that **D** is finite, etc. It may be thought that normal moral theories always are restricted, even when they reject (U_A). A non-universalist usually is interested in some special minimal kind, say, the set of *persons*. He claims that *this* set is divisible into different moral categories, but, at the same time, he normally assumes, at least implicitly, that *other* minimal kinds are morally homogeneous. Can we, then, treat restrictedness as a condition of normality?

We do not think so. For one thing, there may be non-universalists who divide persons into a number of different minimal kinds, and *then* divide some of these kinds into different moral categories. Secondly, one can be a non-universalist with respect to both persons and some other individuals, say, other sentient beings. Thirdly, the idea that particular objects such as houses, personal belongings, etc., have a special 'sentimental' value for some persons, may, perhaps, be interpreted along non-universalistic lines (although this is doubtful). But then it may be necessary to assume that both the set of persons and those minimal kinds which contain the sentimentally valued objects constitute morally heterogeneous collections.

Here, however, it will be convenient to concentrate on *restricted* non-universalistic theories. Given our definitions D7.9–D7.14, we can classify them as follows:

Restricted non-universalistic theories

	Individualistic			Collectivistic
Dichotomous		(a)		(b)
Finite, non-dichotomous	(c)	(d)	(e)	(f)
Non-finite	(g)	(h)	(i)	(j)
	Strongly individual- istic	Centered	Non-centered, not strongly individual- istic	

Let X_T be that minimal kind which lacks **D**-homogeneity according to a given restricted non-universalistic theory T. In the above classification, we have assumed that any such X_T contains at least three members. This explains why we have not divided dichotomous individualistic theories into strongly individualistic, centered and non-centered. Our assumption implies that any dichotomous individualistic theory must be centered. Also, if we assume that X_T is *infinite*, then we do not have to consider theories of type (c). If X_T is infinite, a finite T cannot be strongly individualistic. And even if we do not make this assumption, the distinction between (c)- and (g)-theories does not seem to be especially important. The choice between (c) and (g) does not depend on any moral considerations, but only on our opinions concerning the cardinality of X_T. Therefore, in further discussion, we shall ignore the difference between types (c) and (g). We shall refer to them jointly as (c–g)-theories.

It should be noted, that not every restricted non-universalistic theory must exemplify one of the types (a)–(j). Such a theory does not have to be *fully specific*. For instance, a non-universalist may assume that D is individualistic without having any clear opinion concerning the issue of dichotomy.

It could be asked whether our classification is a 'realistic' one. In other words, can we give more or less 'realistic' examples of non-universalistic theories which instantiate the types (a)–(j)? (The scare-quotes around 'realistic' become understandable if one considers that non-universalistic theories are apt to avoid publicity. Even if they have followers, they are less likely to be found in print.)

Although we have not been able to find such examples for types (h), (i) and (j), these are easily forthcoming as far as our other types are concerned.

Consider an egoist (or an altruist, for that matter) who thinks that there is an irreducible moral distinction between himself and every other person. For example, he claims to have certain moral rights which adhere to him in every possible world, and which no other persons shares. If 'irreducible' stands here for 'irreducible to pure properties', and if our egoist takes all *other* persons to be morally homogeneous with each other, then he is a follower of an (a)-type non-universalistic theory (provided, of course, that he treats every other minimal kind as morally homogeneous).

If he makes an exception for his family (friends, nation, etc.) and thinks that they hover somewhere between himself and all the rest, then he moves to type (d). Note that if his only reason for making the exception is that they are *his* family, then he has not yet left type (a). Clearly, the members of his family may have right to special favors and still be morally homogeneous with ordinary human beings. Type (d) demands that our egoist gives his family members 'inalienable' moral rights, which in no possible world are transferable to anybody else, quite independently of whether they still are members of his family or not.

If he, in addition, treats every member of his family as morally unique (that is, if he thinks that they are morally heterogeneous individuals), then he has moved to type (e)—he has become a follower of a non-centered finite individualistic theory.

Consider now a 'collective' egoist who thinks that he is a member of some special moral category of people (a family, a clan, a nation, etc.). If he thinks that all other people constitute a morally homogeneous class, then category (b) is the right place for him. But if he wants to make some finer moral distinctions (say, first comes The Family, then The Nation, and then all the rest), then we should place him in category (f).

In an influential article, Ernest Gellner has coined the term 'existential ethics' in order to refer to a theory according to which *every* person is morally *unique*.[13] What is right for one does not have to be right for another, even if we cannot point to any (pure) difference between them or between their situations. While Gellner's existentialist ethics' seems to have little in common with the moral doctrines actually put forward by existentialist philosophers,[14] it still constitutes a good example of a (c–g)-theory. Obviously, the slogan 'every person is morally unique, irreplaceable, irreducible' can be understood in radically different ways. While it may be taken as an expression of an extreme variant of non-universalism, it has also found its way into classically universalistic ethical systems such as Kant's. Extremes often meet.

Note that (c–g)-theories represent the moral equivalent of Leibnizianism. While Leibnizians put every individual into a different minimal kind, (c–g) theories place every person in a different moral category.

7.7. *Other normality conditions*

After this rather brief discussion of different non-universalistic theories, let us return to our previous problem. We have formulated one (possibly) non-trivial condition on A and D, which every moral theory, universalistic or not, should obey. We refer, of course, to the principle (N1). Now, can we find *other* conditions of this kind? Let us consider two possibilities:

(N2)   If $p \in A$ is D-homogeneous in $I_w \cup I_v$, then $D(w, v)$ iff $D(p(w), p(v))$.

(Recall that p is D-homogeneous in $X \subseteq I$ iff p assigns to each a in X an individual D-homogeneous with a.)

---

[13] E. Gellner, 'Ethics and Logic', *Proceedings of Aristotelian Society, 1954–5*, pp. 157–178. Also, see A. MacIntyre, 'What Morality is Not', *Philosophy, 32* (1957), pp. 325–335.
[14] Concerning this issue, cf. F. Olafson, *Principles and Persons*, Baltimore 1967, pp. 174–187; D. Locke, 'The Trivializability of Universalizability', *Philosophical Review, 77* (1968), pp. 25–44 (esp. pp. 30–32); and R. T. Garner & B. Rosen, *Moral Philosophy*, New York 1967, pp. 94–95.

(N 3) If **D** stays invariant under an automorphism p, then p is **D**-homo-
geneous.

Both these conditions are related to the principle (N 1): (N 3) is the
converse of (N 1) and (N 1) is simply a special instance of (N 2). Obviously, if (N 2) holds, then (N 1) must hold as well. An automorphism
p is **D**-homogeneous iff p is **D**-homogeneous in $\mathbf{I}_w \cup \mathbf{I}_v$, for every $w, v \in \mathbf{W}$.
And **D** is invariant under p iff, for every $w, v \in \mathbf{W}$, $\mathbf{D}(w, v)$ iff $\mathbf{D}(p(w), p(v))$.

As far as we can judge, there is nothing wrong with (N 2). If p sends
any individual existing in w or v to some **D**-homogeneous individual,
then, it seems, the pairs $\langle w, v \rangle$ and $\langle p(w), p(v) \rangle$ ought to be indistinguishable in terms of **D**, quite independently of whether or not p is
D-homogeneous in $\mathbf{I}{-}(\mathbf{I}_w \cup \mathbf{I}_v)$.

(N 3), on the other hand, is much less convincing. According to it, an
automorphism is **D**-homogeneous if it keeps **D** invariant. But why
should it be so? Perhaps, in some cases, **D** may stay invariant even under
a non-**D**-homogeneous automorphism, providing that the latter has been
constructed in a right way. Here is one example:

Suppose that individuals a, b, c and d all belong to the same minimal kind.
Assume, also, that $\{a, b\}$ and $\{c, d\}$ constitute maximal **D**-homo-
geneous sets. Now, if we have such distinct maximal **D**-homogeneous
groups, which are included in the same minimal kind, then two cases
are possible: either one group ranks 'higher' than the other one, so that
its members have special privileges which the members of the other
group lack, or both groups may be on the same level in the moral
hierarchy. Suppose, for instance, that you are a follower of a non-universalistic 'family' theory: every family constitutes a maximal **D**-homo-
geneous set, but no family ranks higher than any other family. The
moral division between different families depends on the fact that
members of each family have *special* moral claims on other members
of *the same* family. Think now of $\{a, b\}$ and $\{c, d\}$ as two such families.
And suppose that moral relations between a and b are exactly the same
as those between c and d. Then it seems that any automorphism p
which transforms $\{a, b\}$ into $\{c, d\}$ and vice versa, and is fixed on
other individuals, will keep **D** invariant. At the same time, such an
automorphism is obviously not **D**-homogeneous. If this example makes
sense, then we have found an argument against (N 3).

Two problems remain open:

(a) Can we find other non-trivial conditions on A and $\mathbf{D}$, which follow from (U_A), but which should be obeyed by every moral theory, universalistic or not?

(b) *Is* it actually the case that (N1) and (N2) are non-trivial? Can we show that they do not follow from our general theory of automorphisms?

PART III

Beyond Similarity

CHAPTER 8

The Universalizability Dilemma

8.1. *Presentation of the dilemma*

Anyone who discusses the problem of universalizability must, sooner or later, consider the following difficulty:

The universalizability rule "tells you that if an act done by someone else is wrong (or right), it is also wrong (or right) if done by you, *provided* that you are in *exactly the same circumstances*. But, of course, you are never in exactly the same circumstances as other people, so the rule seems to be useless. To make it useful, it would have to be relaxed somewhat: If something is wrong for them, it is also wrong for you, provided your circumstances are sufficiently similar, or similar in relevant respects. But this introduces a new set of problems: When are the circumstances sufficiently similar? And when are they similar in relevant respects? What constitutes a relevant respect? Until these difficult questions are answered, the rule gives us no clear guidance."[1]

In our framework, this difficulty, which we shall call the Universalizability Dilemma, may be formulated as follows:

The Universalizability Principle depends on the concept of similarity. It refers either to exactly similar, indiscernible cases (as when we use such notions as **C**, **Ind** or $\mathcal{A}$) or to relevantly similar ones (the relation **R**). Now it seems undisputable that no two individuals are exactly alike. And perhaps there is nothing contingent about that. One could plausibly

---

[1] J. Hospers, *An Introduction to Philosophical Analysis*, second revised ed., London, 1967, pp. 597 f. For other formulations of the same difficulty see, for instance, C. D. Broad, *Five Types of Ethical Theory*, London, 1930, pp. 223 f.; M. Singer, *Generalization in Ethics*, New York, 1961, p. 18; R. M. Hare, *Freedom and Reason*, London, 1963, p. 12.

argue that, in *any* possible world, indiscernibility amounts to identity. Earlier, we have referred to this position as *local Leibnizianism*. As we already know, such a view does not make the exact similarity variant(s) of the Universalizability Principle totally useless: we can still apply the principle in *hypothetical* arguments, which involve comparing individuals *across* the worlds. ("Supposing that our positions were reversed, ...").[2] However, the strict, fullfledged Leibnizianism deprives us even of this possibility: according to it, indiscernibility *always* amounts to identity, regardless of whether the comparison is made *within* a world or *across* the worlds.[3]

If we now turn to the relevant similarity variant(s) of the universalizability principle, we encounter another difficulty: the concept of relevant similarity seems essentially unclear. What does it *mean* to say that X is a morally relevant aspect of a situation, w?[4]

We could try the following analysis:

(1) X is a morally relevant aspect of w iff X is an aspect of w such that, in its absence, w would have a different obligation-structure. That is, in the absence of X, w would have different deontic alternatives.

For the sake of argument, assume that the counterfactual element in this definition can be made more precise. The real problem lies elsewhere. It seems, namely, that even *irrelevant* changes in w may lead to corresponding, irrelevant changes in w's deontic alternatives. Thus, to give an example, if some person in w has brown eyes (we are assuming that this aspect of w is morally irrelevant), then if his eyes had been of a

---

[2] The role of such hypothetical reasoning in moral deliberation has been stressed by R. M. Hare: "The fact that no two actual cases are ever identical has no bearing on the problem. For all we have to do is to imagine an identical case in which the roles are reversed." (Op. cit., p. 107.) Cf. also op. cit., pp. 93 f., 106, 120, 126 f., 223.
[3] This standpoint may be expressed in a number of ways. For example:

For all worlds w, v, if wCv, then $w = v$;

For all worlds w, v and all individuals a, b, if $\mathbf{Ind}(a_w, b_v)$, then $a = b$;

The identity permutation on individuals and worlds, p_i, is the only automorphism.
[4] Sometimes it is claimed that the Universalizability Dilemma arises because we lack a workable *criterion* of relevance. Thus, it is thought that the difficulty consists in our inability to determine *which* aspects of a situation are morally relevant, rather than in the *analytical* problem concerning the very concept of relevance. It seems, however, that such a position rests on a misunderstanding. Assuming that we have at our disposal a clear concept of relevance *and* a sufficiently rich moral theory, we may expect that this theory will provide us with appropriate relevance criteria.

different colour, this same difference would carry over to all situations which are causally accessible from w, and, in particular, to the set of w's deontic alternatives.

To avoid the difficulty, the definition should be modified:

(2) X is a relevant aspect of w iff X is an aspect of w such that, in its absence, w would have relevantly different deontic alternatives.

But then we end up with a circle: we define relevance in terms of relevance.

This is not the only difficulty with (2). It seems that (2) is not only unsatisfactory *as a definition*, but also simply *false*. To see this, it is sufficient to note that, in some cases, the obligation-structure of a situation may be 'overdetermined'. Thus, it may be the case that the removal of *one* relevant aspect of w will not relevantly change w's deontic alternatives. But would we not say then that the aspect in question was, after all, irrelevant in w? It is doubtful if we would. If I promise my friend that I will go to a party and if I make the same promise to another friend, then both promises seem morally relevant, even though each of them alone would sufficiently determine my obligations.

We could meet this difficulty by making (2) weaker:

(3) X is a relevant aspect of w iff X is an aspect of w and also of some situation v such that, in the absence of X, v would have relevantly different deontic alternatives.

(3) takes care of the relevant aspects which are 'redundant' in w; for any such aspect X there is, hopefully, a situation v in which X is no longer redundant.

However, (3) is clearly *too* weak. It implies that, for any aspect X, if X is relevant in *some* situation, then it is relevant in *all* situations which instantiate X. And this is obviously unacceptable. We would like to say that, if two situations are sufficiently different, then the same aspect may be relevant in one of them and irrelevant in the other. Thus, (3) does not constitute any improvement.

Is there any satisfactory analysis of the concept of relevance? This is a difficult question. However, as long as no such analysis has been presented, one could claim that the concept in question should be treated with the greatest suspicion. Of course, this suspicion will then carry over to the relevant similarity variant(s) of the Universalizability Principle.

Thus, we are confronted with a dilemma. If we make use of the concept of exact similarity, the Universalizability Principle is trivialized by Leibnizianism. On the other hand, if we employ the concept of relevant similarity, it is no longer clear whether we know what we are talking about.

8.2. *A third way out: the condition* (uu)

Can this difficulty be avoided? Of course, we can attack one horn of the dilemma and argue that there is no need to assume anything stronger than *local* Leibnizianism. Or, we can try to come up with some satisfactory analysis of the concept of relevance. But is there no other way out? There certainly is, provided that we can find some non-standard formulation of the Universalizability Principle, a formulation which is *not* made trivial by (strict) Leibnizianism and which does *not* use the notion of relevant similarity. It will develop that such a formulation is, in fact, available, but that it also is quite unconventional. In particular, it does not make use of any concept of *similarity* at all. Thus, we shall not try to replace **C** and **R** by some new kind of similarity relation. Instead, we shall introduce the concept of a *universal* (non-individual) aspect of a situation. We shall argue that this concept is already presupposed by our notions of **C** and **R**, so that it is no less clear than either of them (Chapters 9 and 10). Then, in terms of this concept and the relation **D**, we shall formulate a certain condition on **W** (section 11.1). It will be seen that this condition, which we shall refer to as (uu), is not trivialized by Leibnizianism. At the same time, it will develop that, from an *anti*-Leibnizian point of view, (uu) is equivalent to the condition with which we are already acquainted:

(u) $w\mathbf{C}v \ \& \ w\mathbf{D}u \ \rightarrow \ \exists z(v\mathbf{D}z \ \& \ u\mathbf{C}z)$.

Thus, for an anti-Leibnizian at least, (uu) embodies the universalizability idea precisely as (u) does (section 11.2). But what about Leibnizians? It will be shown below (section 11.3) that, given the definition of **R** in terms of the relation **R**[+] and the concept of a universal aspect,[5] (uu), in

---

[5] As we may remember, **R**[+] is the relation of similarity in *all* morally relevant respects, while **R** is to be understood as the relation of similarity in all *universal* (non-individual, qualitative) morally relevant respects (cf. sections 1.3 and 2.2).

conjunction with some relatively innocent assumptions, is sufficient for the derivation of the **R**-variant of (u):

(ur) $w\mathbf{R}v$ & $w\mathbf{D}u \rightarrow \exists z(v\mathbf{D}z$ & $u\mathbf{R}z)$.

Since, as we shall see, Leibnizianism is unable to trivialize (ur), the derivability of (ur) from (uu) suggests that the latter condition, even from the Leibnizian point of view, represents a way of expressing the universalizability idea.

However, this argument is not wholly conclusive. While (ur) is derivable from (uu), the derivation does not work in the opposite direction. As a matter of fact, we can strengthen this result: In Part I, we have shown that there are many possible universalistic conditions on **R** and **D** aside from (ur). It will emerge that not even the strongest condition of this kind is sufficient for the derivation of (uu) (section 11.3).

Thus, a universalistically-minded Leibnizian *could* claim that the condition (uu) is not really adequate for his purposes. Even though (uu) somehow involves the idea of universalizability in that it implies (ur), it is not *reducible* to the latter condition nor to any other relevant similarity variant of the Universalizability Principle.

However, as long as such a claim of inadequacy is not backed by any additional considerations, it should not cause us too much consternation. A Leibnizian who rejects (uu) as inadequate *because of* its irreducibility to universalistic conditions formulated in terms of relevant similarity cannot, at the same time, consider the concept of relevance as hopelessly suspect and unclear. But then he is not confronted with the dilemma which has led us to (uu) in the first place. Therefore, his objection may be disregarded by anyone who feels that this dilemma is real.

8.3. (uu) *and the extensions of Leibnizianism*

Unfortunately, there is another line of reasoning which may cast suspicion on the condition (uu). We have pointed out earlier,[6] that any universalistic condition, α, on **R** and **D** may be 'split up' into two associated conditions which together entail α:

---

[6] Cf. section 2.2.

(1) $R \subseteq R^+$ (We have been referring to this condition as (RR^+).);

(2) the R^+-variant of α, i.e., the condition which differs from α only in that each occurrence of 'R' has been replaced by 'R^+'.

Since the converse of (RR^+) is trivial, it follows from (1) that R and R^+ coincide with each other. But then (2) and α turn out to be equivalent conditions.

Now, we have argued that (RR^+) is that 'component' of α which embodies the idea of universalizability. That is, non-universalists will reject α *because* they reject (RR^+). Their quarrel is not with principles such as (2). Thus, it seems that the Principle of Universalizability in its relevant similarity version(s) stands and falls together with (RR^+).

In this connection, we have pointed out that, to an *opponent* of Leibnizianism, (RR^+) seems to be equivalent to its C-variant:

(CR^+) $C \subseteq R^+$.

For such a person, both conditions appear to express the same universalistic insight.[7] We have seen[8] that this intuitive equivalence could be formally derived if the following principle were at our disposal:

(CRR^+) $R = R^+/C$.

That is, for any w and v, wRv iff, for some u, wR^+u and uCv.

But is (CRR^+) an acceptable principle to an anti-Leibnizian? We shall prove below (section 10.2) that this question, which previously has been left open, must receive an *affirmative* answer.

Thus, for an anti-Leibnizian, (CR^+) and (RR^+) are demonstrably equivalent. From the Leibnizian point of view, however, the situation is obviously different. While (CR^+) constitutes a trivial consequence of Leibnizianism (given the fact that R^+ is a reflexive relation), (RR^+) is made of a sturdier material. Leibnizianism is perfectly consistent with the claim that $R \nsubseteq R^+$.

Now let us consider the following question: Is it not possible that some appropriate *strengthening* of the Leibnizian position will prove sufficient for the derivation of (RR^+)? Perhaps there is some plausible extension of

---

[7] Ibid.
[8] Cf. section 3.8.

Leibnizianism, call it T, which succeeds where Leibnizianism has failed. Thus, T not only entails that **C** is an identity relation and thereby trivializes all exact-similarity variants of the Universalizability Principle, but it also implies that **R** is included in **R**⁺. But if we are right it our assumption that (**RR**⁺) constitutes *the* universalistic component in all universalistic conditions on **R** and **D**, then it follows that T provides a foundation for all standard formulations of ethical universalism. It suffices for both the **C**- and **R**-versions of the Principle of Universalizability.

We presuppose here, of course, that T is not just a conjunction of Leibnizianism and (**RR**⁺). What we have in mind is rather an extension of Leibnizianism which does not make use of the concept of relevant similarity at all. Nor should it use any other specifically moral concepts. To put it in another way, T is thought to be a purely *metaphysical* principle, of the same kind as Leibnizianism.

Suppose, now, that T, despite all its strength, is quite compatible with the negation of (uu). As a matter of fact, we shall see below (section 12.3) that the possibility of (uu) being derivable from some purely metaphysical extension of Leibnizianism is rather unlikely.

These facts could now be given two different interpretations.

On the one hand, it may be argued that, when all the traditional variants of ethical universalism turn out to be trivial consequences of some metaphysical principle such as T, the condition (uu) becomes especially interesting. Here, at last, we have a version of the Universalizability Principle which successfully asserts its independence when confronted with Leibniz-type metaphysics.

On the other hand, another interpretation seems equally possible. If all the standard variants of the Universalizability Principle are entailed by T, and if T is a plausible extension of Leibnizianism, then it may seem reasonable to claim that Leibniz-type metaphysics provides a proper foundation for ethical universalism. But then the fact that neither T nor any other plausible extension of Leibnizianism entails (uu) tells *against* (uu)'s being an adequate expression of the universalistic standpoint.

Obviously, if a principle like T actually exists, and if our second interpretation is not unreasonable, then the status of (uu) is rather suspect.

What we have just been talking about is not purely hypothetical. Below (sections 12.1 and 12.2), we shall present two extensions of Leibnizianism both of which have the same characteristic: they entail (**RR**$^+$) without entailing (uu). Nor do either of them make use of any specifically moral concepts. But do they constitute *plausible* strengthenings of the Leibnizian standpoint? We shall argue that this question should be given a *negative* answer (section 12.4). This argument, if correct, should provide additional support for our thesis that (uu), after all, represents a genuine way out of the Universalizability Dilemma.

CHAPTER 9

Universal Aspects

9.1. *Universality vs. individuality*

Often we explain what we mean by exact similarity by saying that two objects are exactly similar iff they differ solely in their 'individual' aspects. Thus, for instance, two situations (worlds) are exactly similar iff they involve different individuals but otherwise are exactly the same. In other words, $w\mathbf{C}v$ iff w and v do not differ in their 'universal' ($=$ non-individual) aspects.

This explanation suggests that the concept of a universal aspect is already presupposed by our notion of exact similarity. In particular, in order to understand the relation $\mathbf{C}$ which connects exactly similar worlds, we must have some previous understanding of the distinction betwen universal and individual aspects of worlds.

The distinction in question is equally crucial for our understanding of the relation $\mathbf{R}$. Two worlds are said to be $\mathbf{R}$-connected iff they share all their *universal* relevant characteristics. That is, iff the differences between them are either irrelevant or purely 'individual'.

Here we shall assume the concept of a universal aspect as our primitive and we shall define the concepts $\mathbf{C}$ and $\mathbf{R}$ in terms of it.

By an aspect of a world we shall understand any state of affairs which occurs in that world or, what amounts to the same, any proposition which is instantiated by the world in question. Thus, the distinction between universal and individual world aspects reduces to a distinction between *two types of propositions—universal* and *individual*. In our framework, propositions are identified with sets of possible worlds, i.e., with subsets of $\mathbf{W}$ (cf. section 1.3).

The distinction between individual and universal propositions is thought to be a dichotomy. A proposition is universal iff it is not individual. Or, equivalently,

D9.1 $X \subseteq \mathbf{W}$ is *individual* $= X$ is not universal.

As we have stated above, two worlds are **C**-connected iff they share all their universal aspects. Thus, the definition of **C** is immediately forthcoming:

D9.2 wCv = For every universal $X \subseteq \mathbf{W}$, $w \in X$ iff $v \in X$.

How are we to characterize the set of universal propositions? First of all, it seems necessary to assume that the set in question is non-empty. If all propositions were individual, then D9.2 would imply that any two possible worlds are exactly similar to each other. Obviously, this is an unacceptable position. At the same time, we must assume that the set of universal propositions is not all-inclusive. It seems that *any* non-contradictory proposition which entails the existence of some particular (contingent) individual must, *ipso facto*, be individual. Examples of such propositions are easy to find.[9]

Therefore, we shall consider the following to be true:

The Principle of Division: There are X, $Y \subseteq \mathbf{W}$ such that X is universal and Y is individual.

The following are examples of universal and individual propositions:

(1) Some philosophers are mathematicians; The creator of the Theory of Forms was an outstanding political thinker; Some people never repay their debts.

(2) Frege was a mathematician; Plato was an outstanding political thinker; John never repaid his debt to Mary.

What happens when we negate a universal proposition? Can we get an individual proposition as a result? It is difficult to see any reason why we should allow for such a possibility. Therefore we shall assume that the complements of universal propositions are themselves universal.

The Principle of Complements: Universal propositions have universal complements.

---

[9] Note that the criterion which we have just presented constitutes only a sufficient and not a necessary condition of individuality. A proposition $X \subseteq \mathbf{W}$ may be individual even if there is no individual a such that a exists in every $w \in X$. Thus, for instance, the sentences, 'Plato exists or Socrates exists' and 'Plato does not exist' seem to express individual propositions, even though they do not imply the existence of Socrates nor the existence of Plato.

Given this assumption, the definition of C may be somewhat simplified:

T9.1 $w\mathbf{C}v$ iff, for every universal X, if $w \in X$, then $v \in X$.

To put it differently: $\mathbf{C}(w)$, i.e., the set of all v such that $w\mathbf{C}v$, is the product of the set of all universal propositions instantiated by w.

Proof: T9.1 will follow from D9.2 if we can show that for any v which instantiates every universal proposition instantiated by w, and for any universal $X \subseteq \mathbf{W}$, if $v \in X$, then $w \in X$. Now, suppose that $v \in X$ but $w \notin X$. Then w instantiates $\overline{X} = \mathbf{W}-X$, the complement of X. But, by the Principle of Complements, $\overline{X}$ is universal, so that v must belong to $\overline{X}$. Thus, we get a contradiction: $v \in X$ and $v \in \overline{X}$. **Q.E.D.**

The set of universal propositions is closed under complements. Is it also closed under products and unions?[10] Unfortunately, we cannot make this assumption. Or, rather, we cannot do it as long as we wish to allow for Leibnizianism. The argument is as follows: We shall say that a proposition X is a *u-product* (a *u-union*) iff X is the product (the union) of a set of universal propositions. Now, we can easily derive the following equivalence:

T9.2 Leibnizianism (i.e., the claim that $\mathbf{C}$ is an identity relation) $\Leftrightarrow$ For every $w \in \mathbf{W}$, $\{w\}$ is a u-product.

Proof: By T9.1, $\mathbf{C}(w)$ is a u-product, for every $w \in \mathbf{W}$. And by Leibnizianism, $\mathbf{C}(w) = \{w\}$. Thus, T9.2 from left to right is satisfied. Of course, given D9.1, Leibnizianism follows immediately from the right-hand side of T9.2. **Q.E.D.**

Now T9.2 leads directly to

T9.3 Leibnizianism $\Leftrightarrow$ Every proposition is the union of a set of u-products.

---

[10] Note that any set closed under complements and products is automatically closed under unions. And vice versa: closure under complements and unions entails closure under products.

Proof: (1) From left to right. Consider any $X \subseteq \mathbf{W}$. Clearly, X is the union of the set $\{Y \subseteq \mathbf{W}: \exists w \in X(Y = \{w\})\}$. In other words, X is the union of a set of unit-sets. At the same time. Leibnizianism entails that every unit-set is a u-product (cf. T9.2).

(2) From right to left. If every proposition is the union of a set of u-products, then, for every $w \in \mathbf{W}$, $\{w\}$ must be such a union. Therefore, $\{w\}$ must be a u-product itself. But then, by D9.1, $\{w\} = \mathbf{C}(w)$. Thus, it follows that $\mathbf{C}$ is an identity relation. Q.E.D.

According to the Principle of Division, some propositions are individual. This fact, in conjunction with T9.3, entails the following theorem:

T9.4 Leibnizianism $\Rightarrow$ The set of universal propositions is *not* closed under products (nor under unions).

Proof: By the Principle of Division, there exists some $X \subseteq \mathbf{W}$ such that X is individual. By Leibnizianism and T9.3, there is some set Γ of u-products such that $X = \cup \Gamma$. Suppose now, for *reductio ad absurdum*, that the set of universal propositions is closed under products. Then, given the Principle of Complements, this set is also closed under unions. Consequently, Γ must be a set of universal propositions and the union of Γ, X, proves to be a universal proposition, contrary to the hypothesis. Q.E.D.

In other words, Leibnizianism entails that the distinction between universal and individual propositions is not a *radical* one. If Leibnizianism is true, then *every* proposition, universal or not, results from universal propositions by appropriate Boolean concatenations (cf. T9.3).

However, while Leibnizianism implies that all individual propositions are Boolean concatenations of universal propositions, even Leibnizians may agree that *some* types of such concatenations never lead from universal propositions to individual ones. In particular, the following principle seems eminently plausible:

The Principle of Disjointness: If Γ is a set of *disjoint* universal propositions, then the union of Γ is universal.

It is easy to show that *this* principle of closure is perfectly consistent with Leibnizianism.

Example A: Suppose that **W** consists of four worlds and that the following propositions are universal: **W**, ∅, and all *pairs* of worlds. Obviously, such a model satisfies the principles of Complements, Division and Disjointness. At the same time, Leibnizianism is satisfied, since, for every two worlds in **W**, each of them belongs to some pair to which the other one does not belong. Thus, **C** is an identity relation on **W**.

In what follows, we shall assume that the Principle of Disjointness is satisfied by our model. However, nothing of substance depends on this assumption. Most of what we shall say below will still be acceptable to anyone who thinks that even disjoint u-unions sometimes may be individual propositions.

9.2. *Anti-Leibnizianism*

D9.2 implies that every universal proposition is closed under **C**. That is, for every $w, v \in \mathbf{W}$ and every universal $X \subseteq \mathbf{W}$, if $w\mathbf{C}v$ and $w \in X$, then $w \in X$. What about the converse of this thesis? Is every proposition closed under **C** universal? Obviously, the Leibnizians would deny it, since, according to them, *every* proposition, universal or not, is closed under **C**. But what about *anti*-Leibnizians? Can we not simply identify anti-Leibnizianism with the claim that closure under **C** entails universality? In fact, this is what we propose to do.

Anti-Leibnizianism: Every proposition closed under **C** is universal.

Is this condition a correct explication of anti-Leibnizianism? We think it is, for the following reasons:

Previously, when discussing the concept of automorphism, we suggested that, for an opponent of Leibnizianism, universality and *purity* coincide with each other (section 6.8). In particular, such a person would accept the following thesis:

(a) A proposition is universal iff it is pure (=invariant under automorphisms).

It should be noted that the set of pure propositions is closed under complements, non-empty, not all-inclusive (providing that there are some automorphisms distinct from the identity permutation p_i, that is, providing that Leibnizianism is false), and that it obviously satisfies the Principle of Disjointness. In fact, this set is closed under *all* unions, not only under disjoint ones.

Given (a), T9.1 transforms into

(b) wCv iff v belongs to every pure proposition to which w belongs.

From (b) we can derive the following condition:

(c) A proposition is pure iff it is closed under **C**.

Proof: Assume that $X \subseteq \mathbf{W}$ is pure, $w \in X$ and wCv. Then, by (b), $v \in X$. Thus, closure under **C** immediately follows. Suppose, now, that X is closed under **C**, and consider any $w, v \in \mathbf{W}$ and $p \in \mathcal{A}$ such that $p(w) = v$. If $p(w) = v$, then v belongs to every pure proposition to which w belongs and vice versa. Thus, by (b), wCv and vCw. But then, if X is closed under **C**, $w \in X$ iff $v \in X$. Thus, X is invariant under automorphisms, i.e., X is pure. Q.E.D.

Now, (a) and (c), taken together, entail that

(d) A proposition is universal iff it is closed under **C**.

Given D9.2, (d) is equivalent to our formulation of Anti-Leibnizianism. Thus, the principle of Anti-Leibnizianism turns out to be a direct consequence of the identification of universality with purity.[11]

Observe that Anti-Leibnizianism and Leibnizianism are not simple contradictories. The two principles are incompatible with each other (given the Principle of Division), but it is possible to construct a model which satisfies neither of them.

Example B: Suppose that $\mathbf{W} = \{w_1, w_2, w_3, w_4, w_5\}$ and assume that the following propositions are universal: $\mathbf{W}$, $\{w_1, w_2, w_3\}$, $\{w_1, w_2, w_4\}$, and

---

[11] The reader may remember that, in connection with the theory of automorphisms, we proposed the following definition of **C**:

D6.1 $wCv = \exists p \in \mathcal{A}(p(w) = v)$.

How does this definition relate to principle (b)? Can we prove that

(e) $\exists p \in \mathcal{A}(p(w) = v)$ iff v belongs to every pure proposition to which w belongs?

This can be readily done. (e) from left to right follows immediately from the fact that every pure proposition is closed under automorphisms. Since the proposition $\{u \in \mathbf{W}: \exists p \in \mathcal{A}(p(w) = u)\}$ is pure and contains w, the right-hand side of (e) entails its left-hand side.

all their complements. In such a model, Leibnizianism fails, since $w_1 C w_2$. At the same time, Anti-Leibnizianism is falsified by the fact that the unit-propositions $\{w_3\}$, $\{w_4\}$ and $\{w_5\}$ are all closed under C without being universal.

However, it seems to us that any such 'intermediate' position is extremely difficult to defend. If one denies that C is an identity relation, then why should one be content with anything less than the identification of universality with purity? Therefore, we shall assume that the intermediate position does not constitute any real alternative.

The Principle of Simplification: If some individual propositions are closed under C, then C is an identity relation.

This principle is obviously equivalent to the disjunction of Anti-Leibnizianism and Leibnizianism.

According to T9.4, Leibnizianism entails that some u-products are not universal. Anti-Leibnizianism, on the other hand, leads to the opposite conclusion. Clearly, the set of propositions closed under C must be closed under products (and unions). In fact, we can prove the following equivalence:

T9.5 Anti-Leibnizianism $\Leftrightarrow$ The set of universal propositions is closed under products.

Proof: Since T9.5 from left to right is trivial, we shall only show that the opposite entailment holds. Suppose that $X \subseteq W$ is closed under C. Since, by T9.1, the equivalence classes with respect to C are u-products, X must be the union of a set of u-products. By the right-hand side of T9.5, (1) all u-products are universal. Thus, X is a u-union. At the same time, given the Principle of Complements, (1) entails that (2) all u-unions are universal. Thus, X is a universal proposition.   Q.E.D.

In other words, Anti-Leibnizianism is equivalent to the claim that there exists a *radical* division between universal and individual propositions. To be an anti-Leibnizian is to believe that no individual proposition is reducible to a concatenation of universal components.[12]

---

[12] Observe that the opposite is *not* true: universal propositions may well be constructible from individual components. In fact, given the principles of Division, Complements and Disjointness, it may be shown that *every* proposition is the union or the product of some set of individual propositions.

CHAPTER 10

Universality and Relevance

10.1. *Definition of* **R** *and the first principle of relevance*

In section 8.2, we suggested that $\mathbf{R}^+$ and the concept of a universal aspect are sufficient for the definition of the relation **R**. Now it is time to construct such a definition.

As we know, **R** is the relation of similarity in all universal relevant aspects. Thus, our task is first to define the concept of a relevant aspect or, what amounts to the same, the concept of a relevant proposition. As a matter of fact, we are able to distinguish between two concepts of relevance—one relative (to a situation), the other absolute.

D 10.1 $X \subseteq \mathbf{W}$ is *relevant in* $w = \mathbf{R}^+(w) \subseteq X$.

That is, X is relevant in w iff X is instantiated by every v which is relevantly similar to w. $(\mathbf{R}^+(w) = \mathrm{df} \{v \in \mathbf{W}: w\mathbf{R}^+v\})$

D 10.2 $X \subseteq \mathbf{W}$ is *relevant* = For every $w \in X$, X is relevant in w.

To put it differently: a proposition is relevant iff it is closed under $\mathbf{R}^+$. As we may remember (section 2.2), $\mathbf{R}^+$ is thought to be an equivalence relation. Therefore, D 10.2 could also be formulated as follows: X is relevant iff, for every world w, either X or $\overline{X}$ is relevant in w.

How are we now to define the relation **R**? Unfortunately, it seems that no definition of **R** will be wholly satisfactory, at least not without some additional assumptions. It would seem that any such definition should have the following implications:

(1) **R** is an equivalence relation (providing that the same applies to $\mathbf{R}^+$);

(2) If v instantiates every universal proposition relevant in w, then $w\mathbf{R}v$;

(3) If $w\mathbf{R}v$, then v instantiates every universal proposition relevant in w.

Consider, now, three different definition proposals:

D 10.3 a wRv = For every universal $X \subseteq W$, X is relevant in w iff X is relevant in v.

D 10.3 b wRv = For every universal $X \subseteq W$, if X is relevant in w, then $v \in X$.

D 10.3 c wRv = For every universal relevant $X \subseteq W$, if $w \in X$, then $v \in X$.

While D 10.3 a entails (1) and (3), it fails to imply (2). Analogously, D 10.3 b implies (2) and (3) but not (1). Finally, D 10.3 c takes care of (1) and (2) but is compatible with the negation of (3).

In fact, it may be proved that *no* possible definition of **R** is, by itself, sufficient for the derivation of *all* the conditions (1)–(3).

Proof: Suppose that there *is* such a definition:

D 10.3 $wRv = \alpha$.

Now, since D 10.3 entails (2) and (3), α must be equivalent to the right-hand side of D 10.3 b. But then, since D 10.3 is assumed to entail (1), the same must apply to D 10.3 b. However, this cannot be true, as may be seen from the following example:

Example C: Let $W = \{w_1, w_2, w_3, w_4\}$ and suppose that the set of universal propositions consists of **W**, $\{w_1, w_2, w_3\}$, $\{w_2, w_3\}$, $\{w_2, w_3, w_4\}$ and all their complements. Assume now that the following sets are equivalence classes with respect to R^+: $\{w_1, w_3\}$ and $\{w_2, w_4\}$. Then, by D 10.3 b, it follows that $w_1 R w_2$ and $w_2 R w_3 R w_1$, but not $w_2 R w_1$. Thus, **R** is neither symmetric nor transitive. Consequently, D10.3 b does not entail (1), and therefore D 10.3 cannot entail (1) either. (It will be noted that the model used in this example is anti-Leibnizian. However, a Leibnizian model would do just as well. For instance, let $W = \{w_1, w_2, w_3, w_4, w_5\}$ and assume that the following propositions are universal: **W**, $\{w_1, w_5\}$, $\{w_2, w_5\}$, $\{w_4, w_5\}$ and all their complements. Let $\{w_1, w_3\}$ and $\{w_2, w_4, w_5\}$ be the equivalence classes with respect to R^+. Then it follows that $w_2 R w_1$ but not $w_1 R w_2$. Thus, once more, (1) fails to hold.) Q.E.D.

How are we to solve this problem? Obviously, we could retract one of our adequacy conditions and thereby avoid the whole difficulty. There is, however, another possibility which seems to us much more plausible. Perhaps we should make some additional assumption which would entail the equivalence of all of our three definitions and thereby remove the necessity of choice. As a matter of fact, such an assumption is easily forthcoming. If X is a proposition, then we shall say that a proposition Y is the *relevance closure of X* iff Y is the set of all w such that $\mathbf{R}^+(w) \subseteq X$. Thus, the relevance closure of X is the proposition true in exactly those worlds in which X is relevant.

Consider, now, the following condition:

The First Principle of Relevance (RP1):
The relevance closures of universal propositions are themselves universal.

First, we shall show that, given this principle, all our definitions of **R** prove to be equivalent to each other. Then we shall consider the plausibility of (RP1).

Note that the definiens in D10.3a immediately entails the definiens in D10.3b, and that the latter in its turn entails the definiens in D10.3c. Thus, in order to prove the equivalence, it will be sufficient to show that the definiens in D10.3c entails the definiens in D10.3a.

Proof: Suppose that (a) for every universal relevant $X \subseteq \mathbf{W}$, if $w \in X$, then $v \in X$. Consider any universal $X \subseteq \mathbf{W}$. Case 1: X is relevant in w. Then, if Y is the relevance closure of X, $w \in Y$. And, by (RP1), Y is universal. Since the relevance closure of any proposition is relevant (given the fact that $\mathbf{R}^+$ is symmetric and transitive), (a) entails that $v \in Y$. But then $\mathbf{R}^+(v) \subseteq X$. That is, X is relevant in v. Case 2: X is relevant in v. Then, by similar reasoning as above, the relevance closure Y of X is universal, relevant and contains v. Now, by the symmetry of $\mathbf{R}^+$, the complements of relevant propositions are themselves relevant, and, by the Principle of Complements, the complements of universal propositions are universal. Thus, $\overline{Y}$ is relevant and universal. Suppose, now, that X is not relevant in w. Then $w \in \overline{Y}$. But, in such a Case, (a) implies that $v \in \overline{Y}$, contrary to hypothesis. Thus, X must be relevant in w. Q.E.D.

But is (RP1) a plausible condition? We do not have any conclusive answer to this question. It will be shown, however, that (RP1) is extremely plausible to an anti-Leibnizian, and that it is perfectly consistent with Leibnizianism.

It seems undisputable that the relation **R** should have the following property:

(**CR**) $C \subseteq R$.

Surely, if two situations are identical in *all* universal respects, relevant or not, then they should be **R**-connected.

Consider, now, the following strengthening of our adequacy condition (3):

(4) If $w\mathbf{R}v$, then every universal proposition relevant in w is relevant in v.

Note that (4) follows from D10.5a. As a matter of fact, (4) seems to be a very intuitive condition. Surely, if there is some universal proposition which is relevant in w but not in v, then the situations in question cannot be **R**-connected.

Now, we shall prove that, from the anti-Leibnizian point of view, (RP1) represents a direct consequence of (**CR**)&(4).

Proof: By Anti-Leibnizianism, universality and closure under **C** coincide. Thus, (RP1) is equivalent to

(a) If X is closed under **C**, then the same applies to the relevance closure of X.

That is:

(b) If $w\mathbf{C}v$, then, if X is closed under **C** and relevant in w, X must be relevant in v.

Applying Anti-Leibnizianism once more, (b) transforms into

(c) If $w\mathbf{C}v$, then every universal proposition relevant in w is relevant in v.

Obviously, (c) follows from the conjunction of (**CR**) and (4). Q.E.D.

Thus, for any anti-Leibnizian, universalistically minded or not, (RP1) must be as intuitive as (**CR**) and (4). As for the consistency of (RP1) with Leibnizianism, it is easy to construct Leibnizian models in which universality is preserved by the operation of relevance closure. For instance, consider our model given in Example A. Thus, let $\mathbf{W} = \{w_1, w_2, w_3, w_4\}$ and assume that the set of universal propositions consists of $\mathbf{W}$, $\varnothing$, and all pairs of worlds. Suppose, now, that $\{w_1, w_2\}$ and $\{w_3, w_4\}$ constitute the equivalence classes with respect to $\mathbf{R}^+$. Then it immediately follows that the relevance closure of every universal $X \subseteq \mathbf{W}$ equals either X or $\varnothing$. Thus, every such relevance closure is universal.

In what follows, we shall assume the validity of (RP 1). This means that there is no need to choose between different variants of D 10.3. Any of them will do, since they are all equivalent to each other.

10.2. *The equivalence of* (CR$^+$) *and* (RR$^+$)

In section 8.3, we promised to show that, for an anti-Leibnizian, (CR$^+$) and (RR$^+$) are demonstrably equivalent. The proof consists of two parts. First, we note that, providing that $\mathbf{R}^+$ is reflexive and transitive, the equivalence of (CR$^+$) and (RR$^+$) immediately follows from

(CRR$^+$) $\mathbf{R} = \mathbf{R}^+/\mathbf{C}$.

The next step will be to prove that (CRR$^+$) is derivable from Anti-Leibnizianism:

T 10.1 Anti-Leibnizianism $\Rightarrow$ (CRR$^+$).

Proof: (a) Suppose that $w\mathbf{R}v$. It follows from D 10.3a and from D 10.3b that v belongs to every universal proposition which is relevant in w. By Anti-Leibnizianism, $\mathbf{R}^+/\mathbf{C}(w) = \{v \in \mathbf{W}: \exists u(w\mathbf{R}^+u\mathbf{C}v)\}$ is universal. And obviously, $\mathbf{R}^+/\mathbf{C}(w)$ is relevant in w. Thus, $w\mathbf{R}^+/\mathbf{C}v$. But this means that $\mathbf{R} \subseteq \mathbf{R}^+/\mathbf{C}$. (b) Suppose that $w\mathbf{R}^+/\mathbf{C}v$. Both D 10.3b and D 10.3c entail that $\mathbf{C} \subseteq \mathbf{R}$, and all variants of D 10.3 imply that $\mathbf{R}^+ \subseteq \mathbf{R}$. Consequently, $w\mathbf{R}/\mathbf{R}v$. Since $\mathbf{R}$ is transitive (according to D 10.3a and D 10.3c), $w\mathbf{R}v$. Thus, $\mathbf{R}^+/\mathbf{C} \subseteq \mathbf{R}$. Q.E.D.

10.3. *The second principle of relevance*

We proceed now to a different problem. Suppose that Γ is a set of propositions each of which is universal and relevant. What can we say about the product of Γ? Obviously, $\cap \Gamma$ is relevant, but is it universal? To put it differently, we want to know whether the following principle holds:

The Second Principle of Relevance (RP 2):

The set of universal relevant propositions is closed under products.

Given Anti-Leibnizianism, (RP 2) is trivially true, since, according to anti-Leibnizians, all u-products are universal (cf. T9.5). On the other hand, Leibnizianism is compatible with the negation of (RP 2), as may be seen from the following example:

Example D: Let $W = \{w_1, w_2, w_3, w_4, w_5, w_6, w_7, w_8\}$ and assume that the following propositions are universal: W, $X_1 = \{w_1, w_2, w_3, w_4\}$, $X_2 = \{w_1, w_2, w_5, w_6\}$, $X_3 = \{w_1, w_2, w_7, w_8\}$, $X_4 = \{w_1, w_3, w_5, w_7\}$, and all their complements. Note that this model is Leibnizian (since, for every $w \in W$, $\{w\}$ is a u-product) and that it satisfies the principles of Division, Complements and Disjointness. Let $\{w_1, w_2\}$, (w_3, w_4), $\{w_5, w_6\}$ and $\{w_7, w_8\}$ be the equivalence classes with respect to R^+. Observe that, given this specification of R^+, the relevance closure of every universal $X \subseteq W$ is either identical with X itself or with $\varnothing$. Thus (RP 1) is satisfied. However, (RP 2) fails to hold: For instance, while X_1 and X_2 are both universal and relevant, their product, $\{w_1, w_2\}$, is not universal.

But even though Leibnizians are not *committed* to (RP 2), they may well think it to be a principle worthy of acceptance. According to Leibnizianism, there is no 'iron curtain' between universal and individual propositions. But, as we shall presently argue, a Leibnizian may still claim that such an iron curtain exists as far as *morally relevant* propositions are concerned.

Imagine a universalistically minded Leibnizian who assumes that R and R^+ coincide with each other. That is, he accepts the condition (**RR⁺**), according to which two situations which are similar in all *universal* morally relevant respects must, *ipso facto*, be similar in *all* relevant respects. Now, how would he react, if we confronted him with the following principle?

Irrelevance of Individual Aspects (IIA):

No individual $X \subseteq W$ is relevant.

Probably, he would claim that (IIA) already follows from the universalistic insight embodied in (**RR⁺**).

It should be noted that (IIA) entails (RR$^+$).[13] Moreover, given *Anti-Leibnizianism*, (IIA) is derivable from (RR$^+$).[14] However, (RR$^+$) *alone* is not sufficient for the derivation of (IIA). This is shown by our Example D above.[15]

What (RR$^+$) does imply is only that every relevant proposition is a Boolean concatenation of universal relevant propositions. To be more precise, given (RR$^+$) every relevant proposition proves to be the union of some set Γ such that every member of Γ is the product of a set of universal relevant propositions.[16] At this point we cannot go any further and it is here that (RP2) may help us. Given the Principle of Complements, the set of universal relevant propositions is closed under complements. Additionally, given (RP2), this set is closed under products. Now, every set closed under complements and products is closed under all Boolean concatenations. Thus, it follows that every relevant proposition is universal. In other words, given (RP2), (RR$^+$) entails (IIA).

We have seen, then, that the intuitively felt equivalence of (RR$^+$) and (IIA) can be formally demonstrated by means of (RP2).[17] This suggests that (RP2) should be accepted not only by anti-Leibnizians but also by the proponents of Leibnizianism. Without this principle, a universalistically minded Leibnizian, who claims that **R** reduces to **R$^+$**, would still have to allow for the possibility that some *individual* aspects of situations may turn out to be *morally relevant*—a possibility which must be rather disagreeable from the universalistic point of view.

In order to prevent any misunderstandings, let us stress that the mere acceptance of (RP2) does not in any way commit us to ethical uni-

---

[13] Since **R$^+$** is transitive, **R$^+$**(w) is relevant, for every $w \in$ **W**. But then **R$^+$**(w) is universal, by (IIA). Therefore, every variant of D10.3 implies that **R**(w)$\subseteq$**R$^+$**(w). Thus, **R**$\subseteq$**R$^+$**.

[14] We already know that Anti-Leibnizianism entails (RP2), and we shall see subsequently that (RR$^+$) & (RP2) $\Rightarrow$ (IIA).

[15] One can verify that, in this example, every equivalence class with respect to **R$^+$** is the product of two universal relevant propositions. Therefore, every variant of D10.3 implies that **R** and **R$^+$** coincide with each other. Thus, our model satisfies (RR$^+$). But (IIA) fails to hold: all equivalence classes with respect to **R$^+$** and all their complements are individual relevant propositions.

[16] For the proof, note that, by D10.3c, every equivalence class with respect to **R** is the product of a set of universal relevant propositions. And every relevant proposition is the union of a set of equivalence classes with respect to **R$^+$**. But then, since (RR$^+$) entails that **R** = **R$^+$**, the conclusion follows.

[17] As a matter of fact, (IIA) may be represented as the conjunction of (RR$^+$) and (RP2). To see this, note that (IIA) immediately entails (RP2).

versalism. The same applies to the conjunction of (RP1) and (RP2). In particular, we may accept both these principles and still deny that **R** and **R**$^+$ coincide with each other. The following example will illustrate this point:

Example E: Let $\mathbf{W} = \{w_1, w_2, w_3, w_4, w_5\}$, and assume that the following propositions are universal: $\mathbf{W}$, $X_1 = \{w_1, w_2\}$, $X_2 = \{w_3, w_4\}$, $X_3 = \{w_5\}$, $X_4 = \{w_1, w_3\}$, $X_5 = \{w_2, w_4\}$, and all their complements. Suppose that **R**$^+$ divides **W** into three equivalence classes: $\{w_1, w_4\}$, $\{w_2, w_3\}$ and $\{w_5\}$. In this model, $\mathbf{W}, \varnothing, \{w_1, w_2, w_3, w_4\}$ and $\{w_5\}$ are the only relevant universal propositions, and they also constitute the set of all the relevance closures of universal propositions. Thus, (RP2) and (RP1) are satisfied. At the same time, for any $w \neq w_5$, **W** and $\{w_1, w_2, w_3, w_4\}$ are the only universal propositions relevant in w. Therefore, by any variant of D10.3, $\{w_1, w_2, w_3, w_4\}$ and $\{w_5\}$ constitute the equivalence classes with respect to **R**. Thus, for instance, $w_1 \mathbf{R} w_2$, even though $\langle w_1, w_2 \rangle \notin \mathbf{R}^+$. Consequently, (RR$^+$) fails.[18]

---

[18] Note that the model used in this example is Leibnizian. However, Anti-Leibnizianism would lead us to the same results. To see this, remove X_4 and X_5, together with their complements, from the list of universal propositions. You may verify that this new model is anti-Leibnizian and that it still satisfies (RP1) and (RP2) without satisfying (RR$^+$).

CHAPTER 11

Universality and Universalizability

11.1. *The condition* (uu)

While the relevance closure of a proposition, X, is the set of all w such that $\mathbf{R}^+(w) \subseteq X$, we shall define *the deontic closure of* X as the set of all w such that $\mathbf{D}(w) \subseteq X$. ($\mathbf{D}(w) = \{v \in \mathbf{W}: w\mathbf{D}v\}$.) Thus, the deontic closure of X is the proposition true in exactly those worlds in which X is obligatory. In other words, the deontic closure of X is nothing other than the proposition that X is obligatory.

Consider, now, the following principle:

(uu) Deontic closures of universal propositions are universal.

That is, for any proposition X, if X is universal, then the same applies to the proposition that X is obligatory. The formal similarity between this principle and (RP1) is easily noted.

We shall see below that, for an anti-Leibnizian, (uu) is simply another formulation of the condition (u). But, in distinction from (u), (uu) is *not* trivialized by Leibnizianism. Furthermore, it will be seen that (uu), together with some additional assumptions, is sufficient for the derivation of (ur)—the relevant-similarity variant of (u).[19] But, in distinction from (ur), (uu) does *not* make any use of the presumably suspect concept of relevance. Thus, it seems that in (uu) we have found a formulation of the Universalizability Principle which avoids both horns of the traditional Universalizability Dilemma.

11.2. (uu), (u) *and Leibnizianism*

According to (uu), if a proposition X is universal, then the same applies to the proposition that X is obligatory. But what about the proposition that X is permitted ($=$ the set of all w such that $\mathbf{D}(w)$ overlaps X)? It is

---

[19] The assumptions in question are (RP2), the $\mathbf{R}^+$-variant of (ur), and, indirectly, (RP1).

easy to see that this proposition also must be universal if (uu) is true. If X is universal, then, by the Principle of Complements, the same applies to $\overline{X}$. Therefore, (uu) entails that $\overline{X}$'s being obligatory is a universal proposition. Thus, applying the Principle of Complements once again, it follows that $\overline{X}$'s not being obligatory = X's being permitted is a universal proposition. As a matter of fact, we can strengthen this one-way entailment to an equivalence. Let (uu') be the condition to the effect that, for every universal $X \subseteq W$, the proposition that X is permitted = $\{w \in W : D(w) \cap X \neq \varnothing\}$ is universal. Then,

T11.1 (uu) $\Leftrightarrow$ (uu').

Proof: Above, we have shown that T11.1 holds from left to right. In order to see that it also holds from right to left, it is sufficient to note that the deontic closure of X is the complement of the proposition that $\overline{X}$ is permitted. Thus, (uu) follows from (uu') by two applications of the Principle of Complements.   Q.E.D.

We shall prove now that, for an anti-Leibnizian, (uu) and (u) are equivalent conditions.

T11.2 Anti-Leibnizianism $\Rightarrow$ ((uu) $\Leftrightarrow$ (u)).

Proof: By T11.1, it will be sufficient to show that Anti-Leibnizianism entails the equivalence of (uu') and (u). Now, for an anti-Leibnizian, (uu') reduces to

(1) If X is closed under C, then $\{w \in W : D(w) \cap X \neq \varnothing\}$ is closed under C.

(1) can also be represented as follows:

(2) If $w D u$ and $u \in X$ and X is closed under C, then, if $w C v$, there is some z such that $v D z$ and $v \in X$.

Since C is transitive and reflexive, $C(u)$ is closed under C and contains u. Thus, (2) implies the condition (u), according to which the conjunction $w D u \& w C v$ entails that $\exists z (v D z \& z \in C(u))$. Since every $X \subseteq W$ closed under C must include $C(u)$ if it contains u, (u) implies (2).   Q.E.D.

That (uu) does *not* follow from Leibnizianism may be seen from the example below.

Example F: Let $\mathbf{W} = \{w_1, w_2, w_3, w_4\}$ and suppose that the set of universal propositions consists of $\mathbf{W}$, $\varnothing$ and all the world-pairs. Let $\mathbf{D} = \{\langle w_1, w_2 \rangle, \langle w_2, w_3 \rangle, \langle w_3, w_4 \rangle, \langle w_4, w_4 \rangle\}$. Clearly, this model is Leibnizian. (uu), however, does not hold. While $\{w_1, w_2\}$, $\{w_2, w_4\}$ and $\{w_3, w_4\}$ are universal, their deontic closures, $\{w_1\}$, $\{w_1, w_3, w_4\}$ and $\{w_2, w_3, w_4\}$, are individual propositions.

11.3. (uu) *and* (ur)

We proceed now to the derivation of (ur) from (uu). As we may remember, the condition (ur⁺) constitutes the $\mathbf{R}^+$-variant of (ur). That is, (ur⁺) asserts that $\mathbf{R}^+$-similar worlds have $\mathbf{R}^+$-similar deontic alternatives. To put it formally,

(ur⁺) $w\mathbf{R}^+v \ \& \ w\mathbf{D}u \ \rightarrow \ \exists z(v\mathbf{D}z \ \& \ u\mathbf{R}^+z).$

As we pointed out in sections 2.2 and 8.3, such $\mathbf{R}^+$-variants of the universalistic conditions on $\mathbf{R}$ and $\mathbf{D}$ are relatively uncontroversial. They assert only that $\mathbf{D}$ is a *supervenient* relation, but not that $\mathbf{D}$ is universalizable. Similar remarks apply to the principle (RP2). This condition is perfectly acceptable to an opponent of ethical universalism. Therefore, if we can prove that (uu), (ur⁺) and (RP2), taken together, entail (ur), then it seems reasonable to claim that the 'universalistic' content of (ur) is due to (uu) and *not* to the other premisses.

T11.3 (uu) & (ur⁺) & (RP2) $\Rightarrow$ (ur).

Proof: Suppose that (1) $w\mathbf{R}v$ and (2) $w\mathbf{D}u$. Consider $\mathbf{R}(u)$. Define X^* as $\{v \in \mathbf{W}: \mathbf{D}(v) \cap \mathbf{R}(u) \neq \varnothing\}$. We are to show that (3) $v \in X^*$. By D10.3c, $\mathbf{R}(u)$ is the product of a set of universal relevant propositions. Thus, by (RP2), (a) $\mathbf{R}(u)$ itself is universal. By any variant of D10.3, $\mathbf{R}^+(u) \subseteq \mathbf{R}(u)$. Therefore, (ur⁺) and (2) entail that $\mathbf{R}^+(w) \subseteq X^*$. This means that (b) X^* is relevant in w. According to T11.1, (uu) and (uu′) are equivalent conditions. And (uu′), together with (a), entails that (c) X^* is universal Finally, by D10.3a or D10.3b, (1), (b) and (c) entail (3).   Q.E.D.

It should be noted that in this proof we have made use of different variants of D10.3. This means that, in our reasoning, we have been implicitly presupposing the principle (RP1), which guarantees that D10.3a, D10.3b and D10.3c are equivalent definitions. But this should not perturb us too much. Like (RP2), (RP1) is a condition without universalistic implications. In fact, we can show that the conjunction (RP1) & (RP2) & (ur+) is fully consistent with the negation of (ur).

Example G: Assume that W, R^+ and the set of universal propositions are as in our Example E in section 10.3. Thus, W consists of five worlds, $w_1, ..., w_5$, R^+ divides W into three equivalence classes: $\{w_1, w_4\}$, $\{w_2, w_3\}$ and $\{w_5\}$, and the set of universal propositions consists of W, $\{w_1, w_2\}$, $\{w_3, w_4\}$, $\{w_5\}$, $\{w_1, w_3\}$, $\{w_2, w_4\}$, and all their complements. We already know that this model satisfies (RP1) and (RP2). Suppose, now, that $D = \{\langle w_1, w_5 \rangle, \langle w_2, w_2 \rangle, \langle w_3, w_3 \rangle, \langle w_4, w_5 \rangle, \langle w_5, w_5 \rangle\}$. This means that (ur+) is satisfied: R^+-similar worlds have R^+-similar deontic alternatives. At the same time, pairs such as w_1 and w_2, or w_3 and w_4, are R-similar, even though their deontic alternatives are *not* R-connected. Thus, (ur) fails to hold.

While (uu) entails (ur), the derivation does *not* work in the opposite direction—even in the presence of (ur+), (RP1), (RP2) and (**RR+**). Thus, a universalistically minded Leibnizian, who accepts (ur) because he has accepted (**RR+**) and (ur+), is not thereby *committed* to the acceptance of (uu). The following simple example will illustrate this point.

Example H: Let W, D, and the set of universal propositions be as in Example F in section 11.2. Thus, Leibnizianism holds, but (uu) is not satisfied. Suppose, now, that every two members of W are R^+-connected with each other. In consequence, for any $w, v \in W$, wRv. But then the conditions (RP1), (RP2), (**RR+**), (ur+) and (ur) follow trivially.

Incidentally, it is to be noted that our model in Example H satisfies not only (ur) but also *any* universalistic condition on R and D. Clearly, any such condition is trivially satisfied, if all the members of W are R-similar to each other. Thus, no condition of this kind implies (uu).

This independence of (uu) from the relevant-similarity variants of the Universalizability Principle suggests that some Leibnizians may have doubts about the status of (uu). They may try to argue that (uu) does not constitute an adequate expression of the principle of universalizability. An argument against (uu) constructed along these lines will be discussed in the next chapter.

CHAPTER 12

Extensions of Leibnizianism

12.1 *Absolute Leibnizianism*

Leibnizianism reduces exact similarity to identity. In section 8.3, we suggested that there may exist stronger variants of Leibnizianism, which reduce **R** to **R**+. Such a reduction must consist in the derivation of the condition (**RR**+), according to which **R**+ includes **R**. This is sufficient, because the converse of this condition trivially follows from any variant of D10.3. Before we start searching for such extensions of Leibnizianism, let us recall that Leibnizianism, taken by itself, is fully compatible with the negation of (**RR**+). This is shown by our Example E in section 10.3.

In section 9.1, we have seen (cf. T9.3) that Leibnizianism is equivalent to the following assertion:

(a) Every proposition is the union of a set of u-products.

Or, what amounts to the same,

(b) Every proposition is the product of a set of u-unions.[20]

This means that, according to Leibnizianism, we can always get from the set of universal propositions to any $X \subseteq W$ in two steps: any such X is a concatenation of concatenations of universal propositions. But then a stronger version of Leibnizianism immediately suggests itself: Perhaps we do not really need *two* steps but only *one*. Why not assume that every proposition is a simple, first-level concatenation of universal propositions?

The following condition expresses this idea:

Absolute Leibnizianism: Every $X \subseteq W$ is a u-product or a u-union.

---

[20] The equivalence of (a) and (b) follows from the fact that the union of a set Γ of u-products always equals the product of the set Γ' defined as follows:

Γ' is the set of all $X \subseteq W$ such that, for some set Σ of universal propositions, X is the union of Σ, and the union of Γ is included in the union of Σ.

Such a claim is obviously stronger than Leibnizianism. Example E, referred to above, shows that Leibnizian models do not need to be 'absolutely Leibnizian'. In this example, the propositions $\{w_1, w_4\}$ and $\{w_2, w_3\}$ are neither u-products nor u-unions. At the same time, the derivation of Leibnizianism from Absolute Leibnizianism is straightforward. If X is a u-product, then X is the (degenerate) union of a set of u-products. If X is a u-union, then X is the union of a set of (degenerate) u-products. Thus, Absolute Leibnizianism entails that every proposition is the union of a set of u-products. And we already know that the latter condition is equivalent to Leibnizianism.

But is not Absolute Leibnizianism *too* strong? Is it compatible with our general conditions on the set of universal propositions? Example F in Section 11.2 confirms that it is. There, we assumed that $\mathbf{W}$ consists of four worlds, $w_1, ..., w_4$, and that $\mathbf{W}$, $\varnothing$, and all pairs of worlds exhaust the list of universal propositions. It is easy to ascertain that such a model is absolutely Leibnizian and that it satisfies the principles of Division, Complements, and Disjointness. Incidentally, the same Example F shows that (uu) does *not* follow from Absolute Leibnizianism. If $\mathbf{D} = \{\langle w_1, w_2 \rangle, \langle w_2, w_3 \rangle, \langle w_3, w_4 \rangle, \langle w_4, w_4 \rangle\}$, then the deontic closure of the universal $\{w_1, w_2\}$ equals $\{w_1\}$, which is an individual proposition.

We shall prove now that, given Absolute Leibnizianism, $\mathbf{R}$ and $\mathbf{R}^+$ must coincide with each other:

T 12.1 Absolute Leibnizianism $\Rightarrow$ ($\mathbf{RR}^+$).

Proof: We have to show that, for an arbitrary $w \in \mathbf{W}$, $\mathbf{R}(w) \subseteq \mathbf{R}^+(w)$. By Absolute Leibnizianism $\mathbf{R}^+(w)$ is a u-product or a u-union. Case 1: $\mathbf{R}^+(w) = \cap \Gamma$, where every $Y \in \Gamma$ is universal. Obviously, every such $Y \in \Gamma$ is relevant in w. But then, by D 10.3a or D 10.3b, $\mathbf{R}(w) \subseteq \cap \Gamma = \mathbf{R}^+(w)$ Case 2: $\mathbf{R}^+(w) = \cup \Gamma$, where every member of Γ is universal. Let Γ' be the set of the complements of members of Γ. By the Principle of Complements, every $Y \in \Gamma'$ is universal. It should be noted that the complement of $\mathbf{R}^+(w)$, $\overline{\mathbf{R}^+(w)}$, equals $\cap \Gamma'$. Assume, for *reductio ad absurdum*, that there is some $v \in \mathbf{W}$ such that (a) $w\mathbf{R}v$, but (b) $\neg (w\mathbf{R}^+v)$. By the symmetry and transitivity of $\mathbf{R}^+$, $\overline{\mathbf{R}^+(w)} = \cap \Gamma'$ is closed under $\mathbf{R}^+$. This means that every member of Γ' is not only universal but also relevant. Therefore, by D 10.3a or D 10.3b, (b) implies that (c) $\cap \Gamma' = \overline{\mathbf{R}^+(w)}$

is relevant in v. In other words, (d) $\neg(v\mathbf{R}w)$. Since $\mathbf{R}$ is symmetric (cf. D 10.3a or D 10.3c), (d) contradicts (a). Thus, $\mathbf{R}(w)\subseteq\mathbf{R}^+(w)$.   Q.E.D.

12.2. *Radical Leibnizianism*

According to Leibnizianism, exact similarity between worlds amounts to identity. But what about exact similarities between *sets* of worlds, i.e., between propositions? Does it follow from Leibnizianism that exactly similar propositions are identical with each other? The answer depends on how this new exact similarity relation is defined. Two propositions may be said to be exactly similar iff there is an automorphism which transforms one of them into another. But then, as long as one adheres to Leibnizianism, it must be claimed that no two distinct propositions are exactly similar. This is so because, given Leibnizianism, there are no automorphisms other than the identity permutation. However, the concept of exact similarity between propositions may also be defined in a different way. As we know, two worlds are exactly similar iff one cannot distinguish them by pointing to some universal proposition instantiated by one of them but not by the other (cf. D9.2). We could generalize this idea and say that two *propositions* are exactly similar iff they are *indistinguishable in terms of universal propositions*. That is, for any X, $Y\subseteq\mathbf{W}$, X and Y are exactly similar iff every universal $Z\subseteq\mathbf{W}$ which includes (overlaps, is included in) one of them includes (overlaps, is included in) the other. We shall see below that Leibnizianism alone cannot transform *this* similarity relation into identity.

Propositions which are indistinguishable in the sense just described shall be said to be $\mathbf{C}^*$-connected. Thus, for all X, $Y\subseteq\mathbf{W}$,

D 12.1 $\mathbf{C}^*(X, Y)$ = For every universal $Z\subseteq\mathbf{W}$,

(a) $X\subseteq Z$ iff $Y\subseteq Z$,
(b) $Z\subseteq X$ iff $Z\subseteq Y$,
(c) $X\cap Z\neq\varnothing$ iff $Y\cap Z\neq\varnothing$,

and

(d) $\overline{X}\cap Z\neq\varnothing$ iff $\overline{Y}\cap Z\neq\varnothing$.

Note that the last clause is, strictly speaking, redundant, since it already follows from clause (b). Additionally, given the Principle of Complements, we can derive (c) from (a). Therefore, D 12.1 may be given a simpler formulation:

T 12.2 $\mathbf{C}^*(X, Y)$ iff, for every universal $Z \subseteq \mathbf{W}$,

(a) $X \subseteq Z$ iff $Y \subseteq Z$,

and

(b) $Z \subseteq X$ iff $Z \subseteq Y$.

That is, two propositions are **C**-connected iff they include and are included in precisely the same universal propositions.

The following theorems indicate some properties of $\mathbf{C}^*$:

T 12.3 $\mathbf{C}^*(X, Y)$ iff $\mathbf{C}^*(\overline{X}, \overline{Y})$;

T 12.4 $\mathbf{C}^*$ is an equivalence relation;

T 12.5 $w \mathbf{C} v$ iff $\mathbf{C}^*(\{w\}, \{v\})$.

It is also important that the following equivalence should be noted:

T 12.6 $w \mathbf{R} v$ iff $\mathbf{C}^*(\mathbf{R}^+(w), \mathbf{R}^+(v))$.

Proof: According to D 10.3a, $w \mathbf{R} v$ iff

(a) for every universal $Z \subseteq \mathbf{W}$, $\mathbf{R}^+(w) \subseteq Z$ iff $\mathbf{R}^+(v) \subseteq Z$.

Now, suppose that some universal Z is included in $\mathbf{R}^+(w)$. If Z is empty, then, of course, Z is included in $\mathbf{R}^+(v)$ as well. If Z is non-empty, then Z overlaps $\mathbf{R}^+(w)$. But then (a) together with the Principle of Complements imply that Z overlaps $\mathbf{R}^+(v)$. Since Z is included in $\mathbf{R}^+(w)$, this must mean that $\mathbf{R}^+(w)$ and $\mathbf{R}^+(v)$ overlap each other. Given that $\mathbf{R}^+$ is transitive and symmetric, $\mathbf{R}^+(w)$ and $\mathbf{R}^+(v)$ cannot overlap unless they coincide with each other. Thus, it follows that every universal Z included in $\mathbf{R}^+(w)$ is included in $\mathbf{R}^+(v)$. And, of course, vice versa. Therefore, (a) is equivalent to the following, seemingly stronger assertion:

(b) for every universal $Z \subseteq \mathbf{W}$, $\mathbf{R}^+(w) \subseteq Z$ iff $\mathbf{R}^+(v) \subseteq Z$, and $Z \subseteq \mathbf{R}^+(w)$ iff $Z \subseteq \mathbf{R}^+(v)$.

Given T 12.2, (b) amounts to the claim that $\mathbf{R}^+(w)$ and $\mathbf{R}^+(v)$ are $\mathbf{C}^*$-connected. Q.E.D.

Now, consider the following principle:

Radical Leibnizianism: C^* is an identity relation.

Obviously, in view of T 12.6,

T 12.7 Radical Leibnizianism $\Rightarrow$ (RR^+).[21]

Since we already know that Leibnizianism is too weak for the derivation of (RR^+), T 12.7 and T 12.5 entail that Radical Leibnizianism constitutes a proper extension of Leibnizianism.

Are Radical and Absolute Leibnizianisms *independent* of each other? We must admit that we do not know the answer to this question. In fact, they may well prove to be equivalent conditions, provided, of course, that we keep to our general assumptions about the concept of universal proposition—the principles of Division, Complements, and Disjointness.[22]

Precisely as was the case with Absolute Leibnizianism, Radical Leibnizianism does *not* imply (uu). This is shown by our Example F. (The model used in this example is both absolutely and radically Leibnizian.) As we shall see presently, this independence of (uu) is not particularly surprising.

12.3. (uu) *and Leibnizian metaphysics*

Let us use the term 'up-condition' in order to refer to any condition on W which, for its formulation, depends only on the concept of a universal proposition together with the standard set-theoretical machinery. Since the concept of a universal proposition is entirely sufficient for the definition of C and C^*, we may conclude that Leibnizianism, as well as its Absolute and Radical extensions, are examples of up-conditions. This is why we said in section 8.3 that the extensions in question are 'purely metaphysical', that they do not rely on any specifically moral concepts. What we shall presently prove is that *no* up-extension of Leibnizianism is sufficient for the derivation of (uu), provided that such

---

[21] By T 12.6 and Radical Leibnizianism, wRv iff $R^+(w) = R^+(v)$. And, since R^+ is reflexive, $R^+(w) = R^+(v)$ only if wR^+v.

[22] For instance, without the Principle of Disjointness, mutual independence of the conditions in question would be easily provable.

an extension is compatible with our general assumptions about the set of universal propositions.

Let T be any up-extension of Leibnizianism and assume that our model satisfies T along with the principles of Division, Complements, and Disjointness. Since T is an extension of Leibnizianism, our model is Leibnizian.

Lemma. For some X, $Y \subseteq W$ such that X is universal and Y is individual, X is non-empty and Y includes X.[23]

Let X and Y be any subsets of **W** which satisfy the Lemma. Thus X is universal and non-empty, Y is individual, and $X \subseteq Y$. Assume that **D** has been specified as follows:

For any $v \in Y$, $\mathbf{D}(v) = X$, and, for any $v \notin Y$, $\mathbf{D}(v) = \{v\}$.

In section 1.3, we stipulated that every world has some deontic alternatives. That is, **D** is thought to be serial. Sometimes, it is also claimed that **D** should be transitive. It is easy to see that both these demands are satisfied in our model. At the same time, (uu) fails to hold. While X is universal, its deontic closure, Y, is individual.

It should be noted that this argument is applicable not only to the up-extensions of Leibnizianism. In fact, it applies to *all* up-conditions which are compatible with the Lemma. The class of such conditions is, obviously, very large. For instance, it contains Anti-Leibnizianism and many of its possible extensions.

However, it could plausibly be claimed that the argument above is not really satisfactory. It rests on a tacit assumption that the relation **D** may be specified *independently* of the specification of the set of universal propositions. That is, we have assumed that the concept of a universal proposition is not an inherent part of our concept of moral obligation. Now, some philosophers might question this assumption.

---

[23] By Division and Complements, **W** includes some non-empty individual subset Z. Since Z is the disjoint union of the set consisting of all the unit-sets included in Z, the Principle of Disjointness implies that, for some $w \in Z$, $\{w\}$ is individual. Consider any such w and let $Y = \mathbf{W} - \{w\}$. By Complements, Y is individual. By Division and Complements, **W** contains at least two worlds. Thus, Y is non-empty. Consider any $v \in Y$. By Leibnizianism and Complements, there is some universal $X \subseteq \mathbf{W}$ such that $v \in X$ but $w \notin X$. This means that X is non-empty and that Y includes X. Q.E.D.

They might claim that the relation **D** is to be defined in terms of universal propositions. We have shown above that both Absolute and Radical Leibnizianism entail (**RR+**). But they do this only in the presence of the definition of the relation **R**, the definition which makes reference to universal propositions. It may be thought that the situation is similar as far as (uu) is concerned. Perhaps (uu) may also be shown to follow from some up-condition (compatible with the Lemma) *via an appropriate definition of* **D**.

As is well known, R. M. Hare and a number of other philosophers take the Principle of Universalizability, in its exact similarity formulations, to be analytically true (cf. section 1.2). Thus, the principle in question is thought to follow from the analysis of the concept of moral obligation. If I ought to perform an act, *A*, then—by the very meaning of 'ought'—every person placed in exactly similar circumstances, and who is also otherwise exactly similar to me, ought to perform an act exactly similar to *A*. In our terminology, we could express this idea of Hare's as follows:

Hare's Principle: The condition (u), according to which **C**-connected situations have **C**-connected deontic alternatives, follows from the correct definition of **D**.

Since, as we already know, **C** in its turn is definable in terms of the concept of a universal proposition, Hare's Principle establishes the existence of an analytical connection between the latter concept and the relation *D*. If this principle is true, then we may expect that (uu) will be derivable from some up-conditions (compatible with the Lemma) via the definition of **D**. In fact, we do not have to look very far in order to find such a up-condition. As we may remember, *Anti-Leibnizianism* entails that (uu) and (u) are equivalent to each other. Thus, if Hare's Principle is true, then (uu) constitutes an analytical consequence of Anti-Leibnizianism.

But the situation is different as far as Leibnizians are concerned. The condition (u) is just a trivial corollary of Leibnizianism. Therefore, Hare's Principle cannot be of any help to someone who wants to derive (uu) from some version of Leibniz-type metaphysics. Nothing is gained if we modify Hare's Principle and demand that not only (u) but also (uu) is to be immediately derivable from the definition of **D**. If such a modified principle were correct, then the whole issue of Leibnizianism versus Anti-Leibnizianism would loose its relevance as far as the status of (uu) is concerned. If we are to show that (uu) derives its support from Leibniz-type metaphysics, then what we need is a definition of **D** which does *not* entail (uu) but makes it instead an analytical consequence of some up-extension of Leibnizianism. But, it seems to us, no such definition is available.[24]

Assume that we are right in our conjecture. That is, assume that (uu) is a condition which we cannot trace back to any version of Leibniz-type metaphysics. At the same time, we know that there are up-extensions of Leibnizianism, which entail *all* the standard formulations of the Principle of Universalizability—those in terms of **C** as well as those in terms of **R**. It might be thought that these facts cast some suspicion on our thesis that (uu) constitutes an adequate expression of the universalizability idea.

Should we take this difficulty seriously? *Only* in the event that at least one of the up-extensions in question—Radical or Absolute Leibnizianism—has a sufficiently high degree of plausibility. That is, they should not turn out to be much less plausible that Leibnizianism itself. Otherwise, they could not serve as a proper foundation for the Principle of Universalizability.

Now, we doubt whether this provision can be satisfied. It is difficult to see what kind of arguments would persuade us that the 'radicalization' or 'absolutization' of Leibnizianism constitutes a plausible development of the original position. At the same time, there is at least one consideration which tells *against* such a move. In the next section we shall argue that Leibnizianism is invulnerable to a certain type of criticism which may be made against its radical and absolute extensions.

---

[24] That is, at least as long as we do not consider purely *artificial* constructions, like the following one: First, define some binary relation, **E**, on **W**. Let T be some up-extension of Leibnizianism, compatible with our general assumptions about the set of universal propositions, and let (uue) be the **E**-variant of (uu). Thus, (uue) is the condition to the effect that, for any universal $X \subseteq W$, $\{w \in W: E(w) \subseteq X\}$ is universal. Now, define **D** as follows:

$w\mathbf{D}v = $ df $w\mathbf{E}v$ & (T $\rightarrow$ (uue)).

Clearly, this definition, while not entailing (uu), makes it an analytical consequence of T.

12.4. *Critique of Absolute and Radical Leibnizianism*

To begin with, it should be noted that Radical and Absolute Leibniz-ianism have a common consequence: they both imply that mutually independent propositions are not C^*-connected. (Two propositions are independent from each other iff neither of them entails [= is included in] the other.)

T 12.8 Radical or Absolute Leibnizianism $\Rightarrow$

$\Rightarrow$ For any X, $Y \subseteq W$, if $X \nsubseteq Y$ and $Y \nsubseteq X$, then not $C^*(X, Y)$.

Proof: The consequent of T 12.8 immediately follows from Radical Leibnizianism. Thus, it remains to show that it also follows from Absolute Leibnizianism.

For any $X \subseteq W$, let $U(X)$ be the union of the set of universal proposi-tions included in X, and define $P(X)$ as the product of the set of universal propositions which include X. Note that $U(X) \subseteq X \subseteq P(X)$. Also, X is a u-product iff $X = P(X)$, and X is a u-union iff $X = U(X)$. Finally, observe that $C^*(X, Y)$ iff $U(X) = U(Y)$ and $P(X) = P(Y)$. By Absolute Leibnizian-ism, X and Y are either both u-unions or both u-products or one of them is a u-union while the other is a u-product. Assume that $C^*(X, Y)$. Then it follows that either (1) $X = U(X) = U(Y) = Y$, or (2) $X = P(X) = P(Y) = Y$, or (3) $X = U(X) \subseteq P(X) = P(Y) = Y$, or (4) $X = P(X) \subseteq U(X) = U(Y) = Y$. Thus, if $C^*(X, Y)$, then either $X \subseteq Y$ or $Y \subseteq X$.   Q.E.D.

Now, consider any individual proposition. For instance,

(1) There is an x such that $x =$ Plato.

Compare (1) with the following individual proposition:

(2) There is an x such that $x =$ Aristotle.

(1) and (2) are, so to speak, 'copies' of each other. They differ only in that they refer to distinct individuals. Otherwise, they are exactly identical.[25]

---

[25] Some other examples of such propositional 'copies' are:

Plato is a man.   Aristotle is a man.
Plato was a disciple of Socrates.   Aristotle was a disciple of Plato.

Suppose, now, that you are an absolute or a radical Leibnizian. Since (1) and (2) are, obviously, independent propositions, T 12.8 shows that you cannot treat (1) and (2) as C*-connected. In other words, you are committed to the claim that there is some universal proposition Z such that either (a) Z follows from (=includes) (1) or from (2) but not from both, or (b) Z entails (=is included in) either (1) or (2) but not both.

This existential claim, however, will be rather unconvincing, if one is not prepared to back it with *examples*. Thus, the question arises: Can we find some universal Z which satisfies one of the clauses (a) or (b)?

Suppose, first, that Z satisfies the clause (a). For instance, assume that Z follows from (1) but not from (2). Can we find an example of such a proposition? Clearly, a proposition such as *There is an x such that x is the author of a number of dialogues* will not do in this context. While this proposition does not follow from (2), it does not follow from (1) either. It is a contingent fact about Plato that he wrote dialogues. The same argument applies to all propositions of the form *There is an x such that x is P*, where P is some contingent property of Plato. But what if P belongs to Plato with necessity, in all possible worlds in which Plato exists? For every such P, it seems, it will either be the case that P also constitutes a necessary property of Aristotle, so that the corresponding proposition will follow from both (1) and (2), or it will turn out that P is an 'individual' property of Plato, so that the resulting proposition will not be universal. Thus, for instance, if the proposition *There is an x such that x is a person* follows from (1), then it will also follow from (2). And the proposition *There is an x such that x ≠ Aristotle*, which follows only from (1), is individual.

We will have the same difficulties in finding a universal Z entailed by (2) but not by (1). But what about the second possibility? Is there any universal Z which satisfies clause (b)? In our opinion, this seems highly unlikely. Note should be taken of the fact that such a Z must be consistent (since it does not entail both (1) and (2)), and that it has to entail the existence of some particular contingent individual—either Plato or Aristotle. But, if our criterion of individuality for propositions given in section 9.1. was correct, every consistent Z which entails the existence of some particular contingent individual must be an individual proposition.

Thus, neither (a) nor (b) seem to be satisfied by any universal Z.

If this is true, then (1) and (2) are C*-connected, even though they are mutually independent. Therefore, both Absolute and Radical Leibnizianism prove to be false.

Clearly, this objection rests heavily on the assumption of the C*-connection between propositional 'copies' such as (1) and (2). Our argument for the existence of such a connection is, partly, rhetorical in nature. It *seems* that (1) has no universal consequences which it does not share with (2) (and vice versa), but, of course, we have not proved this claim. Thus, our objection is not wholly conclusive. Still, to assume the C*-connection between (1) and (2) is much more plausible than to *reject* it, as Absolute and Radical Leibnizianism would have us do.

We cannot use the same or a similar argument against *Leibnizianism*. The C*-connection between mutually independent propositions such as (1) and (2) is perfectly compatible with C's being an identity relation.[26]

The difficulty would arise only if, *per impossibile*, (1), or (2), were a unit-proposition (that is, a proposition true in only one world). Leibnizianism is equivalent to the claim that, for any unit-proposition X, X has C* to nothing but itself. And of course, if we instead of (1) had started with some unit-proposition (1'), then the Leibnizian would deny that there is any proposition (2') which is related to (1') in the same way as (2) is related to (1). (As we may recall, (2) is independent of (1), but both propositions are exactly the same as far as their 'universal' components are concerned.) Therefore, the objection would never get off the ground.

Thus, it seems that both Absolute and Radical Leibnizianism are essentially less plausible than Leibnizianism proper. But, if this is true, then we can no longer claim that *all* the standard formulations of the Universalizability Principle are derivable from some sufficiently, but *not unreasonably* strong version of a Leibniz-type metaphysics. Therefore, the objection against (uu) fails.

----

[26] This is shown, for instance, by our Leibnizian Example E in section 10.3. There, the propositions $\{w_1, w_4\}$ and $\{w_2, w_3\}$ are C*-connected while being independent of each other.

PART IV

Individuals Do Not Matter

CHAPTER 13

Universalizability in Morals and Elsewhere

13.1. *Propositional operations*

By an n-place operation on propositions we shall understand a function which transforms n-tuples of propositions into propositions. In particular, deontic closure is a 1-place operation on propositions. The same applies to the operations of complement and relevance closure. As additional illustrations, let us consider the following:

Unavoidability. If $X \subseteq W$, then Y shall be said to be *the unavoidability closure of X* iff Y is the set of worlds in which X is unavoidable, i.e., iff Y is the set of worlds in which X is the case and in which nothing can be *done*—no actions can be performed—which would prevent X's being the case. In section 3.2, we introduced the alternative-relation **A** on **W**. **D** was thought to be included in **A** and perhaps even to be definable in terms of this relation. Clearly, the precise nature of **A** may be fixed in a number of different ways, and different interpretations of **A** will result in different specifications of **D**. However, the following interpretation of **A** seems to be especially natural: $w\mathbf{A}v$ iff everything that is unavoidable in w obtains in v. Given this interpretation, the unavoidability closure of X turns out to be identical with $\{w \in \mathbf{W}: \forall v \in \mathbf{W}(w\mathbf{A}v \to v \in X)\}$—just as the deontic closure of $X = \{w \in \mathbf{W}: \forall v(w\mathbf{D}v \to v \in X)\}$.

Causal necessity. Y shall be said to be *the causal closure of* a proposition X iff Y is the set of worlds in which X's being the case is causally necessary. Admittedly, the concept of causal necessity is not very clear, but it seems reasonable to distinguish it from the concept of unavoidability. For instance, according to the so-called soft determinists, the existence of avoidable states of affairs is perfectly compatible with the assumption that no state of affairs is causally contingent. Thus, according to this position, causal necessity does not entail unavoidability. Obviously, this opinion may also be shared by some indeterminists. Nor does unavoidability entail causal necessity. If some states of affairs which obtain in a given world are causally contingent, then it may well happen that some such causally contingent states of affairs are unavoidable—nothing can be *done* to prevent their occurrence.

Implication. If $X, Y \subseteq \mathbf{W}$, then we shall say that *the implication closure of* $\langle X, Y \rangle$ is the set of all worlds w satisfying the condition: $w \notin X$ or $w \in Y$. Implication closure is a 2-place operation on propositions.

13.2. *Universalizability conditions and their common background*

An n-place operation on propositions shall be said to be *universalizable* iff it transforms n-tuples of universal propositions into universal propositions. That is, universalizability is the property of operations which yield universal values when applied to universal arguments.

According to (uu), deontic closure is a universalizable operation. Analogously, the Principle of Complements and (RP1) ascribe universalizability to the operations of complement and relevance closure, respectively. We can continue to formulate universalizability conditions for unavoidability, causal necessity, implication, etc. Such conditions seem to be at least as convincing as (uu) itself. This leads us to a rather natural question: Can we trace all these different universalizability claims back to some underlying *general intuition*?

To be sure, the claims in question are independent of each other. In particular, an ethical non-universalist, who rejects (uu), will, in all probability, still ascribe universalizability to such ethically neutral operations as complement, implication, or causal closure. However, the situation may be different for someone who considers (uu) to be valid, just as valid as the other universalizability conditions which we have mentioned. It may well be the case that, from such a viewpoint, different universalizability claims are closely connected with each other. They all appear to be different applications of the same fundamental intuition, different consequences of the same general idea.

But, one may ask, if this is true, then what is the content of this idea? How can it be expressed? The proposed answer is already suggested by the title of this part. It seems to us that the common intuition behind different universalizability claims consists in a more or less vague belief that individuals 'do not matter', that individual aspects of things are 'irrelevant', 'unimportant', 'of no consequence'. We should note that 'irrelevance' here means something more than just moral irrelevance. But *what* does it mean then? What does it mean that individuals do not matter, if it means anything at all? Obviously, the intuition in question needs clarification. Additionally, we must clarify the connection between this intuition and the different universalizability claims. Assuming that 'individuals do not matter', how does it follow that operations such as deontic closure, complement, unavoidability closure, etc., are universalizable? We shall try to answer these questions in Chapter 15. In Chapter 14, we shall prepare the ground by introducing some new concepts into our framework.

To avoid possible misunderstandings, it has to be pointed out that a proper explication of the idea that individuals do not matter must allow for the existence of *non*-universalizable propositional operations, along with universalizable ones.[1]

In the last section of Chapter 15 (section 15.4), we shall consider the claim that the exact similarity variant of the Universalizability Principle is empty of any interesting content even from the point of view of someone who does not accept Leibnizianism. This claim has already been touched upon in section 1.1 (footnote 2). It will be seen that this impression of emptiness disappears as soon as we make a clear distinction between different concepts of exact similarity.

In Chapter 16, we shall see that our explication of the Individuals-do-not-matter idea leads to some rather unexpected results. Earlier in this work, we considered the standard claim that Leibnizianism trivializes the Universalizability Principle in all its formulations which do not have recourse to the concept of moral relevance. We have argued that this claim is erroneous. The condition (uu) represents a 'relevance-

---

[1] As an example, consider the operation which transforms each $X \subseteq W$, universal or not, into the proposition true in exactly those worlds in which Socrates exists. Obviously, even if, in some general sense, individuals 'do not matter', they still do matter very much as far as such non-universalizable operations are concerned.

free' formulation of the Universalizability Principle which is perfectly independent of Leibnizianism. Now we shall go even further. It will develop that there is a sense in which the general intuition that individuals do not matter, the intuition which may be thought to underlie our universalizability claims with respect to different propositional operations, is *incompatible* with Leibnizianism. To be more precise, we shall show that our explication of this intuition, when conjoined with certain additional assumptions, entails *Anti*-Leibnizianism. Admittedly, the assumptions needed for this derivation are not undisputable. But they are not wholly farfetched either. Thus, a Leibnizian who is prepared to accept these assumptions will have to admit that, contrary to our intuition, individuals do matter. Of course, he may still claim that such operations as deontic closure, causal closure, etc., are all universalizable. But he will not be able to relate all these universalizability claims to each other by deriving them from the general assumption of the fundamental unimportance of the individual aspects of things. Thus, we end up with a rather paradoxical result. It is not at all true that the Universalizability Principle is made trivial by Leibnizianism. On the contrary, it is only when we take the Leibnizian point of view that this principle, as expressed by (uu), may become really interesting *in its own right*. For then it is no longer obvious that the proper defence of (uu) consists in tracing it back to something more general, to the same general intuition which underlies other, ethically neutral, universalizability claims.

CHAPTER 14

Intensions and Extensions

14.1. *Intensional propositions*

Consider two sentences:

(a) Every father is a parent

(b) Either Socrates is a philosopher or it is not the case that Socrates is a philosopher.

How many propositions do these sentences express? Up to now, we have been identifying propositions with sets of possible worlds. Thus, the proposition that every father is a parent was thought to be identical with the set of worlds in which every father is a parent. Given this interpretation, (a) and (b) express the same proposition: the set of all possible worlds. However, such an approach is not the only possible one. In many contexts, we would like to say that different sentences express the same proposition only insofar as they are synonymous. But (a) does not seem to be synonymous with (b). This would suggest that the proposition expressed by (a) is distinct from the one expressed by (b), even though these two propositions are 'necessarily equivalent'—they are true in the same worlds. To put it differently, the propositions in question are distinct from each other, but they have the same 'extension' —they correspond to the same subset of **W**. In what follows, we shall call such propositions *intensional*, and we shall reserve the term 'proposition' for sets of worlds. At times, we shall also refer to such sets as '*extensional propositions*'.

What we propose to do, then, is to add to our framework the following new components:

(1) the set of intensional propositions (for convenience, we shall denote this set with the symbol '**IP**' and we shall refer to its members as *A*, *B*, *C*, etc.) and (2) the extension-function, **ex**, which assigns to every intensional

proposition some subset of **W**. For any $A \in$ **IP**, **ex**(A) is thought to be the set of worlds in which A is true.

It follows from what we have said above that the function **ex** is not one–one. There may be A, B in **IP** such that **ex**(A) = **ex**(B), even though A and B are distinct from each other.

How many intensional propositions are there? What is the size of **IP**? Can we assume that every $X \subseteq$ **W** is the extension of some $A \in$ **IP**? Or is it at least true that, for every two distinct worlds in **W**, there is some $A \in$ **IP** such that exactly one of these worlds belongs to **ex**(A)? It is better to leave such questions aside, if we want to keep our theory as neutral as possible.

14.2. *Intensional operations and the Principle of Extensionality*

In section 13.1, we considered different operations on (extensional) propositions. Clearly, we can also talk about different operations on *intensional* propositions. Let us say that an *n*-place operation on intensional propositions (or, for short, an *n*-place *intensional operation*) is a function from *n*-tuples of members of **IP** into **IP**. The following are examples of such operations:

Ought. For every $A \in$ **IP**, **Ought**(A) is the intensional proposition that it ought to be the case that A. **ex(Ought**(A)) is thought to be identical with the deontic closure of **ex**(A).

Non. If $A \in$ **IP**, **Non**(A) is the intensional proposition that it is not the case that A. **ex(Non**(A)) = the complement of **ex**(A).

Unavoidable. **Unavoidable** (A) is the intensional proposition that it is unavoidable that A. Its extension coincides with the unavoidability closure of **ex**(A).

Causally Necessary. **Causally Necessary**(A) is the intensional proposition that it is causally necessary that A. Its extension is thought to be identical with the causal closure of **ex**(A).

IfThen. If A, $B \in$ **IP**, **IfThen**(A, B) is the intensional proposition that, if A, then B. **ex(IfThen**(A, B)) = the implication closure of $\langle$**ex**(A), **ex**(B)$\rangle$.

We have assumed that the intensional propositions have extensions. It is natural to think that the same applies to intensional operations.

Just as the extensions of intensional propositions are extensional propositions, the extensions of intensional operations may be thought to be 'extensional operations'. That is, operations on extensional propositions. This suggests that we may extend the function **ex** to intensional operations. Thus, for instance, **ex(Ought)**, **ex(Non)**, **ex(Unavoidable)**, **ex(Causally Necessary)**, and **ex(IfThen)** may be identified with, respectively, the operations of deontic closure, complement, unavoidability closure, causal closure, and implication closure.

Unfortunately, this way of extending **ex** from intensional propositions to intensional operations leads to certain difficulties. In order to see this, let us consider what kind of connection there should exist between the extensions of intensional operations and the extensions of intensional propositions. The following proposal seems to be eminently plausible: Let o^n be any n-place intensional operation, for which **ex** has been defined. And let $A_1, ..., A_n$ be members of **IP**. Then,

The Extensionality Principle:

$$\mathbf{ex}(o^n(A_1, ..., A_n)) = \mathbf{ex}(o^n)(\mathbf{ex}(A_1), ..., \mathbf{ex}(A_n)).$$

According to this proposal, the extension of the intensional proposition which results by applying o^n to $A_1, ..., A_n$ should be identical with the extensional proposition which results by applying the extension of o^n to the extensions of $A_1, ..., A_n$. To put it somewhat informally, the extension of $o^n(A_1, ..., A_n)$ should be determined by the extensions of o^n and $A_1, ..., A_n$.

It is easy to see that the Extensionality Principle does not create any difficulties as far as our extension-assignments to **Ought, Non, Unavoidable**, etc., are concerned. Thus, to take **Ought** as an example, if **ex(Ought)** = deontic closure, then it follows from the Extensionality Principle that, for any intensional proposition A, the extension of **Ought**(A) equals the deontic closure of the extension of A—and this is precisely what we have assumed from the start.

However, we shall see in a moment that the acceptance of the Extensionality Principle essentially restricts the domain of the function **ex**.

Let us say that an intensional operation o^n is *regular* iff, for any $A_1, ..., A_n, B_1, ..., B_n \in \mathbf{IP}$, if

$$ex(A_1) = ex(B_1) \text{ and } ... \text{ and } ex(A_n) = ex(B_n),$$

then

$$ex(o^n(A_1, ..., A_n)) = ex(o^n(B_1, ..., B_n)).$$

That is, o^n is regular if the *extensions* of its values depend only on the *extensions* of its arguments. In other words, o^n is regular if extension-preserving replacements of its arguments invariably result in extension-preserving replacements of values. (We shall say that o^n is *irregular* iff o^n is not regular.)[2]

Now, consider any intensional operation o^n, for which ex has been defined. We shall prove that the Extensionality Principle entails that o^n is a regular operation.

Proof: Suppose that $A_1, ..., A_n, B_1, ..., B_n$ are intensional propositions such that

(1) $ex(A_1) = ex(B_1), ..., \text{ and } ex(A_n) = ex(B_n)$.

By the Extensionality Principle,

(2) $ex(o^n(A_1, ..., A_n)) = ex(o^n)(ex(A_1), ..., ex(A_n))$,

and

(3) $ex(o^n(B_1, ..., B_n)) = ex(o^n)(ex(B_1), ..., ex(B_n))$.

By (1), the right-hand sides of (2) and (3) coincide with each other. But then the same must be true of the left-hand sides. Thus,

(4) $ex(o^n(A_1, ..., A_n)) = ex(o^n(B_1, ..., B_n))$.   Q.E.D.

Many intensional operations are *irregular*. It will be easy to see this if we consider just one example: Let **Believes**$_a$ be the operation which to every $A \in \mathbf{IP}$ assigns the intensional proposition that a believes that A

[2] Our regularity-irregularity distinction corresponds to an essentially similar distinction introduced by S. Kanger in 'Entailment', *Modality, Morality and Other Problems of Sense and Nonsense. Essays dedicated to Sören Halldén*, Lund, 1973, pp. 168–179. Kanger distinguishes between *normally intensional* (=regular) and *ultraintensional* (=irregular) propositional operations.

(where a is some fixed individual). Now, it is well-known that we may believe that a given intentional proposition, A, is true, without believing the same of some other intensional propositions which are necessarily equivalent to A. Thus, for instance, we may believe that two and two are four, without having any belief about some complicated mathematical theorem. (As a matter of fact, we may even lack the concepts which are necessary for the *understanding* of the theorem in question.[3] But this means that, for any non-omniscient a, **Believes**$_a$ is an irregular operation.[4]

The moral to be drawn from this argument may be put as follows: the function **ex** is only *partially* defined on the set of intensional operations. As far as irregular operations are concerned, it is meaningless to ask about their extensions.

14.3. *Proper and infinitary intensional operations*

We shall say that an intensional operation o is *proper* iff **ex** is defined for o. Above, we have shown that, given the Extensionality Principle, only regular intensional operations are proper. It may be tempting to assume that regularity is not only a necessary but also a sufficient condition of propriety. However, we think that such an assumption would be rather unreasonable. Suppose, for instance, that o is a regular, but otherwise extremely 'arbitrary' operation on intensional propositions. That is, the assignments made by o do not follow any recognizable pattern. Thus, for instance, if o is *1*-place, assume that it assigns **Ought**(A_1) to A_1, A_2 to A_2, **Non**(A_3) to A_3, **Unavoidable**(A_6) to A_4, A_5 to A_5, etc. How are we to determine the extensional operation, o_e, which constitutes the extension of o? We get *some* help here from the Extensionality Principle: For any $X \subseteq W$ and $A \in IP$ such that $ex(A) = X$, $o_e(X)$ must coincide with $ex(o(A))$. But what about those $X \subseteq W$ which are not extensions of any intensional propositions? As we may recall,

---

[3] Compare Alvin Plantinga, 'Actualism and Possible Worlds', *Theoria*, *42* (1976), pp. 139–160, and 'The Boethian Compromise', *American Phil. Quart.*, *15* (1978), pp. 129–138.

[4] In fact, the sufficient and necessary condition of some operations on **IP** being irregular is that **IP** contains some members A, B, C, and D, such that $A \neq B$, $C \neq D$, $ex(A) = ex(B)$ and $ex(C) \neq ex(D)$. The necessity of this condition immediately follows from the definition of regularity. And its sufficiency may be seen by considering any *1*-place operation o on **IP** such that o assigns C to A and D to B. Any such operation o is irregular, since $ex(o(A)) = ex(C) \neq ex(D) = ex(o(B))$, even though $ex(A) = ex(B)$.

we have not made any assumptions about the size of **IP**. In particular, we have allowed for the possibility that, for some $X \subseteq W$, there is no $A \in \mathbf{IP}$ such that $\mathbf{ex}(A) = X$. Obviously, we cannot specify $o_\mathbf{e}$ for *such* X as long as we cannot discern any pattern in the assignments made by o. It seems that, under these circumstances, there is no non-arbitrary way of assigning extensions to 'arbitrary' intensional operations like o.

Fortunately, the assumption that all regular operations are proper is not necessary for our purposes. What we need is something much weaker. In what follows we shall simply assume that **Ought** is a proper operation and that its extension is identical with deontic closure. If necessary, we shall also make analogous assumptions about **Non, Unavoidable, Causally Necessary** and **IfThen**. This move should not lead to any difficulties. We already know that the intensional operations in question are all regular, and it is clear that none of them is 'arbitrary'— the patterns which they exhibit are immediately discernible.

Until now, we have spoken only of operations with a *fixed* and *finite* number of arguments. However, these restrictions may be easily removed. Let us say that o is an *operation* on **IP** (or, for short, an *intensional operation*) iff there is a set K such that (1) every element of K is a (possibly infinite and even uncountable) sequence of members of **IP** (that is, elements of K are functions from ordinals into **IP**); (2) for every $s \in K$, and every sequence s' consisting of members of **IP**, if s and s' are of the same length (that is, if they have the same domain), then $s \in K$; and (3) o is a function from K into **IP**.

Given this new, broader definition, the set of intensional operations will contain members which take as their arguments proposition-sequences of a variable and even infinite length. Of course, there is nothing that hinders an analogous broadening of the concept of *extensional* operation. Thus, we may assume that the function **ex** is defined not only for intensional operations with a fixed and finite number of arguments, but, possibly, also for some intensional operations whose number of arguments is variable and/or infinitary.[5] To illustrate:

Let A be some fixed member of **IP**. Define o as the operation which assigns A to each sequence of intensional propositions. Since o is regular

---

[5] Note that it is easy to modify the definition of regularity and the Extensionality Principle so that they will accommodate operations of this new type.

and since it exhibits a simple pattern, it may be assumed that o is proper and that, in particular, $ex(o)$ is the operation which assigns $ex(A)$ to each sequence of extensional propositions.

In what follows, we shall use the term 'operation' in the broad sense. The reason for this will become clear in Chapter 16, where we shall have to consider certain infinitary intensional operations.

CHAPTER 15

Universality and Intensions

15.1. *Intensional propositions: universal and individual*

Consider two groups of intensional propositions:

1. (a) Every father is a parent; (b) The discovery of radioactivity was made by a woman; (c) There are people who are professional politicians.

2. (a) Either Socrates is a philosopher or it is not the case that Socrates is a philosopher; (b) Marie Curie-Sklodowska is a woman; (c) Jimmy Carter is a professional politician.

All propositions in the second group contain particular individuals as their 'constituents'. On the other hand, no such particular individuals appear in the propositions belonging to the first group. In Part III, we divided extensional propositions into universal and individual. Now we propose to make an analogous, though by no means identical, distinction in the field of intensional propositions. Generally speaking, an intensional proposition is individual iff it contains at least one particular individual among its constituents;[6] and it is universal iff it is not individual. Thus, the intensional propositions in the first group are all universal, while the members of the second are examples of individual intensional propositions.

It is very important to note that this new distinction is *not* just a simple replica of our old universality-individuality distinction in the field of extensional propositions. In particular, it is *not* the case that, for any $A \in$ **IP**, A is individual iff **ex**(A) is individual. Thus, for instance, **ex**(2a) equals **W**, the set of all possible worlds. At the same time, given the

---

[6] Obviously, this characteristic, which, by the way, will be somewhat modified in what follows, is to be looked upon as a presystematic explication, and not as a proper *analysis* of the concept of individuality as applied to intensional propositions. To analyze this concept we would first have to define the notion of constituent and this is beyond the purview of the present work.

principles of Division, Complements and Disjointness, **W** must be a universal proposition. This means that some individual intensional propositions, such as (2a), have universal extensions. In fact, we can go even further. Assume that, for any $A \in$ **IP**, **IP** also contains the proposition (2a)&A—the conjunction of (2a) and A. Although A and (2a)&A are distinct intensional propositions, they have precisely the same extension. Now, since (2a) is individual, it seems clear that (2a)&A has to be individual as well.[7] This means that, for any $X \subseteq$ **W**, universal or not, if X is the extension of some $A \in$ **IP**, then X is the extension of some individual member of **IP**. This also means that any $A \in$ **IP**, universal or not, has the same extension as some individual member of **IP**.

Our explanation of the concept of individuality as applied to intensional propositions needs some qualification.

(i) An intensional proposition was said to be individual if it contains some particular individual among its constituents. But what if we allow for the possibility that some of our individuals are *non-contingent* entities, say numbers? Should we say then that the (intensional) proposition that $2+2=4$ is individual because it contains such particular individuals as 2 and 4? Perhaps it is better to take the opposite view and restrict the set of individual intensional propositions to those which have *contingent* particular individuals as their constituents.

(ii) Assume that **IP** contains propositions which refer to *particular worlds*. Thus, for instance, let 'w_0' denote the actual world and assume that the following proposition belongs to IP:

(α) There exists an x such that x is the person who, in w_0, discovered the law of gravitation.

Shall we say that (α) is an individual intensional proposition or not? Clearly, (α) has the same extension as the proposition

(β) Newton exists.

But, in distinction from (β), (α) does not contain Newton, nor any other particular individual, among its constituents. On the other hand, it does contain a particular world, w_0. For reasons which will become

---

[7] Since Socrates appears in (2a), he will also appear in any complex intensional proposition which contains (2a) as a part.

clear below, we shall stipulate that such world-constituents are to be treated on a par with individuals. Thus, an intensional proposition will be said to be individual iff it contains among its constituents a particular (contingent) individual or a particular world.

15.2. *Universalizable intensional operations.*
Universalizability of **Ought**

As we know, an extensional operation is universalizable if it always yields universal values when applied to universal arguments. This concept of universalizability is immediately extendible to intensional operations. An intensional operation o shall be said to be *universalizable* iff, for any sequence s of intensional propositions such that s belongs to the domain of o, if every member of s is universal, then $o(s)$ is universal as well.

We have seen above that individual intensional propositions may well have universal extensions. The situation is perfectly similar as far as intensional operations are concerned. Thus, consider that operation on **IP** which to every A assigns the proposition $(2a)\&A$. We already know that this operation is non-universalizable. If we now define its extension as that operation on subsets of **W** which to every $X \subseteq$ **W** assigns $\mathbf{ex}(2a) \cap X = \mathbf{W} \cap X = X$, then it follows that this non-universalizable intensional operation has a universalizable extension. This result can be generalized. Assuming that for every operation o on **IP**, for which the function **ex** has been defined, o has the same extension as the operation o' such that (1) o and o' have the same domain, and (2) for every s in the domain of o', $o'(s) = (2a)\&o(s)$, it follows that every intensional operation, for which **ex** has been defined, shares its extension with some non-universalizable operation. It also follows that every extensional operation which constitutes the extension of some operation o on **IP** is the extension of some non-universalizable operation on **IP**.

Consider, now, the following condition:

(uu$_{\mathrm{int}}$) **Ought** is a universalizable operation.

That is, for any universal intensional proposition A, **Ought**(A) also is universal.

Clearly, (uu$_{\mathrm{int}}$) constitutes the 'intensional' variant of (uu). It seems obvious that any ethical universalist—any person who accepts (uu)—

will accept (uu$_{int}$) as well. But what about ethical *non*-universalists? Will they reject (uu$_{int}$), just as they reject (uu)? We doubt it very much. In fact, we think that everyone *will accept* (uu$_{int}$) as a true condition. In particular, ethical non-universalists most probably will agree that **Ought** is universalizable, even though they consider deontic closure, the extension of **Ought,** to be a non-universalizable operation.

We shall try to argue for this claim by means of an example. Suppose that John is an ethical egoist, of the non-universalizable kind. He is convinced that, from the moral point of view, nothing matters but his own happiness. (We assume that John is a hedonist.) To be more definite, let us assume that, in John's view, there is a direct connection between the proposition that a certain A ought to be the case and the proposition that either A is simply unavoidable or John's happiness presupposes A. We shall refer to this whole disjunctive proposition as '**Maximizes-John's-Happiness(A)**'. Instead of trying to determine the precise meaning of the intensional operation involved, let us assume that the following is true:

(a) **Maximizes-John's-Happiness** is a non-universalizable operation. (In fact, for *every* $A \in$ **IP**, **Maximizes-John's-Happiness(A)** is an individual proposition, since it contains John among its constituents.)

(b) **Maximizes-John's-Happiness** is proper, and its extension is a non-universalizable operation on extensional propositions.

We shall also assume that, in John's view,

(c) The operations **Ought** and **Maximizes-John's-Happiness** have the same extension.

Clearly, it follows from (b) and (c) that deontic closure, the extension of **Ought,** is a non-universalizable operation. This means that John may properly be called an ethical non-universalist.

Now, we know that, for any $A \in$ **IP**, John considers the intensional propositions

(1) **Ought(A)**

and

(2) **Maximizes-John's-Happiness(A)**

to be necessarily equivalent. But does he also *identify* these propositions with each other? Surely not, or at least not if he deserves to be taken seriously. If he did, then we would say that he lacks a proper understanding of the operation **Ought** or that he is thinking of an operation other than the one we have in mind. It is only when John distinguishes between (1) and (2), but still thinks them to be necessarily equivalent, that there is any weight to his position.

The argument which we have just used is a variant of the standard objection against ethical naturalism. However, we do not want to claim that this objection is effective against *all* possible naturalistic analyses of moral concepts. What we do claim is only that this objection certainly is effective when the proposed analysis is of a very radical, 'revolutionary' kind—when most people would even deny that the analysans and analysandum are *equivalent* to each other, not to say anything about their alleged identity. It seems, therefore, that ethical naturalism and ethical non-universalism are incompatible positions.

But if (1) and (2) are distinct from each other, then the individuality of (2) does not carry over to (1). There is no reason to think that John, the individual constituent of (2), also is a constituent of (1). Just as there is no reason to think that Socrates is a constituent of the (intensional) proposition that every father is a parent, even though this proposition is true in exactly the same worlds in which it is true that either Socrates is a philosopher or it is not the case that Socrates is a philosopher. Thus, providing that the intensional proposition A, which appears in (1), is universal, the same will apply to (1) itself. This means that even ethical non-universalists will consider **Ought** to be a universalizable operation.

We shall assume, therefore, that (uu_{int}) is a perfectly uncontroversial condition. But what is the connection between this condition and its extensional variant, (uu)? As we already know, (uu_{int}), by itself, is insufficient for the derivation of (uu). Otherwise, ethical non-universalists would be unable to accept (uu_{int}). Perhaps, however, we can find some *additional* condition which, when conjoined with (uu_{int}), will make the derivation of (uu) possible. This is what we shall try to do in the next section.

15.3. *Individuals do not matter*

According to (uu$_{int}$), **Ought** is universalizable. Clearly, analogous assumptions may be made about many other intensional operations. The universalizability of **Ought** is just as obvious as the universalizability of **Non, Unavoidable, Causally Necessary,** or **IfThen.** Everyone who understands the operations in question will have to concur in this. But the claim that a given (proper) intensional operation is universalizable does not, by itself, entail the corresponding claim about the *extension* of this operation. Thus, if it is the extensions we are interested in, if we want to derive the universalizability claims about different extensional operations (deontic closure, complement, unavoidability closure, etc.), then we shall have to identify some *general* principle which will make all such derivations possible.

Above, we have seen that there is no perfect parallelism between the universality-individuality distinction in the field of intensions and the corresponding distinction in the domain of extensions. In particular, it developed that some individual intensional propositions have universal extensions, and the extensions of some non-universalizable intensional operations were found to be universalizable. But these observations do not preclude the two distinctions in question being connected at least in the following manner:

Individuals-do-not-matter: Universal intensional propositions always have universal extensions. Analogously, the extensions of universalizable (proper) intensional operations always are universal.[8]

Given this principle, the universalizability of deontic closure immediately follows from the universalizability of **Ought** (together with the assumption that **ex(Ought)** = deontic closure). The same holds true with regard to other extensional operations. The universalizability of complement follows from the universalizability of **Non,** the universalizability of causal closure follows from the universalizability of **Causally Necessary,** etc. Thus, quite generally, Individuals-do-not-matter makes it possible to derive different extensional universalizability claims from their uncontroversial intensional variants.

---

[8] The name chosen for this principle already suggests that we consider it to be the explication of the idea that 'individuals do not matter'.

But is Individuals-do-not-matter a plausible principle? In so far as it allows the derivation of (uu), it certainly is implausible to ethical non-universalists. This is, however, as it should be. What we are interested in is whether this principle constitutes a plausible option for someone who *accepts* different extensional universalizability claims, but wishes to anchor them in some general intuition.

In the next chapter, we shall show that the plausibility of Individuals-do-not-matter may well be challenged by some Leibnizians. Here, we shall only clear up one source of possible misunderstanding.

It is not too difficult to find examples of intensional propositions which lack individual constituents, but whose extensions nevertheless are individual. This applies, for instance, to the intensional proposition

(α) There exists an x such that x is the person who, in w_0, discovered the law of gravitation.

$ex(\alpha)$, i.e., the set of worlds in which Newton exists, is a paradigmatic example of an individual extensional proposition.[9] At the same time, (α) itself does not have any particular individuals among its constituents. Instead, it contains a particular world. Thus, the plausibility of Individuals-do-not-matter depends on our previous stipulation that, as far as the distinction between universal and individual intensional propositions is concerned, the world-constituents and the individual constituents are to be treated in precisely the same way. Without this assumption, (α) would be an example of a universal proposition with an individual extension.

In what way, one may ask, does Individuals-do-not-matter constitute an explication of the idea that individuals do not matter? Or, to put it differently, what shall we say now about the following questions: In which contexts are individuals 'irrelevant'? And what does it mean that they are 'irrelevant' in these contexts?

The answer is obvious. According to our principle, individuals are irrelevant to universal (and universalizable) intensional entities—propositions and operations. And *that* they are irrelevant means that the *extensions* of such entities always are universal (universalizable), never

---

[9] Note that $ex(\alpha)$ entails the existence of a particular contingent individual.

individual. One could say that Individuals-do-not-matter is an optimistic principle. If expresses a belief that, in some respects at least, appearances are not deceptive. According to this principle, individuals do not matter whenever they do not *seem* to matter. That is, whenever we have to do with an intensional entity which, on the face of it, is non-individual, then non-individuality will also apply to this entity on its deeper, extensional level.

Perhaps this is what is meant by some people when they claim that individual aspects of things are not any 'real' properties. To be Newton is not a 'real' property of Newton, nor is it a 'real' property of a situation w that Newton (and not someone like him) exists in w. One way of interpreting this claim would be to say that there is no need to consider such intensional properties, not even on the extensional level, as long as we describe things in purely universal terms, that is, as long as we keep to intensional propositions and concepts in which particular individuals (or particular worlds) do not appear explicitly, as constituents. And this is simply to say that Individuals-do-not-matter.

15.4. *Exact similarity: intensional and extensional*

In section 1.1 (footnote 2), we formulated the following problem: According to the Universalizability Principle in its exact-similarity version, objects which are exactly similar must exhibit exactly similar moral properties. But is it not a perfectly obvious, and therefore, uninteresting claim? How could two objects be exactly similar if they did not have exactly similar properties, whether moral or not?

We are now in a position to show that this argument depends on a certain ambiguity in the concept of exact similarity, an ambiguity which has to do with the distinction between intensional and extensional propositions.

In Chapter 9, we defined the exact-similarity relation $\mathbf{C}$ in terms of universal extensional propositions. Thus, for every w, v in $\mathbf{W}$, w and v are copies iff, for every universal $X \subseteq \mathbf{W}$, $w \in X$ iff $v \in X$. Consider now the intensional analogue of $\mathbf{C}$—the relation $\mathbf{C}^i$ of 'intensional copyhood':

D15.1 $w\mathbf{C}^iv = $ For every universal $A \in \mathbf{IP}$, $w \in \mathbf{ex}(A)$ iff $v \in \mathbf{ex}(A)$.

$\mathbf{C}^i$, in distinction to $\mathbf{C}$, is defined in terms of intensional propositions. Thus, we may refer to $\mathbf{C}^i$ as the intensional concept of relevant similarity.

What is the relation between C^i and C?

(a) Is it the case that $C^i \subseteq C$? In other words, is it the case that, for every pair of worlds which are not copies of each other, there is some universal intensional proposition A such that exactly one of these worlds belongs to the extension of A? Nothing that we have said above commits us to such an assumption, but the assumption itself does not seem to be implausible.

Nevertheless, it is best not to take a definite stand on this matter as long as there is no compelling reason for us to do so.

(b) Is it the case that $C \subseteq C^i$? Clearly, this question should be given an affirmative answer not only by all Leibnizians, but *also* by anyone who claims that Individuals-do-not-matter.

Proof: Assume that wCv and consider any universal $A \in \mathbf{IP}$. Since Individuals-do-not-matter, $\mathbf{ex}(A)$ is universal. But then the definition of C in terms of universal extensional propositions implies that $w \in \mathbf{ex}(A)$ iff $v \in \mathbf{ex}(A)$. Thus, by D 15.1, wC^iv. Q.E.D.

On the other hand, a person who rejects both Leibnizianism and the thesis that Individuals-do-not-matter may well *deny* that C is included in C^i. In order to see this, let us review once again our example in section 15.2. There, we considered a person, John, according to whom the intensional operations **Ought** and **Maximizes-John's-Happiness** have the same extension, even though only one of them is universalizable. Thus, for every universal $A \in \mathbf{IP}$, the intensional propositions

(1) **Ought**(A)

and

(2) **Maximizes-John's-Happiness**(A)

are, according to John, necessarily equivalent, even though (1) is universal while (2) is individual. In fact, it is reasonable to assume that, for some such universal A, (2) is not only individual but also has individual extension. Now, if John is an anti-Leibnizian, then, in his view, the individuality of $\mathbf{ex}(2)$ entails that $\mathbf{ex}(2)$ is not closed under C. That is, A maximizes John's happiness in some w but, in a certain copy v of w, A is instead conducive to the happiness of another individual, b, such that b in v is indiscernible from John in w. Since $ex(2) = ex(1)$, it follows that w, but not v, belongs to $ex(1)$. Therefore, the universality of (1) implies that the copies w and v are not C^i-connected. Thus, according to some ethical non-universalists, C will *not* be included in C^i.

Let us now consider the following condition:

(u*) If wCv and $X \subseteq W$ is universal, then w belongs to the deontic closure of X only if the same applies to v.

In other words, for any pair of copies and any universal extensional proposition X, X is obligatory in one of them iff it is obligatory in the other.[10]

We shall prove that (u*) is just another formulation of the condition (u). Therefore, in our model, (u*) represents the exact-similarity variant of the Universalizability Principle just as (u) does.

Proof: By the Principle of Simplification (cf. section 9.3), either Leibnizianism or Anti-Leibnizianism is true. Given Leibnizianism, both (u) and (u*) become trivially valid, and therefore equivalent to each other. Thus, we only have to prove that they will still remain equivalent on the assumption of Anti-Leibnizianism. As we may recall, Anti-Leibnizianism entails the equivalence of (u) and (uu) (cf. T11.2). At the same time, (uu), together with the definition of C in terms of universal extensional propositions (D9.1), immediately implies (u*): If $X \subseteq W$ is universal, then, by (uu), the same applies to the deontic closure of X. Therefore, if w belongs to the deontic closure of X and wCv, D9.1 implies that the deontic closure of X will also contain v.

As for the derivation of (u) from (u*), it should be noted that, by Anti-Leibnizianism and the Principle of Complements, $\overline{C(u)}$ is universal, for every $u \in W$. Assume now that (u) is false. Then, for some $w, v, u \in W$ such that wCv and wDu, there is no z such that vDz and uCz. This means that v belongs to the deontic closure of $\overline{C(u)}$. Since $\overline{C(u)}$ is universal and C is symmetric, (u*) implies that w also belongs to the deontic closure of $\overline{C(u)}$. However, this contradicts our assumption that wDu. Q.E.D.

Consider now the 'intensional' analogue of (u*)—a condition in which C has been replaced by the relation C^i of intensional copyhood, exten-

---

[10] As we may remember, X is obligatory in w iff $D(w) \subseteq X$, that is, iff w belongs to the deontic closure of X.

sional propositions have been substituted by the intensional ones and deontic closure by the intensional operation **Ought**:

(u_{int}^*) If $wC^i v$ and $A \in IP$ is universal, then w belongs to $ex(Ought(A))$ only if the same applies to v.

Since C^i is symmetric, we may also express this condition as follows: For any pair of intensional copies and any universal intensional proposition A, **Ought**(A) is true in one of them iff it is true in the other.

It should be noted that, if we had replaced C^i by C in (u_{int}^*), then we would have obtained a condition which is unacceptable to ethical non-universalists, insofar as they are anti-Leibnizians. Thus, the C-variant of (u_{int}^*) would be unacceptable to John in our above example. Such persons would also reject (u^*) and (u). But what would they say about (u_{int}^*)?

As we pointed out above (section 15.2), the condition (uu_{int}), in distinction from its extensional variant (uu), is quite uncontroversial and will be accepted even by ethical non-universalists. We shall see now that the same applies to (u_{int}^*). In fact, the latter condition follows immediately from (uu_{int}):

Proof: Assume the antecedent of (u_{int}^*). By (uu_{int}), the universality of A implies the universality of **Ought**(A). Therefore, by the definition of C^i (D 15.1), w belongs to $ex(Ought(A))$ only if the same applies to v. Q.E.D.

We may conclude, then, that the relation between (u_{int}^*) and (u^*), and therefore between (u_{int}^*) and (u), mirrors the relationship between (uu_{int}) and (uu). While (u_{int}^*), which utilizes the *intensional* interpretation of exact similarity, is an uncontroversial condition, the same does not apply to (u) (nor to the conditions such as (u^*) or the C-variant of (u_{int}^*)). It would seem therefore, that the impression of self-evidence which accrues to the exact-similarity version of the Universalizability Principle depends, at least partly, on the fact that we do not clearly distinguish between the intensional and the extensional interpretations of exact similarity, between relations such as C^i and C. While it is obvious that C^i-similar situations will be exactly similar in their intensional properties, whether moral or not, the C-similar situations may exhibit intensional dissimilarities (*if* 'individuals do matter'). At the same time, C-similar situations must be exactly similar in their extensional properties, but this fact is compatible with the assumption that they will have dissimilar deontic alternatives.[11]

---

[11] If $X \subseteq W$ is a 'property' of w, that is, if $w \in X$, and, in particular, if $X = D(w)$, then, of course, any C-similar v will have a 'property' Y which is exactly similar to X. To put it in the language of automorphisms: there exists an automorphism p such that $p(X) = Y$. But from this it does *not* follow that $D(v)$ equals Y, nor that $D(v)$ is exactly similar to X.

CHAPTER 16

Leibnizianism Once Again

16.1. *Individuals-do-not-matter and Leibnizianism.*
Are these two principles incompatible?

What about Leibnizians? Do individuals matter in their view? In a sense, they do matter very much. According to Leibnizians, the individuals involved in a situation can never be replaced without changing some of the universal aspects of the situation. Leibnizianism amounts to the claim that individual differences between situations always imply some universal differences. To put it formally, for any w, $v \in W$, and any individual $X \subseteq W$ such that $w \in X$ and $v \notin X$, there is some universal $Y \subseteq W$ such that $w \in Y$ and $v \notin Y$. (It is easy to ascertain that this condition is equivalent to the assumption that C is an identity relation.)

But does this mean that Leibnizianism and Individuals-do-not-matter are incompatible with each other? There is no direct incompatibility here because one can construct models in which both these principles are satisfied. But the picture may change if we enrich our theory with additional assumptions. To illustrate, consider the following condition:

The Principle of Finiteness: For every $w \in W$, if Γ is the set of all universal extensional propositions to which w belongs, then Γ contains some finite subset Γ' such that the product of Γ' equals the product of Γ.

In other words, for every world w, there exists a *finite* set of universal (extensional) aspects of w whose product entails *all* the universal (extensional) aspects of w. In section 9.1, it was shown that the product of the set of universal aspects of a world w coincides with $C(w)$—the set of copies of w (cf. T9.1). Therefore, the Principle of Finiteness may also be formulated as follows:

For every $w \in W$, $C(w)$ is the product of some *finite* set of universal extensional propositions.

This finiteness assumption could be accepted even by those who would claim that the total number of universal extensional propositions instantiated by w is infinite.

We shall see that, given the Principle of Finiteness, Individuals-do-not-matter leads to Anti-Leibnizianism.

Proof: As we already know, the intensional operation **IfThen** is universalizable. But then, if Individuals-do-not-matter, the universalizability of **IfThen** carries over to its extensional equivalent—the operation of implication closure. This fact, together with the Principle of Complements, implies that

(a) For any universal X, $Y \subseteq W$, $X \cap Y$ is universal.

($X \cap Y$ equals the complement of the implication closure of $\langle X$, the complement of $Y \rangle$.)

It follows from (a) that

(b) The set of universal (extensional) propositions is closed under finite products.

Thus, given the Principle of Finiteness,

(c) For every $w \in W$, $C(w)$ is universal.

By the Principle of Disjointness, (c) entails Anti-Leibnizianism:

Every (extensional) proposition closed under **C** is universal.

(Note that, if $X \subseteq W$ is closed under **C**, then X is the disjoint union of the set $\{Y \subseteq W: \exists w \in X(C(w) = Y)\}$.)   Q.E.D.

Above, we have shown how to derive the incompatibility of Individuals-do-not-matter and Leibnizianism by making a certain *finitude* assumption about *extensional* propositions. The same incompatibility result could also be obtained in a different way—by making a certain assumption of *infinitude* about *intensional* propositions.

Consider the following principle:

Existence of Infinitary Conjunction: **IP** is closed under an operation which assigns to each sequence s of intensional propositions the (intensional) proposition which is the conjunction of the members of s. (Since this operation is assumed to apply even to infinite sequences, we shall refer to it as '*infinitary conjunction*'.)

Thus, for instance, if s is the proposition-sequence $\langle 1+1=2, 2+2=4, 4+4=8, ...\rangle$, then the infinitary conjunction of s is the (intensional) proposition that $1+1=2$ and $2+2=4$ and $4+4=8$ and ....

For every proposition-sequence s, the extension of the infinitary conjunction of s equals the product of the set of extensions of the members of s. Thus, infinitary conjunction is a regular operation. At the same time, it exhibits an easily discernible pattern. Therefore, we may take it to be proper. In particular, we shall define ex(infinitary conjunction) as the operation on extensional propositions which assigns to each sequence s of such propositions the product of the set consisting of all the members of s. We shall refer to this operation as 'infinitary extensional conjunction'. This extension-assignment satisfies the Extensionality Principle: For every sequence s of intensional propositions, if s' is the corresponding sequence of extensions of the members of s, then ex(the infinitary conjunction of s) = the infinitary extensional conjunction of s'.

Suppose that all members of a sequence s are universal intensional propositions. What is the status of the infinitary conjunction of s? Is it universal or individual? The answer seems obvious. If no proposition in s contains any particular (contingent) individuals or particular worlds among its constituents, then the same must apply to their conjunction. Thus, we may conclude that the infinitary conjunction is a universalizable intensional operation.

But then, if Individuals-do-not-matter, it follows that

(a) Infinitary extensional conjunction is universalizable.

Given the Axiom of Choice, (a) is equivalent to the condition:

(b) The set of universal extensional propositions is closed under products.[12]

---

[12] Let Γ be any set of universal extensional propositions. By the Axiom of Choice, Γ can be well-ordered. That is, there is a sequence s such that, for every $X \subseteq W$, X is a member of s iff $X \in \Gamma$. By (a), it follows that the infinitary extensional conjunction of $s = \bigcap \Gamma$ is universal.

We have shown in section 9.2 that (b) is just another formulation of Anti-Leibnizianism (cf. T9.5). Thus, Anti-Leibnizianism follows from Individuals-do-not-matter, if **IP** is closed under infinite conjunctions.[13]

16.2. Discussion of the assumptions used in the derivation of incompatibility

Clearly, neither the Principle of Finiteness nor the Existence of Infinitary Conjunction are especially intuitive conditions. In fact, both of them may easily be questioned. Thus, to consider the Principle of Finiteness first, one may claim that there are worlds w whose universal aspects are 'inexhaustible', in the sense that no finite group of such aspects is sufficient for the determination of $C(w)$. That is, there is no finite group of such aspects whose product entails *all* the universal aspects of w. In other words, there may be worlds whose universal aspects are not only infinitely many, but also are so different and complicated that they cannot be reduced to any finite number. As a matter of fact, it may be claimed that *all* possible worlds are of this kind. Whether this is a reasonable position or not will, of course, depend on our interpretation of the concept of a possible world. The Principle of Finiteness becomes less and less plausible when we take worlds to be more and more 'all-inclusive' entities.

What about the Existence of Infinitary Conjunction? Is it reasonable to assume that, for *any* sequence s of intensional propositions, **IP** contains the conjunction of the members of s, quite independently of whether s is finite or not? Well, it may seem justified to assume that, for *some* infinite proposition-sequences, **IP** also contains their conjunctions. In particular, this may be the case whenever the sequence in question is 'effectively constructible', that is, whenever there exists a finite rule which specifies the first member of the sequence and allows the determination of the *next* member at every stage of the sequence-construction. $\langle 1+1=2, \ 2+2=4, \ 4+4=8, \ ...\rangle$ is a sequence of this kind. But, of course, there will be many sequences of intensional propositions which do not satisfy the condition of effective constructibility. Can we assume

---

[13] Or, if you wish, under infinite *dis*junctions. Given the Principle of Complements, (b) is equivalent to the claim that all u-unions are universal. And this claims follows, via Individuals-do-not-matter, from the assumption that the infinitary disjunction is ι universalizable operation on **IP**.

that IP also contains conjunctions which correspond to *such* sequences? The answer must depend on our interpretation of IP or, what amounts to the same thing, on our interpretation of the concept of an intensional proposition. Thus, for instance, if we assume that, for every intensional proposition A, there is a possible world w such that A is understood in w by some finite subject, then the closure of IP under infinitary conjunction will have to be rejected. The same result will follow, if we define IP by reference to some fixed finitary language L, so that intensional propositions are identified with the meanings of sentences of L. On the other hand, the interpretations which relate IP to infinitary languages or to the powers of understanding displayed by hypothetical infinitely intelligent beings point in the opposite direction.

What are the conclusions that may be drawn from this discussion? We have seen that neither the Principle of Finiteness nor the Existence of Infinitary Conjunction are uncontroversial conditions. Therefore, it is still possible that Leibnizianism and the idea that Individuals-do-not-matter are compatible with each other. Nevertheless, the fact remains that this idea is much easier to accept from the Anti-Leibnizian point of view. Thus, there is a sense in which ethical universalism is more of a problem for Leibnizians than for their opponents. The latter may consider the Universalizability Principle to be just a special instance of the general metaphysical claim about the unimportance of the individual aspects of things. But this way of reducing an ethical principle to a metaphysical one may not be open for the proponents of Leibnizianism.

Bibliography

Aristotle, *Nicomachean Ethics*, transl. by H. Rackham, Loeb Classical Library, Cambridge, Mass., 1926.
— *Posterior Analytics*, transl. by H. Tredennick, Loeb Classical Library, Harvard-London, 1960.
Bergström, L., "Review of R. M. Hare, 'Freedom and Reason'", *Theoria*, *30* (1964), pp. 39–49.
Broad, C. D., *Five Types of Ethical Theory*, London, 1930.
Fine, K., 'Properties, Propositions and Sets', *Journal of Philosophical Logic, 6* (1977), pp. 135–191.
Garner, R. T. & Rosen, B., *Moral Philosophy*, New York, 1967.
Gellner, E., 'Ethics and Logic', *Proceedings of Aristotelian Society*, *55* (1954–5), pp. 157–178.
Gewirth, A., 'The Non-Trivializability of Universalizability', *Australasian Journal of Philosophy*, *47* (1969), pp. 123–131.
— *Reason and Morality*, Chicago, 1978.
Hare, R. M., 'Universalizability', *Proceedings of Aristotelian Society, 55* (1954–5), pp. 295–312.
— *Freedom and Reason*, London, 1963.
Herstein, I. N., *Topics in Algebra*, Blaisdell International Textbook Series, Waltham, Mass., 1964.
Hilpinen, R. (ed.), *Deontic Logic: Introductory and Systematical Readings*, Synthese Library, Dordrecht, 1971.
Hospers, J., *An Introduction to Philosophical Analysis*, 2nd rev. ed., London, 1967.
Kanger, S., 'Entailment', *Modality, Morality and Other Problems of Sense and Nonsense. Essays dedicated to Sören Halldén*, Lund, 1973, pp. 168–179.
Kant, I., *Groundwork of the Metaphysics of Morals*, in H. J. Paton, *The Moral Law*, London, 1948.
— *Critique of Practical Reason*, transl. by L. W. Beck, Indianapolis-New York, 1958.
Kripke, S. A., 'Naming and Necessity', *Semantics of Natural Language*, ed. by D. Davidson and G. Harman, Synthese Library, Dordrecht, 1972.
Leibniz, G. W., *Philosophical Papers and Letters*, transl. by L. E. Loemker, Synthese Historical Library, Dordrecht, 1969.
Locke, D., 'The Trivializability of Universalizability', *The Philosophical Review, 77* (1968), pp. 25–44.
MacIntyre, A., 'What Morality Is Not', *Philosophy, 32* (1957), pp. 325–335.

Monro, D. H., 'Impartiality and Consistency', *Philosophy*, *36* (1961), pp. 161–176.

— *Empiricism and Ethics*, Cambridge, 1967.

Nakhnikian, G., 'Generalization in Ethics', *The Review of Metaphysics*, *17* (1963–4), pp. 436–461.

Olafson, F. A., *Principles and Persons*, Baltimore, 1967.

Organ, T. W., *An Index to Aristotle in English*, Princeton, 1940.

Paton, H. J., *The Moral Law. Kant's Groundwork of the Metaphysics of Morals*, London, 1948.

Plantinga, A., 'Actualism and possible worlds', *Theoria*, *42* (1976), pp. 139–160.

— 'The Boethian Compromise', *American Philosophical Quarterly*, *15* (1978), pp. 129–138.

Reiner, H. 'Die Goldene Regel', *Zeitschrift für Philosophische Forschung*, *3* (1948), pp. 74–105.

Schrag, B. E., *Universalizability and the Concept of Morality*, doctoral dissertation, 1975. Xerox Univ. Microfilms, Order No. 76–119.

Segerberg, K., 'Some Logics of Commitment and Obligation', *Deontic Logic: Introductory and Systematic Readings*, ed. by R. Hilpinen, Synthese Library, Dordrecht, 1971.

Sidgwick, H., *Methods of Ethics*, 7th ed., London, 1907.

Singer, M. G., 'The Golden Rule', *Philosophy*, *38* (1963) pp. 293–314.

— *Generalization in Ethics*, New York, 1961.

Sobel, J. H., "'Everyone', Consequences and Generalization Arguments' *Inquiry*, *10* (1967), pp. 373 404.

Appendix to Part IV

Professor Dag Prawitz has pointed out that the universality-individuality distinction in the field of *intensional* propositions might be much easier to understand than the corresponding distinction in the field of *extensions*. In fact, one may wonder whether the latter distinction is understandable at all and, consequently, whether our whole discussion, insofar as it presupposes the distinction in question, makes any sense.

This difficulty would be met, however, if we could show that the extensional universality-individuality distinction is *definable* in terms of the same concepts that we have used in our explication of the intensional distinction.

In what follows we shall try to construct such a definition. It is to be noted that our proposal is only tentative. Nevertheless, it seems to us to be on the right track.

As the reader may remember, an intensional proposition is individual if it contains some contingent individual or some particular world among its constituents. In section 15.1 we noted that there are many individual intensional propositions which have universal extensions. Thus, the question arises: What is the distinctive feature of those individual intensional propositions which exhibit *individual* extensions?

In order to answer this question we shall first introduce the notion of a propositional *variant*. Let A be any member of **IP** and let s be the sequence which consists of all the contingent individuals and particular worlds which are the constituents of A. (If A is universal, then the length of s will equal 0.) Let s' be any similar sequence of individuals and worlds such that s and s' are equally long and lack common members. (Both s and s' are assumed to be sequences without repetitions.) We shall say that $B \in$ **IP** is a *variant of A* if B results from A when we in the latter proposition replace the members of s by the corresponding members of s'.

$A \in$ **IP** shall be said to be *essentially individual* if there is *no* variant B of A such that $\text{ex}(A) = \text{ex}(B)$ (i.e., such that A and B are true in exactly the same worlds).

The following are some examples of essentially individual propositions:

(a) Plato is a philosopher; (b) Newton exists; (c) Aristotle is a disciple of Plato, (d) Plato is a philosopher or Aristotle is a philosopher.

Clearly, every replacement of Plato by another individual in (a) will result in a proposition whose extension differs from the extension of (a). There is no individual distinct from Plato who is a philosopher in exactly those worlds in which Plato is a philosopher. Analogous remarks apply to the propositions (b), (c) and (d). It is to be noted, however, that the essential individuality of (d) rests on a certain restriction in our definition of a propositional variant: we have assumed that the sequences s and s' lack common members. In the absence of this restriction, (d) would have the following proposition among its variants:

Aristotle is a philosopher or Plato is a philosopher.

And clearly, the extension of the latter proposition coincides with the extension of (d).

If $A \in \mathbf{IP}$ is individual but not essentially so, then we shall say that A is *non-essentially individual*. The following are examples of such propositions:

(e) Either Socrates is a philosopher or it is not the case that Socrates is a philosopher; (f) Plato is a mountain; (g) Plato $\neq$ Socrates; (h) Someone is a philosopher and Plato $\neq$ Socrates.

To see that neither of these propositions is essentially individual it is sufficient to consider their variants in which Plato and Socrates have been replaced by some other pair of persons, say, Leibniz and Newton.

While the extensions of (a)–(d) are individual, the extensions of (e)–(h) all seem to be universal. Therefore, it might be thought that being essentially individual is the distinctive feature of the individual intensional propositions with individual extensions. Such a conclusion, however, would not be correct. Even though all essentially individual propositions seem to have individual extensions, the same applies to some of the propositions which are non-essentially individual. To see this, consider the intensional proposition which we have already discussed in sections 15.1 and 15.3:

(α) There exists an x such that x is the person who, in w_0, discovered the law of gravitation.

It is easy to see that (α) is non-essentially individual.[1] At the same time, we already know that (α) is a proposition with an individual extension (cf. section 15.3).

Perhaps, however, the following is true: An individual intensional proposition A has an individual extension if, and only if, either A itself is essentially individual or if, at least, A is *extensionally equivalent* to some essentially individual proposition. Thus, (α) has an individual extension because it is extensionally equivalent to the essentially individual proposition (b): Newton exists.

If this suggestion is correct, then it invites the following generalization:

For any $X \in \mathbf{W}$ such that X constitutes the extension of some intensional proposition, X is individual if there is some essentially individual $A \in \mathbf{IP}$ such that $\mathbf{ex}(A) = X$; otherwise such an X is universal.

As the reader will note, this definition of the extensional universality-individuality distinction is only *partial*—nothing is said about those subsets of $\mathbf{W}$ which do *not* constitute the extensions of any members of $\mathbf{IP}$ (insofar as any such subsets exist). This limitation, however, does not seem to be especially troublesome. If our intuitions concerning the distinction in question can be fixed for a large class of extensional propositions, then, perhaps, it will give us some guidance as to how to deal with the remaining cases. Besides, the assumption that the extensional universality-individuality distinction is exhaustive is not really fundamental to our discussion. It is true that, in the absence of this assumption, we would have to introduce some additional axioms,[2] but most of our results would still hold.

---

[1] The replacement of w_0 in (α) by any other particular world in which the discovery of the law of gravitation was also made by Newton will result in an intensional proposition whose extension coincides with the extension of (α).

[2] For example, the Principle of Complements, according to which the set of universal propositions is closed under complements, would have to be appended by the analogous principle for individual propositions.

We have seen that the definition above allows for the existence of individual intensional propositions with universal extensions. But what about the opposite case? Can there exist universal intensional propositions with individual extensions? Even this possibility is not foreclosed by our definition: the extension of a universal $A \in \mathbf{IP}$ may be individual, provided that A is extensionally equivalent to some essentially individual $B \in \mathbf{IP}$. It is only when we assume that Individuals-do-not-matter that this possibility is excluded. Thus our definition does *not* transform the universalistic standpoint into a triviality.

Index of Names and Subjects

SYNTHESE LIBRARY

SYNTHESE LIBRARY

Studies in Epistemology, Logic, Methodology,
and Philosophy of Science

Managing Editor:
JAAKKO HINTIKKA, (Academy of Finland, Stanford University
and Florida State University)

Editors:
ROBERT S. COHEN (Boston University)
DONALD DAVIDSON (University of Chicago)
GABRIËL NUCHELMANS (University of Leyden)
WESLEY C. SALMON (University of Arizona)

1. J. M. Bocheński, *A Precis of Mathematical Logic.* 1959, X + 100 pp.
2. P. L. Guiraud, *Problèmes et méthodes de la statistique linguistique.* 1960, VI + 146 pp.
3. Hans Freudenthal (ed.), *The Concept and the Role of the Model in Mathematics and Natural and Social Sciences. Proceedings of a Colloquium held at Utrecht, The Netherlands, January 1960.* 1961, VI + 194 pp.
4. Evert W. Beth, *Formal Methods. An Introduction to Symbolic Logic and the Study of Effective Operations in Arithmetic and Logic.* 1962, XIV + 170 pp.
5. B. H. Kazemier and D. Vuysje (eds.), *Logic and Language. Studies Dedicated to Professor Rudolf Carnap on the Occasion of His Seventieth Birthday.* 1962, VI + 256 pp.
6. Marx W. Wartofsky (ed.), *Proceedings of the Boston Colloquium for the Philosophy of Science 1961-1962,* Boston Studies in the Philosophy of Science (ed. by Robert S. Cohen and Marx W. Wartofsky), Volume I. 1963, VIII + 212 pp.
7. A. A. Zinov'ev, *Philosophical Problems of Many-Valued Logic.* 1963, XIV + 155 pp.
8. Georges Gurvitch, *The Spectrum of Social Time.* 1964, XXVI + 152 pp.
9. Paul Lorenzen, *Formal Logic.* 1965, VIII + 123 pp.
10. Robert S. Cohen and Marx W. Wartofsky (eds.), *In Honor of Philipp Frank,* Boston Studies in the Philosophy of Science (ed. by Robert S. Cohen and Marx W. Wartofsky), Volume II. 1965, XXXIV + 475 pp.
11. Evert W. Beth, *Mathematical Thought. An Introduction to the Philosophy of Mathematics.* 1965, XII + 208 pp.
12. Evert W. Beth and Jean Piaget, *Mathematical Epistemology and Psychology.* 1966, XII + 326 pp.
13. Guido Küng, *Ontology and the Logistic Analysis of Language. An Enquiry into the Contemporary Views on Universals.* 1967, XI + 210 pp.
14. Robert S. Cohen and Marx W. Wartofsky (eds.), *Proceedings of the Boston Colloquium for the Philosophy of Science 1964-1966, in Memory of Norwood Russell Hanson,* Boston Studies in the Philosophy of Science (ed. by Robert S. Cohen and Marx W. Wartofsky), Volume III. 1967, XLIX + 489 pp.

13–792479 *Rabinowicz*

15. C. D. Broad, *Induction, Probability, and Causation. Selected Papers.* 1968, XI + 296 pp.
16. Günther Patzig, *Aristotle's Theory of the Syllogism. A Logical-Philosophical Study of Book A of the Prior Analytics.* 1968, XVII + 215 pp.
17. Nicholas Rescher, *Topics in Philosophical Logic.* 1968, XIV + 347 pp.
18. Robert S. Cohen and Marx W. Wartofsky (eds.), *Proceedings of the Boston Colloquium for the Philosophy of Science 1966-1968,* Boston Studies in the Philosophy of Science (ed. by Robert S. Cohen and Marx W. Wartofsky), Volume IV. 1969, VIII + 537 pp.
19. Robert S. Cohen and Marx W. Wartofsky (eds.), *Proceedings of the Boston Colloquium for the Philosophy of Science 1966-1968,* Boston Studies in the Philosophy of Science (ed. by Robert S. Cohen and Marx W. Wartofsky), Volume V. 1969, VIII + 482 pp.
20. J.W. Davis, D. J. Hockney, and W. K. Wilson (eds.), *Philosophical Logic.* 1969, VIII + 277 pp.
21. D. Davidson and J. Hintikka (eds.), *Words and Objections: Essays on the Work of W. V. Quine.* 1969, VIII + 366 pp.
22. Patrick Suppes, *Studies in the Methodology and Foundations of Science. Selected Papers from 1911 to 1969.* 1969, XII + 473 pp.
23. Jaakko Hintikka, *Models for Modalities. Selected Essays.* 1969, IX + 220 pp.
24. Nicholas Rescher *et al.* (eds.), *Essays in Honor of Carl G. Hempel. A Tribute on the Occasion of His Sixty-Fifth Birthday.* 1969, VII + 272 pp.
25. P. V. Tavanec (ed.), *Problems of the Logic of Scientific Knowledge.* 1969, XII + 429 pp.
26. Marshall Swain (ed.), *Induction, Acceptance, and Rational Belief.* 1970, VII + 232 pp.
27. Robert S. Cohen and Raymond J. Seeger (eds.), *Ernst Mach: Physicist and Philosopher,* Boston Studies in the Philosophy of Science (ed. by Robert S. Cohen and Marx W. Wartofsky), Volume VI. 1970, VIII + 295 pp.
28. Jaakko Hintikka and Patrick Suppes, *Information and Inference.* 1970, X + 336 pp.
29. Karel Lambert, *Philosophical Problems in Logic. Some Recent Developments.* 1970, VII + 176 pp.
30. Rolf A. Eberle, *Nominalistic Systems.* 1970, IX + 217 pp.
31. Paul Weingartner and Gerhard Zecha (eds.), *Induction, Physics, and Ethics: Proceedings and Discussions of the 1968 Salzburg Colloquium in the Philosophy of Science.* 1970, X + 382 pp.
32. Evert W. Beth, *Aspects of Modern Logic.* 1970, XI + 176 pp.
33. Risto Hilpinen (ed.), *Deontic Logic: Introductory and Systematic Readings.* 1971, VII + 182 pp.
34. Jean-Louis Krivine, *Introduction to Axiomatic Set Theory.* 1971, VII + 98 pp.
35. Joseph D. Sneed, *The Logical Structure of Mathematical Physics.* 1971, XV + 311 pp.
36. Carl R. Kordig, *The Justification of Scientific Change.* 1971, XIV + 119 pp.
37. Milič Čapek, *Bergson and Modern Physics,* Boston Studies in the Philosophy of Science (ed. by Robert S. Cohen and Marx W. Wartofsky), Volume VII. 1971, XV + 414 pp.

38. Norwood Russell Hanson, *What I Do Not Believe, and Other Essays* (ed. by Stephen Toulmin and Harry Woolf), 1971, XII + 390 pp.
39. Roger C. Buck and Robert S. Cohen (eds.), *PSA 1970. In Memory of Rudolf Carnap*, Boston Studies in the Philosophy of Science (ed. by Robert S. Cohen and Marx W. Wartofsky), Volume VIII. 1971, LXVI + 615 pp. Also available as paperback.
40. Donald Davidson and Gilbert Harman (eds.), *Semantics of Natural Language*. 1972, X + 769 pp. Also available as paperback.
41. Yehoshua Bar-Hillel (ed.), *Pragmatics of Natural Languages*. 1971, VII + 231 pp.
42. Sören Stenlund, *Combinators, λ-Terms and Proof Theory*. 1972, 184 pp.
43. Martin Strauss, *Modern Physics and Its Philosophy. Selected Papers in the Logic, History, and Philosophy of Science*. 1972, X + 297 pp.
44. Mario Bunge, *Method, Model and Matter*. 1973, VII + 196 pp.
45. Mario Bunge, *Philosophy of Physics*. 1973, IX + 248 pp.
46. A. A. Zinov'ev, *Foundations of the Logical Theory of Scientific Knowledge (Complex Logic)*, Boston Studies in the Philosophy of Science (ed. by Robert S. Cohen and Marx W. Wartofsky), Volume IX. Revised and enlarged English edition with an appendix, by G. A. Smirnov, E. A. Sidorenka, A. M. Fedina, and L. A. Bobrova. 1973, XXII + 301 pp. Also available as paperback.
47. Ladislav Tondl, *Scientific Procedures*, Boston Studies in the Philosophy of Science (ed. by Robert S. Cohen and Marx W. Wartofsky), Volume X. 1973, XII + 268 pp. Also available as paperback.
48. Norwood Russell Hanson, *Constellations and Conjectures* (ed. by Willard C. Humphreys, Jr.). 1973, X + 282 pp.
49. K. J. J. Hintikka, J. M. E. Moravcsik, and P. Suppes (eds.), *Approaches to Natural Language. Proceedings of the 1970 Stanford Workshop on Grammar and Semantics*. 1973, VIII + 526 pp. Also available as paperback.
50. Mario Bunge (ed.), *Exact Philosophy – Problems, Tools, and Goals*. 1973, X + 214 pp.
51. Radu J. Bogdan and Ilkka Niiniluoto (eds.), *Logic, Language, and Probability. A Selection of Papers Contributed to Sections IV, VI, and XI of the Fourth International Congress for Logic, Methodology, and Philosophy of Science, Bucharest, September 1971*. 1973, X + 323 pp.
52. Glenn Pearce and Patrick Maynard (eds.), *Conceptual Change*. 1973, XII + 282 pp.
53. Ilkka Niiniluoto and Raimo Tuomela, *Theoretical Concepts and Hypothetico-Inductive Inference*. 1973, VII + 264 pp.
54. Roland Fraïssé, *Course of Mathematical Logic – Volume 1: Relation and Logical Formula*. 1973, XVI + 186 pp. Also available as paperback.
55. Adolf Grünbaum, *Philosophical Problems of Space and Time*. Second, enlarged edition, Boston Studies in the Philosophy of Science (ed. by Robert S. Cohen and Marx W. Wartofsky), Volume XII. 1973, XXIII + 884 pp. Also available as paperback.
56. Patrick Suppes (ed.), *Space, Time, and Geometry*. 1973, XI + 424 pp.
57. Hans Kelsen, *Essays in Legal and Moral Philosophy*, selected and introduced by Ota Weinberger. 1973, XXVIII + 300 pp.
58. R. J. Seeger and Robert S. Cohen (eds.), *Philosophical Foundations of Science. Proceedings of an AAAS Program, 1969*, Boston Studies in the Philosophy of

Science (ed. by Robert S. Cohen and Marx W. Wartofsky), Volume XI. 1974, X + 545 pp. Also available as paperback.

59. Robert S. Cohen and Marx W. Wartofsky (eds.), *Logical and Epistemological Studies in Contemporary Physics*, Boston Studies in the Philosophy of Science (ed. by Robert S. Cohen and Marx W. Wartofsky), Volume XIII. 1973, VIII + 462 pp. Also available as paperback.

60. Robert S. Cohen and Marx W. Wartofsky (eds.), *Methodological and Historical Essays in the Natural and Social Sciences. Proceedings of the Boston Colloquium for the Philosophy of Science 1969-1972*, Boston Studies in the Philosophy of Science (ed. by Robert S. Cohen and Marx W. Wartofsky), Volume XIV. 1974, VIII + 405 pp. Also available as paperback.

61. Robert S. Cohen, J. J. Stachel and Marx W. Wartofsky (eds.), *For Dirk Struik. Scientific, Historical and Political Essays in Honor of Dirk J. Struik*, Boston Studies in the Philosophy of Science (ed. by Robert S. Cohen and Marx W. Wartofsky), Volume XV. 1974, XXVII + 652 pp. Also available as paperback.

62. Kazimierz Ajdukiewicz, *Pragmatic Logic*, transl. from the Polish by Olgierd Wojtasiewicz. 1974, XV + 460 pp.

63. Sören Stenlund (ed.), *Logical Theory and Semantic Analysis. Essays Dedicated to Stig Kanger on His Fiftieth Birthday*. 1974, V + 217 pp.

64. Kenneth F. Schaffner and Robert S. Cohen (eds.), *Proceedings of the 1972 Biennial Meeting, Philosophy of Science Association*, Boston Studies in the Philosophy of Science (ed. by Robert S. Cohen and Marx W. Wartofsky), Volume XX. 1974, IX + 444 pp. Also available as paperback.

65. Henry E. Kyburg, Jr., *The Logical Foundations of Statistical Inference*. 1974, IX + 421 pp.

66. Marjorie Grene, *The Understanding of Nature: Essays in the Philosophy of Biology*, Boston Studies in the Philosophy of Science (ed. by Robert S. Cohen and Marx W. Wartofsky), Volume XXIII. 1974, XII + 360 pp. Also available as paperback.

67. Jan M. Broekman, *Structuralism: Moscow, Prague, Paris*. 1974, IX + 117 pp.

68. Norman Geschwind, *Selected Papers on Language and the Brain*, Boston Studies in the Philosophy of Science (ed. by Robert S. Cohen and Marx W. Wartofsky), Volume XVI. 1974, XII + 549 pp. Also available as paperback.

69. Roland Fraïssé, *Course of Mathematical Logic* – Volume 2: *Model Theory*. 1974, XIX + 192 pp.

70. Andrzej Grzegorczyk, *An Outline of Mathematical Logic. Fundamental Results and Notions Explained with All Details*. 1974, X + 596 pp.

71. Franz von Kutschera, *Philosophy of Language*. 1975, VII + 305 pp.

72. Juha Manninen and Raimo Tuomela (eds.), *Essays on Explanation and Understanding. Studies in the Foundations of Humanities and Social Sciences*. 1976, VII + 440 pp.

73. Jaakko Hintikka (ed.), *Rudolf Carnap, Logical Empiricist. Materials and Perspectives*. 1975, LXVIII + 400 pp.

74. Milič Čapek (ed.), *The Concepts of Space and Time. Their Structure and Their Development*, Boston Studies in the Philosophy of Science (ed. by Robert S. Cohen and Marx W. Wartofsky), Volume XXII. 1976, LVI + 570 pp. Also available as paperback.

75. Jaakko Hintikka and Unto Remes, *The Method of Analysis. Its Geometrical Origin and Its General Significance*, Boston Studies in the Philosophy of Science (ed. by Robert S. Cohen and Marx W. Wartofsky), Volume XXV. 1974, XVIII + 144 pp. Also available as paperback.

76. John Emery Murdoch and Edith Dudley Sylla, *The Cultural Context of Medieval Learning. Proceedings of the First International Colloquium on Philosophy, Science, and Theology in the Middle Ages – September 1973*, Boston Studies in the Philosophy of Science (ed. by Robert S. Cohen and Marx W. Wartofsky), Volume XXVI. 1975, X + 566 pp. Also available as paperback.

77. Stefan Amsterdamski, *Between Experience and Metaphysics. Philosophical Problems of the Evolution of Science*, Boston Studies in the Philosophy of Science (ed. by Robert S. Cohen and Marx W. Wartofsky), Volume XXXV. 1975, XVIII + 193 pp. Also available as paperback.

78. Patrick Suppes (ed.), *Logic and Probability in Quantum Mechanics.* 1976, XV + 541 pp.

79. Hermann von Helmholtz: *Epistemological Writings. The Paul Hertz/Moritz Schlick Centenary Edition of 1921 with Notes and Commentary by the Editors.* (Newly translated by Malcolm F. Lowe. Edited with an Introduction and Bibliography, by Robert S. Cohen and Yehuda Elkana), Boston Studies in the Philosophy of Science (ed. by Robert S. Cohen and Marx W. Wartofsky), Volume XXXVII. 1977, XXXVIII+204 pp. Also available as paperback.

80. Joseph Agassi, *Science in Flux*, Boston Studies in the Philosophy of Science (ed. by Robert S. Cohen and Marx W. Wartofsky), Volume XXVIII. 1975, XXVI + 553 pp. Also available as paperback.

81. Sandra G. Harding (ed.), *Can Theories Be Refuted? Essays on the Duhem-Quine Thesis.* 1976, XXI + 318 pp. Also available as paperback.

82. Stefan Nowak, *Methodology of Sociological Research: General Problems.* 1977, XVIII + 504 pp.

83. Jean Piaget, Jean-Blaise Grize, Alina Szeminska, and Vinh Bang, *Epistemology and Psychology of Functions*, Studies in Genetic Epistemology, Volume XXIII. 1977, XIV+205 pp.

84. Marjorie Grene and Everett Mendelsohn (eds.), *Topics in the Philosophy of Biology*, Boston Studies in the Philosophy of Science (ed. by Robert S. Cohen and Marx W. Wartofsky), Volume XXVII. 1976, XIII + 454 pp. Also available as paperback.

85. E. Fischbein, *The Intuitive Sources of Probabilistic Thinking in Children.* 1975, XIII + 204 pp.

86. Ernest W. Adams, *The Logic of Conditionals. An Application of Probability to Deductive Logic.* 1975, XIII + 156 pp.

87. Marian Przełęcki and Ryszard Wójcicki (eds.), *Twenty-Five Years of Logical Methodology in Poland.* 1977, VIII + 803 pp.

88. J. Topolski, *The Methodology of History.* 1976, X + 673 pp.

89. A. Kasher (ed.), *Language in Focus: Foundations, Methods and Systems. Essays Dedicated to Yehoshua Bar-Hillel*, Boston Studies in the Philosophy of Science (ed. by Robert S. Cohen and Marx W. Wartofsky), Volume XLIII. 1976, XXVIII + 679 pp. Also available as paperback.

90. Jaakko Hintikka, *The Intentions of Intentionality and Other New Models for Modalities.* 1975, XVIII + 262 pp. Also available as paperback.

91. Wolfgang Stegmüller, *Collected Papers on Epistemology, Philosophy of Science and History of Philosophy*, 2 Volumes, 1977, XXVII + 525 pp.
92. Dov M. Gabbay, *Investigations in Modal and Tense Logics with Applications to Problems in Philosophy and Linguistics.* 1976, XI + 306 pp.
93. Radu J. Bogdan, *Local Induction.* 1976, XIV + 340 pp.
94. Stefan Nowak, *Understanding and Prediction: Essays in the Methodology of Social and Behavioral Theories.* 1976, XIX + 482 pp.
95. Peter Mittelstaedt, *Philosophical Problems of Modern Physics*, Boston Studies in the Philosophy of Science (ed. by Robert S. Cohen and Marx W. Wartofsky), Volume XVIII. 1976, X + 211 pp. Also available as paperback.
96. Gerald Holton and William Blanpied (eds.), *Science and Its Public: The Changing Relationship*, Boston Studies in the Philosophy of Science (ed. by Robert S. Cohen and Marx W. Wartofsky), Volume XXXIII. 1976, XXV + 289 pp. Also available as paperback.
97. Myles Brand and Douglas Walton (eds.), *Action Theory. Proceedings of the Winnipeg Conference on Human Action, Held at Winnipeg, Manitoba, Canada, 9-11 May 1975.* 1976, VI + 345 pp.
98. Risto Hilpinen, *Knowledge and Rational Belief.* 1979 (forthcoming).
99. R. S. Cohen, P. K. Feyerabend, and M. W. Wartofsky (eds.), *Essays in Memory of Imre Lakatos*, Boston Studies in the Philosophy of Science (ed. by Robert S. Cohen and Marx W. Wartofsky), Volume XXXIX. 1976, XI + 762 pp. Also available as paperback.
100. R. S. Cohen and J. J. Stachel (eds.), *Selected Papers of Léon Rosenfeld*, Boston Studies in the Philosophy of Science (ed. by Robert S. Cohen and Marx W. Wartofsky), Volume XXI. 1978, XXX + 927 pp.
101. R. S. Cohen, C. A. Hooker, A. C. Michalos, and J. W. van Evra (eds.), *PSA 1974: Proceedings of the 1974 Biennial Meeting of the Philosophy of Science Association*, Boston Studies in the Philosophy of Science (ed. by Robert S. Cohen and Marx W. Wartofsky), Volume XXXII. 1976, XIII + 734 pp. Also available as paperback.
102. Yehuda Fried and Joseph Agassi, *Paranoia: A Study in Diagnosis*, Boston Studies in the Philosophy of Science (ed. by Robert S. Cohen and Marx W. Wartofsky), Volume L. 1976, XV + 212 pp. Also available as paperback.
103. Marian Przełęcki, Klemens Szaniawski, and Ryszard Wójcicki (eds.), *Formal Methods in the Methodology of Empirical Sciences.* 1976, 455 pp.
104. John M. Vickers, *Belief and Probability.* 1976, VIII + 202 pp.
105. Kurt H. Wolff, *Surrender and Catch: Experience and Inquiry Today*, Boston Studies in the Philosophy of Science (ed. by Robert S. Cohen and Marx W. Wartofsky), Volume LI. 1976, XII + 410 pp. Also available as paperback.
106. Karel Kosík, *Dialectics of the Concrete*, Boston Studies in the Philosophy of Science (ed. by Robert S. Cohen and Marx W. Wartofsky), Volume LII. 1976, VIII + 158 pp. Also available as paperback.
107. Nelson Goodman, *The Structure of Appearance*, Boston Studies in the Philosophy of Science (ed. by Robert S. Cohen and Marx W. Wartofsky), Volume LIII. 1977, L + 285 pp.
108. Jerzy Giedymin (ed.), *Kazimierz Ajdukiewicz: The Scientific World-Perspective and Other Essays, 1931 - 1963.* 1978, LIII + 378 pp.

109. Robert L. Causey, *Unity of Science.* 1977, VIII+185 pp.
110. Richard E. Grandy, *Advanced Logic for Applications.* 1977, XIV + 168 pp.
111. Robert P. McArthur, *Tense Logic.* 1976, VII + 84 pp.
112. Lars Lindahl, *Position and Change: A Study in Law and Logic.* 1977, IX + 299 pp.
113. Raimo Tuomela, *Dispositions.* 1978, X + 450 pp.
114. Herbert A. Simon, *Models of Discovery and Other Topics in the Methods of Science,* Boston Studies in the Philosophy of Science (ed. by Robert S. Cohen and Marx W. Wartofsky), Volume LIV. 1977, XX + 456 pp. Also available as paperback.
115. Roger D. Rosenkrantz, *Inference, Method and Decision.* 1977, XVI + 262 pp. Also available as paperback.
116. Raimo Tuomela, *Human Action and Its Explanation. A Study on the Philosophical Foundations of Psychology.* 1977, XII + 426 pp.
117. Morris Lazerowitz, *The Language of Philosophy. Freud and Wittgenstein,* Boston Studies in the Philosophy of Science (ed. by Robert S. Cohen and Marx W. Wartofsky), Volume LV. 1977, XVI + 209 pp.
118. Tran Duc Thao, *Origins of Language and Consciousness,* Boston Studies in the Philosophy of Science (ed. by Robert S. Cohen and Marx. W. Wartofsky), Volume LVI. 1979 (forthcoming).
119. Jerzy Pelč, *Semiotics in Poland, 1894 - 1969.* 1977, XXVI + 504 pp.
120. Ingmar Pörn, *Action Theory and Social Science. Some Formal Models.* 1977, X + 129 pp.
121. Joseph Margolis, *Persons and Minds, The Prospects of Nonreductive Materialism,* Boston Studies in the Philosophy of Science (ed. by Robert S. Cohen and Marx W. Wartofsky), Volume LVII. 1977, XIV + 282 pp. Also available as paperback.
122. Jaakko Hintikka, Ilkka Niiniluoto, and Esa Saarinen (eds.), *Essays on Mathematical and Philosophical Logic. Proceedings of the Fourth Scandinavian Logic Symposium and of the First Soviet-Finnish Logic Conference, Jyväskylä, Finland, 1976.* 1978, VIII + 458 pp. + index.
123. Theo A. F. Kuipers, *Studies in Inductive Probability and Rational Expectation.* 1978, XII + 145 pp.
124. Esa Saarinen, Risto Hilpinen, Ilkka Niiniluoto, and Merrill Provence Hintikka (eds.), *Essays in Honour of Jaakko Hintikka on the Occasion of His Fiftieth Birthday.* 1978, IX + 378 pp. + index.
125. Gerard Radnitzky and Gunnar Andersson (eds.), *Progress and Rationality in Science,* Boston Studies in the Philosophy of Science (ed. by Robert S. Cohen and Marx W. Wartofsky), Volume LVIII. 1978, X + 400 pp. + index. Also available as paperback.
126. Peter Mittelstaedt, *Quantum Logic.* 1978, IX + 149 pp.
127. Kenneth A. Bowen, *Model Theory for Modal Logic. Kripke Models for Modal Predicate Calculi.* 1978, X + 128 pp.
128. Howard Alexander Bursen, *Dismantling the Memory Machine. A Philosophical Investigation of Machine Theories of Memory.* 1978, XIII + 157 pp.
129. Marx W. Wartofsky, *Models: Representation and Scientific Understanding,* Boston Studies in the Philosophy of Science (ed. by Robert S. Cohen and Marx W. Wartofsky), Volume XLVIII. 1979 (forthcoming). Also available as a paperback.
130. Don Ihde, *Technics and Praxis. A Philosophy of Technology,* Boston Studies in

the Philosophy of Science (ed. by Robert S. Cohen and Marx W. Wartofsky), Volume XXIV. 1979 (forthcoming). Also available as a paperback.
131. Jerzy J. Wiatr (ed.), *Polish Essays in the Methodology of the Social Sciences,* Boston Studies in the Philosophy of Science (ed. by Robert S. Cohen and Marx W. Wartofsky), Volume XXIX. 1979 (forthcoming). Also available as a paperback.
132. Wesley C. Salmon (ed.), *Hans Reichenbach: Logical Empiricist.* 1979 (forthcoming).
133. R.-P. Horstmann and L. Krüger (eds.), *Transcendental Arguments and Science.* 1979 (forthcoming). Also available as a paperback.

SYNTHESE HISTORICAL LIBRARY

Texts and Studies
in the History of Logic and Philosophy

Editors:

N. KRETZMANN (Cornell University)
G. NUCHELMANS (University of Leyden)
L. M. DE RIJK (University of Leyden)

1. M. T. Beonio-Brocchieri Fumagalli, *The Logic of Abelard.* Translated from the Italian. 1969, IX + 101 pp.
2. Gottfried Wilhelm Leibniz, *Philosophical Papers and Letters.* A selection translated and edited, with an introduction, by Leroy E. Loemker. 1969, XII + 736 pp.
3. Ernst Mally, *Logische Schriften,* ed. by Karl Wolf and Paul Weingartner. 1971, X + 340 pp.
4. Lewis White Beck (ed.), *Proceedings of the Third International Kant Congress.* 1972, XI + 718 pp.
5. Bernard Bolzano, *Theory of Science,* ed. by Jan Berg. 1973, XV + 398 pp.
6. J. M. E. Moravcsik (ed.), *Patterns in Plato's Thought. Papers Arising Out of the 1971 West Coast Greek Philosophy Conference.* 1973, VIII + 212 pp.
7. Nabil Shehaby, *The Propositional Logic of Avicenna: A Translation from al-Shifā: al-Qiyās,* with Introduction, Commentary and Glossary. 1973, XIII + 296 pp.
8. Desmond Paul Henry, *Commentary on De Grammatico: The Historical-Logical Dimensions of a Dialogue of St. Anselm's.* 1974, IX + 345 pp.
9. John Corcoran, *Ancient Logic and Its Modern Interpretations.* 1974, X + 208 pp.
10. E. M. Barth, *The Logic of the Articles in Traditional Philosophy.* 1974, XXVII + 533 pp.
11. Jaakko Hintikka, *Knowledge and the Known. Historical Perspectives in Epistemology.* 1974, XII + 243 pp.
12. E. J. Ashworth, *Language and Logic in the Post-Medieval Period.* 1974, XIII + 304 pp.
13. Aristotle, *The Nicomachean Ethics.* Translated with Commentaries and Glossary by Hypocrates G. Apostle. 1975, XXI + 372 pp.
14. R. M. Dancy, *Sense and Contradiction: A Study in Aristotle.* 1975, XII + 184 pp.
15. Wilbur Richard Knorr, *The Evolution of the Euclidean Elements. A Study of the Theory of Incommensurable Magnitudes and Its Significance for Early Greek Geometry.* 1975, IX + 374 pp.
16. Augustine, *De Dialectica.* Translated with Introduction and Notes by B. Darrell Jackson. 1975, XI + 151 pp.

17. Arpád Szabó, *The Beginnings of Greek Mathematics.* 1979 (forthcoming).

18. Rita Guerlac, *Juan Luis Vives Against the Pseudodialecticians. A Humanist Attack on Medieval Logic.* Texts, with translation, introduction and notes. 1978, xiv + 227 pp. + index.

SYNTHESE LANGUAGE LIBRARY

Texts and Studies
in Linguistics and Philosophy

Managing Editors:

JAAKKO HINTIKKA
Academy of Finland, Stanford University, and Florida State University (Tallahassee)

STANLEY PETERS
The University of Texas at Austin

Editors:

EMMON BACH (University of Massachusetts at Amherst)
JOAN BRESNAN (Massachusetts Institute of Technology)
JOHN LYONS (University of Sussex)
JULIUS M. E. MORAVCSIK (Stanford University)
PATRICK SUPPES (Stanford University)
DANA SCOTT (Oxford University)